CRIMINAL EVIDENCE AND PROCEDURE: AN INTRODUCTION

Alastair N. Brown
Solicitor

Foreword by Charles N. Stoddart
Sheriff of Lothian and Borders at Edinburgh

T&T CLARK
EDINBURGH
1996

T&T CLARK LTD
59 GEORGE STREET
EDINBURGH EH2 2LQ
SCOTLAND

First published 1996

ISBN 0 567 00511 9

British Library Cataloguing-in-Publication Data
A catalogue record for this book is available from the British Library

Typeset by Waverley Typesetters, Galashiels
Printed and bound in Great Britain by Bell & Bain Ltd, Glasgow

For Susan

PREFACE

It was not my original intention to write a preface for this book. Three events have, however, induced me to change my mind. The first of these is that Sheriff Stoddart has read the book and taken the trouble to write a foreword. I should like to take the opportunity to thank him for doing so and for his kind words. I also take the opportunity of thanking the staff of T&T Clark for their support, assistance and encouragement during the writing and publication processes.

The second event was the publication by the Scottish Office Home Department of the White Paper, Crime and Punishment (Cm 3302) in June 1996. It seemed reasonable to suppose, after the massive legislative effort involved in the 1995 consolidation of Scottish criminal justice legislation, that things would go quiet for a while. The White Paper, however, proposes further changes which are of relevance to the subject-matter of this book and I take the opportunity to note some of them. One of these will not require legislation and that is the making of an order, as contemplated by section 175(4) of the 1995 Act, extending to summary cases the Lord Advocate's appeal against sentence (dealt with at p 168 of the book). It is not clear how extensively that right of appeal will be used. The White Paper itself notes (para 8.21) that it is intended to be used 'sparingly' and records that, out of eleven such appeals under solemn procedure considered by the High Court between the introduction of the procedure and the date of the White Paper, sentence was increased in only two. In *HM Advocate v Bell* 1995 SLT 350; 1995 SCCR 244 the High Court said of such appeals that the sentence passed by the judge at first instance would only be interfered with if it fell outside the range of sentences which the judge at first instance, applying his mind to all the relevant factors, could reasonably have considered appropriate. The court stressed that mere leniency is not enough to justify interference with the sentence but that it is leniency which is *undue* which matters. Having regard to the relatively restricted scope for sentencing in summary cases, it might be that summary cases suitable for such appeals will be rare indeed.

The other significant changes, as to which the White Paper promises legislation 'at an early date' (para 16.1), are as follows:

— to enable the courts to impose orders restricting the liberty of movement of offenders in the community;
— to require the courts to impose a life sentence on an offender convicted for the second time of a serious violent or sexual offence;
— to make changes to the appeals criteria (White Paper, paras 15.7 and 15.8), so that, *inter alia*, (*a*) there should be a single ground of appeal in solemn cases, that a miscarriage of justice has occurred, and that this ground should not be qualified or limited (see p 156 *et seq* of the book) and (*b*) the test for fresh evidence on appeal should be 'reasonable explanation' why the evidence was not led at trial, so adopting the

general line taken by the High Court in *Church* v *HM Advocate* and departing from the approach founded on *Salusbury-Hughes* v *HM Advocate* and confirmed in *Elliott* v *HM Advocate*, overturning *Church* (see pp 162–165 of the book).

The White Paper also invites views on possible increases in the sentencing powers of sheriffs.

The third event was the passing of section 73 of the Criminal Procedure and Investigations Act 1996. Parliament has taken the opportunity, in this essentially English Act, to amend section 27 of the 1995 Act by inserting a new subsection (4A) which provides that the fact that an accused person was on bail when a subsequent offence was committed is to be held as admitted unless challenged by preliminary objection under section 72 of the 1995 Act (under solemn procedure) or before the plea is recorded (under summary procedure). This effffectively restores the position to that which obtained when being on bail was a special capacity (see *Aitchison* v *Tudhope* 1981 JC 65; 1981 SLT 231; 1981 SCCR 1). Pages 73 and 98 of the book are affected.

All of this serves to underline Sheriff Stoddart's remark that there is a need for all those professionals who might use the criminal law to become aware of how the system is changing.

My intention has been to provide an introductory account of the subject, but not one which is too basic to be of assistance to the more experienced practitioner. I have made selection among the various aspects of criminal evidence and procedure in a way which I hope meets that need, saying little or nothing about some issues (such as mental health) but devoting significant space to others (such as hearsay). How appropriate that selection has been will be for the reader to judge. I hope, as JF Archbold did in the preface to the first edition of his *Criminal Evidence and Pleading*, that this will prove to be a 'practically useful book'. That hope is the only comparison which I would dare to make with *Archbold*. He provided English law with an indispensable and comprehensive companion to its criminal practice. If I prove to have provided Scots lawyers with a way in to criminal evidence and procedure—I make no greater claim—I shall be well content.

Alastair N Brown
4th July 1996

CONTENTS

Contents

Contents

TABLE OF CASES

TABLE OF STATUTES

FOREWORD

I am delighted to have an opportunity to introduce this new work to all readers interested in Scottish criminal procedure and the related law of evidence. This area has undergone a considerable upheaval recently, with the enactment of the Criminal Justice (Scotland) Act 1995, followed hard on its heels by a consolidation measure which incorporates almost all the current law. It is to the Criminal Procedure (Scotland) Act 1995 to which reference must first be made in a search for the answers to any procedural problem; likewise, evidential difficulties will often be solved by recourse to its terms. Alongside all this statutory material there continues to develop a steady stream of case-law.

In this book Alastair Brown, an experienced member of the Procurator Fiscal Service, provides a highly readable and informative guide to the main areas of the law, all under reference to the new statutory provisions. As cases brought under the previous provisions work their way out of the system, it is becoming increasingly necessary to refer to what the law has become, rather than to what it once was. Many a pitfall awaits the unwary, but most can be avoided by a perusal of this excellent work. Particularly welcome is the repeated discussion of how the law works, and is intended to work, in practice; for this is not just a 'black letter law' book, but far more useful.

I am sure that the book will appeal to a market beyond those immediately interested in the operation of the criminal justice system, such as students and practitioners (including putative Advocate-deputes with no criminal experience); I think it deserves a wider readership among police and related investigatory agencies. As the practice of criminal law becomes more complex, the greater is the need for all those professionals who might use it to become aware of how the system is changing.

I have no hesitation in recommending Alastair Brown's work to all.

Charles N Stoddart
Sheriff of Lothian and Borders
July 1996

1 : INTRODUCTION

The purpose of the book

The Scottish Law Commission has pointed out that the functions of the law of evidence and the law of procedure are very similar.

> '[W]here a court or tribunal has to decide a disputed issue of fact it is the proper function of the law of evidence to assist it by providing intelligible and acceptable rules which will indicate what evidence it may receive in order to elucidate the truth in relation to the matter in dispute. The rules of procedure may be said to have a similar function: they guide the court or tribunal as to the means by which it must arrive at its decision.'[1]

The law of evidence and procedure is, then, the framework within which courts must take their decisions. This book is intended to provide an account of the subject appropriate to the needs of those who have not studied it before or who are relatively unfamiliar with it. It should also be of value for the experienced practitioner who needs a succinct account of the essentials of a particular area of law, but it is not written primarily with the needs of such practitioners in mind. In particular, the object has been to achieve comprehensibility and clarity in relation to the essentials of the subject rather than to provide comprehensive coverage of every last detail of the law.

The law is stated as at 1st April 1996.

The Criminal Procedure (Scotland) Act 1995

The Criminal Procedure (Scotland) Act 1995 is the single most important source for the law of criminal evidence and procedure and a thorough familiarity with its provisions is essential. That Act consolidated the law and it is understood that the drafting intention was to provide in that Act everything necessary for day-to-day work in the criminal courts. Accordingly, although at about the same time Parliament passed a number of other Acts which have a bearing on criminal practice, in this book the expression 'the 1995 Act' refers exclusively to the Criminal Procedure (Scotland) Act 1995. Other Acts are given their full titles.

It must be emphasised, however, that the book does not purport to be a commentary on the 1995 Act as such. The Act is not in itself a comprehensive code of criminal evidence and procedure and to confine consideration to material dealt with in the Act would be to fail to cover important subject-matter. Furthermore, detailed consideration of some of the material in the 1995 Act would tend to make the book too intensive for an introductory text and important themes would be submerged in the detail.

The structure of the book

There is a substantial degree of interpenetration between evidence and procedure. Not only can procedural irregularities have a profound effect

---

[1] Scot Law Com No 149, Evidence: Report on Hearsay Evidence in Criminal Proceedings, para 2.5.

upon the admissibility of evidence but also many questions relating to evidence have consequences for the procedure which is followed. Accordingly, this book sets out to describe evidence and procedure in an integrated way, rather than making the more conventional separation between them. The law of procedure is considered in the general order in which steps occur in prosecutions. Solemn and summary procedure are dealt with together, so far as possible (as has been done in the 1995 Act), since the same principles underlie both and they share many common rules. Where the two must be treated separately, solemn procedure is taken first, again following the pattern of the Act. Matters of evidence are discussed as they become relevant to the topics dealt with. As a result many rules of evidence are treated primarily in the context of solemn procedure. This particular result of the structure may be justified upon the basis that much of the law of evidence has been developed in the context of the jury trial by judges whose experience is overwhelmingly of jury trials. Accordingly, although summary cases account for the great majority of criminal cases in terms of numbers, aspects of the law of evidence are in fact easier to understand if the perceived needs of the jury are kept in mind.

Types of procedure

Some basic material is necessary as a foundation for understanding the first steps in procedure. The first thing to be understood is the division of cases between those dealt with under solemn procedure and those dealt with under summary procedure. Solemn procedure is the procedure under which serious cases are dealt with while summary procedure relates to less serious cases. Solemn procedure involves a jury and summary procedure does not. As Lord Justice-Clerk Macdonald pointed out in *Lamb v Threshie*,[2] the difference is nowhere really defined. Summary procedure is most easily characterised by its omissions and limitations. There is no indictment (though the summary complaint has developed into something not dissimilar), no jury, no requirement for a list of witnesses and productions and a strict limitation on the maximum sentence available. As Trotter put it:

> 'Criminal jurisdiction is exercised by summary procedure when the trial takes place before a judge or judges alone, without a jury, by summary and expeditious process, and without all the formalities and solemnities requisite in solemn procedure. Hence the term "summary" procedure.'[3]

The High Court of Justiciary (as a trial court) exercises jurisdiction under solemn procedure only; the sheriff court exercises jurisdiction under both solemn and summary procedure; and the district court exercises jurisdiction under summary procedure only. The High Court of Justiciary also sits as an appeal court and is in fact the only appeal court for Scottish criminal cases (since the House of Lords has no jurisdiction in relation to Scottish criminal cases).

The essentials of evidence

The other foundational material relates to the basic principles of the law of evidence.

[2] (1892) 3 White 261 at 270.
[3] T Trotter, *Summary Criminal Jurisdiction According to the Law of Scotland* (1936) p 3.

Burden of proof

The most fundamental principle in the law of criminal evidence and procedure is that the burden of proof is at all times upon the prosecution. The prosecution is required to prove its case; the accused does not have to prove anything. Accordingly, the prosecution leads its evidence first and, if at the end of the prosecution case there is insufficient evidence for a conviction the accused is entitled to be acquitted in terms of sections 97 and 160 of the 1995 Act. Insufficiency may arise either because there was never going to be enough evidence for a conviction (in which case the Crown made a mistake when it commenced proceedings) or because essential parts of the prosecution evidence have been ruled inadmissible.

As a result of the principle that the burden of proof is at all times on the prosecution, the hope that some investigators express, that a case will succeed because 'the accused will never be able to explain it at court', is entirely illusory. The accused does not have to explain anything at all, ever, unless the prosecution case is sufficient in itself to justify a conviction. This is the meaning of the presumption of innocence. However guilty the accused may be in fact, he cannot be found guilty by a court unless the prosecution provides evidence to prove his guilt; and, of course, he cannot be punished by a criminal court unless he has first been found guilty.

It would be difficult to improve on Lord Sankey LC's formulation of this in *Woolmington* v *DPP*,[4] an English case, but one which expresses the Scottish principle equally well.

> '[I]t is the duty of the prosecution to prove the prisoner's guilt. . . . If at the end of and on the whole of the case, there is a reasonable doubt, created by the evidence given by either the prosecution or the prisoner . . . the prosecution has not made out the case and the prisoner is entitled to an acquittal. No matter what the charge or where the trial, the principle that the prosecution must prove the guilt of the prisoner is part of the common law . . . and no attempt to whittle it down can be entertained.'

There has been a tendency, particularly on the part of English legal writers, to distinguish what they call the 'legal' burden of proof from what they call the 'provisional' or 'tactical' burden.[5] Although this distinction can be a useful one it can also lead to confusion.

What is meant by the 'legal' burden is the requirement on the prosecution to put enough evidence before the court to entitle it to convict. In other words, when the accused is charged with a crime it is up to the prosecution to lead evidence which shows that the accused did in fact commit the crime charged. There comes a point, however, at which the evidence so led by the prosecution is sufficiently complete and sufficiently convincing that the accused can expect to be convicted unless he leads evidence which casts doubt on the reliability of the evidence led by the prosecution or on the conclusions to be drawn from it. This is the 'provisional' or 'tactical' burden. To say that there is such a burden of proof on the accused is simply a way of expressing a judgment about the strength of the prosecution case which has unfolded against him. Case-law never places a duty on the accused to disprove the case against him and Acts of Parliament only place such a duty on the accused rarely and in relation to

---

[4] [1935] AC 462.
[5] See, eg, Lord Denning, 'Presumptions and Burdens' (1945) 61 LQR 379.

limited aspects of the case. Accordingly, when it was suggested in *Lambie* v *HM Advocate*[6] that an accused who wished to invoke the defence of incrimination (that is, to say that the offence was committed by some particular other person) must prove that defence, the High Court on appeal said that this approach was incorrect and that all that was necessary for the acquittal of the accused was that the evidence left a reasonable doubt in the minds of the jury.

An example of a case in which such a 'tactical' burden did arise is *Milne* v *Whaley*[7] in which an accused person was acquitted by a sheriff on a charge of driving without either a licence or insurance because there was no corroboration of his admissions (corroboration being essential to the proof of the overwhelming majority of crimes). The High Court held on appeal that the sheriff's approach had been incorrect, saying:

'[A]ll the Crown has to do is to demonstrate *prima facie* the absence of an entitlement to drive, and the Crown has amply done that in this case by proving the circumstances in which the charge was brought. Thereafter, if an accused person wishes to displace the *prima facie* inference . . . it is for him to do so.'

Since the position in that case was that Mr Whaley, when stopped by the police and asked to produce his licence and insurance, replied that he had neither and then gave evidence that he had not had a licence or insurance he clearly could not meet the tactical burden. But the need to do so would never have arisen if the prosecution had not put before the court evidence sufficient to establish *prima facie* that he had committed the offences.

The situation in which such a tactical burden had arisen was the context in which Lord Justice-General Emslie once remarked:

'[I]f a sheriff is going to acquit because he entertains a reasonable doubt, there must be, in the material before him in the evidence, a basis upon which such a reasonable doubt can reasonably arise.'[8]

Standard of proof
As in English law, expressed in *Woolmington*, the standard to which the prosecution case must be proved in Scotland is beyond reasonable doubt. Precisely what that expression is intended to convey is very difficult to expound, and Lord Justice-Clerk Thomson counselled against attempts at reformulation in *McKenzie* v *HM Advocate*.[9] The English Court of Appeal expressed similar views in *R* v *Ching*[10] when it said, 'If judges stopped trying to define that which is almost impossible to define there would be fewer appeals.'

Scottish juries are usually told that a reasonable doubt it not a speculative or fanciful doubt but is the kind of doubt which would cause them to hesitate in some important decision in their own affairs such as a decision to marry, to take a particular job or to move house. Before an accused person can be convicted the evidence must be such as to persuade those who have to decide the facts in the case—the jury, sheriff or district court justice— that there is no reason of any substance, no material reason, to doubt his

[6] 1973 JC 53.
[7] 1975 SLT (Notes) 75.
[8] *Tudhope* v *McAllister* 1984 SLT 395 at 396.
[9] 1959 JC 32.
[10] (1976) 63 Cr App R 7.

guilt. The standard to be reached is much higher than a mere balance of probabilities (under which it would be enough if the thing sought to be proved were more probably true than not) but certainty is not required.

A reasonable doubt may exist because the evidence is simply not cogent enough to establish the guilt of the accused to the standard required, perhaps because there are gaps in it or perhaps because important parts of it are either not believed or are regarded as unreliable. In this situation, the prosecution has failed to discharge the burden of proof and the accused must be acquitted. Alternatively, if the accused gives evidence himself, or calls witnesses who give evidence, that evidence may be sufficiently credible to create doubt about the prosecution case on one of the essentials of the charge, even though the judge or the jury might not be prepared to go as far as to say that they actually believed the defence evidence. Of course, if the defence evidence *is* believed, that will certainly be an end of the matter.

Occasionally an Act of Parliament will require an accused to prove facts which amount to a defence to a particular charge. Where that is the case, it is clear from *Neish* v *Stevenson*[11] and *King* v *Lees*[12] that he has only to do so on a balance of probabilities.

Admissibility of evidence

It is a serious matter to charge any person with crime, and it was even more serious over 100 years ago when the principles which underpin the law of evidence were being developed. At that time, capital punishment was available for a wide range of offences and the death penalty was imposed with some frequency. It was (and, since miscarriages of justice remain unacceptable, even if reversible, still is) of considerable importance to ensure that the evidence laid before a court, and especially before a jury of laymen, was evidence which was of a sort which could be regarded as trustworthy. The law developed what is called an 'exclusory' approach to criminal evidence.

Scots law shares this approach (but not the detail of the rules) with English law and those systems derived from it. What it means is that the law as to the admissibility of evidence in Scotland consists in large measure of a set of rules relating to the exclusion of those types of evidence which are perceived as unfair or not tending to assist a just result.

The critical importance of the concept of admissibility is that if pieces of evidence (usually referred to as 'adminicles of evidence') essential to the proof of the case are held to be inadmissible the result will be an insufficiency of evidence and the case will fail without the truth of the allegations ever being considered.

Dickson suggested that the purpose of the law of evidence in Scotland is

'to exclude valueless and deceptive proofs, to secure regularity in the investigations and to confine within reasonable limits the duration and expense of judicial proceedings.'[13]

More recently, Field has expressed the same idea thus:

'Without the law of evidence, all items of information which might conceivably have a bearing on one or more of the issues in a trial, however unreliable, unfair

[11] 1969 SLT 229.
[12] 1993 SCCR 28.
[13] W G Dickson, *A Treatise on the Law of Evidence in Scotland* (3rd edn, 1887) Preface.

or misleading, would be put before the court. Wearisome and time-wasting as such a process might be in an action before a judge or sheriff, it would be positively hazardous when those deciding upon the facts of a case are laymen, sitting either in a jury or a district court.'[14]

It is of assistance in understanding the law on admissibility of evidence if these purposes are borne in mind.

It should also be understood that the courts in deciding any question as to admissibility are likely to have to strike a balance. The nature of that balance was well expressed by Lord Wheatley in *Milne* v *Cullen*,[15] where he said:

'[I]t is the function of the court to seek to provide a proper balance to secure that the rights of individuals are properly preserved, while not hamstringing the police in their investigation of crime with a series of academic vetoes which ignore the realities and practicalities of the situation and discount completely the public interest.'

As a result of the principle that the burden of proof is always on the prosecution, the courts will always prefer the interest of the accused if to do otherwise will involve material unfairness. We may note MacKenna's comment that 'it is thought to be more against the public interest that the innocent should be convicted than that the guilty should go free'.[16]

Notwithstanding the importance which the Scottish courts attach to the acquittal of the innocent, they are very far from subscribing to the view that the defence have what the (English) Criminal Law Revision Committee caricatured as 'a sacred right to the benefit of anything in the law which may give them a chance of an acquittal, even on a technicality, however strong the case is against them.'[17]

Sufficiency of evidence

We have already noted that the importance of the concept of admissibility is that if adminicles of evidence essential to the proof of the case are held inadmissible the case will fail without the truth of the allegations ever being considered. The importance of the concept of sufficiency is that even if all the evidence which is admissible is believed, the case will still fail unless there is evidence sufficient in law to entitle the court to consider the essential allegations proved. Fundamentally, this means that there must be corroboration—that is, there must be two sources of evidence to prove every fact which it is essential for the Crown to prove before the court is entitled to convict.

Corroboration has nothing to do with admissibility of evidence and it is emphatically *not* the case that evidence which is not spoken to by two witnesses is not admissible, as is sometimes thought. But essential facts must be proved by two sources of evidence. Accordingly, the identification of the accused as the person who committed the crime is not proved unless there are two separate sources of evidence to demonstrate that it was him. In an assault, the charge cannot be proved unless there are two sources of evidence to show that an attack took place. Examples could easily be

---

[14] D Field, *The Law of Evidence in Scotland* (1991) p 1.
[15] 1967 JC 21.
[16] Sir Brian MacKenna, 'Criminal Law Revision Committee's Eleventh Report: Some Comments' [1972] Crim LR 605 at 606–607.
[17] Eleventh Report, 1972, Cmnd 4991, para 27.

multiplied and we shall consider the concept of sufficiency in much more detail below in the context of submissions of 'no case to answer'. The basic principle must, however, be borne in mind as the rest of the book is read.

It is necessary at this point to notice an analytical division of evidence into direct and circumstantial. The terms describe a relationship between evidence and the facts in issue. Direct evidence consists of a witness's testimony as to direct observation of a fact in issue, whereas circumstantial evidence is testimony as to facts from which fact in issue may be inferred. Circumstantial evidence is indirect evidence of a fact, consisting of something which is at least consistent with the fact to be proved but which might also be consistent with other possibilities. However, such evidence becomes capable of proving the fact in issue when there is an accumulation of such evidence, perhaps (but not necessarily) in combination with direct evidence of the fact in issue, such that, unless one is to resort to speculation or believe that coincidence has been heaped upon coincidence, the combined effect of the evidence is consistent only with the matter to be proved.

The important point is that both direct and circumstantial evidence are equally valid, at least for purposes of sufficiency of evidence. There is no limit on the ways in which adminicles of admissible evidence can interact to amount to a sufficiency. In *Howden* v *HM Advocate*,[18] for example, it was held that an accused charged with two offences, positively identified by several witnesses as the perpetrator of the first crime but only tentatively identified as the perpetrator of the second, was properly convicted of the second where circumstantial evidence established beyond reasonable doubt that the same person committed both offences.

Little v *HM Advocate*[19] is an example of a murder case proved *inter alia* by circumstantial evidence. In considering the case the High Court pointed out that the question is not whether each of the several circumstances points by itself towards the fact in issue but whether taken together they are capable of supporting the inference that the fact in issue was so. So, for example, in that case unusual transactions on a building society account were of importance in establishing incitement to murder and were relevant even though they did not bear directly on the facts.

An admission can provide one source of evidence. Some other source or sources will be required to corroborate the facts admitted. So in *Innes* v *HM Advocate*,[20] on a charge of theft, the evidence to identify the accused was (i) an admission to a single police officer; (ii) possession of the stolen property, again spoken to by a single witness, not the officer in (i); and (iii) presence at the time of the theft, spoken to by yet another single witness. In upholding the conviction Lord Justice-Clerk Thomson said, 'So long as there are separate sources, each incriminating the accused person it is unnecessary to have more than one witness to each source.'

Heywood v *Smith*[21] provides another illustration. In that case the evidence of one police officer who saw the accused swallow an object thought to be drugs combined with a confession to having done so heard by another officer was sufficient to convict the accused of attempting to pervert the course of justice. The argument in that case was about the admissibility of the

[18] 1994 SCCR 19.
[19] 1983 SCCR 56.
[20] 1955 SLT (Notes) 69.
[21] 1989 SCCR 391.

confession but the point of the argument was to try to reduce the prosecution case to the evidence of a single witness as to seeing the swallowing of the object, which would have been insufficient.

It must be understood that all this relates to proof by the Crown. Where there is an onus on the accused (for example, to displace a presumption) he does not require corroboration. So in *Robertson* v *Watson*[22] Lord Cooper said, 'It is not essential that the evidence tendered by the [accused] should be independently corroborated', and in *King* v *Lees*[23] the Crown conceded that a sheriff had been wrong to refuse to give effect to the accused's evidence that his breath alcohol was attributable to drinking after a road accident and not before it (so giving himself a defence to a drink driving charge). The sheriff's reasoning had been that the accused's evidence was uncorroborated.

The juvenile offender

The final introductory matter relates to the juvenile offender. In terms of section 41 of the 1995 Act it is conclusively presumed that no child under the age of eight years can be guilty of any offence.

Children below the age of sixteen can be prosecuted. However, the whole thrust of Part V of the 1995 Act, which deals with the prosecution of such children, is directed towards their protection so far as that is consistent with the interests of justice and, accordingly, a framework of safeguards is provided for such cases.

These safeguards begin when the child is arrested. Section 43 of the 1995 Act provides that where a person who is apparently a child is arrested and cannot be brought forthwith before a sheriff, a police officer of the rank of inspector or above, or the officer in charge of the police station to which the child is brought, must inquire into the case and liberate the child on a written undertaking by his parent or guardian that he will attend at the hearing of the charge. To this obligation to liberate there are only three exceptions, although the third is rather wide. The first exception relates to homicide or 'other grave crime'; the second applies where it is necessary in the interest of the child to remove him from association with a reputed criminal or prostitute; and the third applies where the officer has reason to believe that the child's liberation would defeat the ends of justice. In the event that one of these exceptions applies and the child is not liberated, the general rule in terms of section 43(4) of the 1995 Act is that the child is to be kept in a place of safety other than a police station unless the officer certifies that one of three sets of circumstances applies. These are that it is impracticable to do so (an example of which would be the unavailability of any such place), that he is of so unruly a character that he cannot safely be so detained, or that his state of health or mental or bodily condition makes it inadvisable so to detain him. Of these, the second accounts for such a large proportion of such certificates that they have become known as 'unruly certificates'. The certificate must be produced to the court when the child appears from custody.

Section 42(1) of the 1995 Act provides that a child below the age of sixteen can only be prosecuted on the instructions of the Lord Advocate or

---

[22] 1949 JC 73.
[23] 1993 SCCR 28.

at his instance, though as *McGuire* v *Dean*[24] makes clear this does not mean that a summary complaint has to refer to the Lord Advocate's instructions on its face. Instead, there is a rebuttable presumption that a complaint raised by a procurator fiscal complies with the Lord Advocate's instructions.

Where the child is not prosecuted, the police are required by section 43(5) of the 1995 Act to inform the Reporter to the Children's Panel. The Reporter might well proceed with a children's hearing but the procedure applying in that event is outwith the scope of this book.

Section 42(1) of the 1995 Act restricts jurisdiction in cases against children to the High Court and the sheriff court. Subsection (3) requires the police to warn the parent or guardian of a child who is arrested to attend court and subsection (7) requires them to notify the local authority. That local authority are required, by subsection (8), to provide the court with a social enquiry report on the child.

Where the child is prosecuted the parent or guardian must, in terms of section 42(2) of the 1995 Act, be required to attend court except where the child has already been removed from the care or charge, of his parent by order of the court.

Section 51 of the 1995 Act makes provision for the situation in which a child accused of crime who either pleads not guilty or pleads guilty and has sentence deferred is to be kept in custody pending trial or sentencing. In general, those under the age of sixteen are to be committed to the local authority to be detained in secure accommodation or a place of safety. However, by subsection (3), if the child is not less than fourteen years old and it appears to the court that he is 'unruly or depraved' he may be committed to a remand centre (if one is available) or to a prison.

[24] 1973 JC 20.

2 : JURISDICTION

If a crime is not within the jurisdiction of the Scottish courts then Scottish rules of procedure and evidence will not apply to it. The converse—that a crime within the jurisdiction of the Scottish courts will *only* be subject to Scottish rules—does not hold true. For a variety of reasons crimes can sometimes be subject to the jurisdiction of the courts of more than one country. We are concerned here only with whether or not the *Scottish* courts will have jurisdiction. Whether the courts of some other country might also take jurisdiction is, for us, immaterial.

The High Court of Justiciary

Territorial jurisdiction

The jurisdiction of the Scottish courts is primarily territorial in its basis. This means that if the crime is committed within the geographical area covered by the court, the court will have jurisdiction to deal with the crime.

The High Court of Justiciary has jurisdiction as a trial court in respect of crimes committed anywhere in Scotland. Section 3(2) of the 1995 Act provides that 'Any crime or offence which is triable on indictment may be tried by the High Court sitting at any place in Scotland.'

All crimes may be tried on indictment except those for which an Act of Parliament prescribes prosecution under summary procedure only. Section 292 of the 1995 Act contains detailed rules for determining when an offence is triable only summarily but in practice such restriction to summary prosecution is usually by implication, where the legislation provides for a penalty only on summary conviction. Many such offences are listed in Schedule 2 to the Criminal Procedure (Consequential Provisions) (Scotland) Act 1995.

Before the jurisdiction of the High Court is excluded in relation to a category of crime that exclusion must be express or necessarily implied. The best authority for this proposition seems to be *McPherson v Boyd*,[1] in which Lord Justice-General Dunedin said:

> '[T]here is an underlying universal jurisdiction in both the Sheriff Court and this Court, and it seems to me, therefore, to be quite settled by long practice that where Parliament is going to give jurisdiction to courts other than the Sheriff Court or the Court of Justiciary it must say so.'

The most obvious—and perhaps the only significant current—example of the exclusion of the jurisdiction of the High Court relates to offences which can only be prosecuted under summary procedure, as a necessary consequence of the fact that the High Court only sits under solemn procedure. The exception to this occurs where a summary offence is, in terms of section 292(6) of the 1995 Act, prosecuted on the same indictment as an offence which can be dealt with under solemn procedure.

---

[1] (1907) 5 Adam 247.

'Scotland' for the purposes of criminal jurisdiction includes the territorial sea, the breadth of which is now twelve nautical miles.[2]

It is, however, not always obvious when a crime has been committed in Scotland. It may be, for example, that a false representation is made by post or telephone from another jurisdiction and takes effect in Scotland in that a person in Scotland is induced to act on that representation. For example, a payment may be sent from Scotland to the other jurisdiction. Alternatively, it may be that the pretence is made from Scotland to another jurisdiction. There are, of course, many possible permutations.

The leading case on this sort of situation is *Laird* v *HM Advocate*.[3] The case involved a fraudulent scheme, hatched in Scotland, under which the accused pretended, by telex and telephone from Scotland to a company in England, that they could supply steel of a particular quality. They delivered steel of a different quality and covered up the difference by uttering (that is, passing) forged documents. The delivery and uttering took place in England. Refusing their appeal against conviction, during which it had been argued that the Scottish court had no jurisdiction, Lord Justice-Clerk Wheatley said:

> '[I]t seems to me that where a crime is of such a nature that it has to originate with the forming of a fraudulent plan, and that thereafter various steps have to be taken to bring that fraudulent plan to fruition, if some of these subsequent steps take place in one jurisdiction and some in another, then if the totality of the events in one country plays a material part in the operation and fulfilment of the fraudulent scheme as a whole there should be jurisdiction in that country.'

This is, of course, expressed with particular reference to a fraudulent scheme but there seems to be no reason why it should not apply to any criminal scheme. The test would seem to be whether the totality of the events in Scotland plays a material part in the scheme as a whole.

Laird proceeded under reference to three much older cases: *HM Advocate* v *Bradbury*,[4] *HM Advocate* v *Allan*[5] and *HM Advocate* v *Witherington*.[6]

In *Bradbury* the accused wrote letters from England to persons in Scotland. In them he made fraudulent representations and induced the recipients to send goods to him in England. The court took the view that there was jurisdiction because the loss occurred in Scotland.

Allan concerned an accused who had, from London, placed fraudulent advertisements in Scottish newspapers. Persons in Scotland were induced to send money to London. It was objected that there was no jurisdiction in the Scottish court because the accused's actings were all in London but the High Court followed *Bradbury* and repelled the objection. Lord Ardmillan said:

> 'If a man, for instance, standing in one country shoots a man across the border, thus committing a crime which takes effect in another country, or if he commences a theft or fraud in one country, *he is amenable in either case to the jurisdiction of the courts of both countries*' (emphasis added).

---

[2] Territorial Sea Act 1987, s 1(1)(a).
[3] 1984 SCCR 469.
[4] (1872) 2 Couper 311.
[5] (1873) 2 Couper 402.
[6] (1881) 8 R (J) 4.

Witherington was a Full Bench decision (that is, a decision by a number of judges greater than the quorum for an appeal and therefore particularly authoritative) on similar facts to *Bradbury* in which the High Court confirmed the approach taken in *Bradbury*.

Although *Bradbury, Allan* and *Witherington* were not cited in *Clements* v *HM Advocate*,[7] it is possible to discern in that case a similar understanding of the concept of territoriality. The facts were that the two appellants had been charged with, and convicted of, being concerned in the supplying of controlled drugs, which were delivered (by others) from the London area to Edinburgh. The two appellants represented the London end of the operation; neither of them had been in Scotland (at least in connection with the offence) and Gouner the second appellant, did not even know that the drugs were destined for Scotland. It was argued on their behalf that the Scottish courts had no jurisdiction. However, the High Court upheld their convictions. Explaining that decision, Lord Justice-General Hope pointed out that where a criminal enterprise of this sort exists there is an obvious connection between the activities of all the participants and the point of supply, where the harmful act is to occur. Lord Hope could see no reason why the courts of one part of the UK should be precluded from exercising jurisdiction in relation to all participants (though he left open the possibility of a different result if international borders were involved). In this he was to some extent influenced by what Lord Griffiths had to say in *Somchai Liangsiriprasert* v *Government of the United States of America*[8] (a Privy Council case relating to extradition from Hong Kong):

> 'Unfortunately in this century crime has ceased to be largely local in origin and effect. Crime is now established on an international scale and the common law must face this new reality. Their Lordships can find nothing in precedent, comity or good sense that should inhibit the common law from regarding as justiciable in England inchoate crimes committed abroad which are intended to result in the commission of criminal offences in England.'

Exceptions to territorial jurisdiction

Limited exceptions exist to the principle that jurisdiction is territorially based. Crimes on board British ships are amenable to the jurisdiction of the Scottish courts by section 686 of the Merchant Shipping Act 1894. Otherwise, the exceptions are set out in section 11 of the 1995 Act. By subsection (1) any British citizen or British subject who, in a foreign country, commits what would have been murder or culpable homicide had it been committed in Scotland is guilty of that crime in Scotland.

Subsection (2) applies only to those British citizens and subjects employed in the service of the Crown. If such a person, in a foreign country, when acting or purporting to act in the course of his employment, does anything which would constitute an offence punishable on indictment had it been done in Scotland, he is guilty of that crime in Scotland.

By subsection (3) persons affected by subsections (1) and (2) can be prosecuted in Scotland.

Finally, by subsection (4) a person who has in his possession in Scotland property which he has stolen in another part of the UK or who in Scotland

[7] 1991 SCCR 266.
[8] [1991] 1 AC 225.

receives property stolen in another part of the UK may be dealt with, indicted, tried and punished as if he had stolen the property in Scotland.

Sheriff court jurisdiction

The jurisdiction of the sheriff court is more restricted than that of the High Court.

Offences

Section 3(6) of the 1995 Act sets out the offences with which the sheriff may deal under solemn procedure.

> 'Subject to any express exclusion contained in any enactment, it shall be lawful to indict in the sheriff court all crimes except murder, treason, rape and breach of duty by magistrates.'

The effect of this is to restrict prosecution of the particular crimes mentioned to the High Court; but all other offences committed within Scotland may be indicted in the sheriff court. The sheriff court also has the extra-territorial jurisdiction established by section 11 of the 1995 Act to the extent that it applies to offences other than those mentioned in section 3(6).

In relation to summary prosecutions, section 4(4) of the 1995 Act gives the sheriff concurrent jurisdiction with all other courts of summary jurisdiction (that is, the district court) and accordingly any matter which can competently be prosecuted on summary complaint can be so prosecuted in the sheriff court.

Territorial jurisdiction

There are six sheriffdoms in Scotland (Grampian, Highland and Islands; Tayside, Central and Fife; North Strathclyde; Lothian and Borders; Glasgow and Strathkelvin; South Strathclyde, Dumfries and Galloway), each of which is divided into sheriff court districts. For example, in the sheriffdom of Lothian and Borders there are district sheriff courts at Edinburgh, Linlithgow, Haddington, Jedburgh, Duns, Peebles and Selkirk.

It is the practice to prosecute crimes within the sheriff court district in which they are committed. The only requirement in law, however, is to try an offence within the sheriffdom in which it is committed. By section 4(2) of the 1995 Act, where an offence is alleged to have been committed in one district in a sheriffdom it is competent to try that offence in any other district in that sheriffdom. It is suggested that *Laird* and the earlier cases which that case followed are good law in relation to the jurisdiction of the sheriff court in cases of crime which involve two (or more) national jurisdictions.

Multiple sheriffdoms

It is suggested that *Laird* is also authoritative as between sheriffdoms and this proposition derives support from *Lipsey* v *Mackintosh*[9] where a letter was sent from one sheriff court district to another and it was held that both sheriff courts had jurisdiction.

Where an offence is committed in a harbour, river, arm of the sea or other water, tidal or otherwise, which runs between or forms the boundary of two or more courts, section 9(1) of the 1995 Act permits the offence to be

[9] 1913 SC (J) 104.

tried by any one of those courts. An offence committed within 500 metres of the boundary of the jurisdiction of two or more courts may be tried by any of those courts in terms of section 9(2) of the 1995 Act. By section 9(3) of the 1995 Act which is expressed in somewhat antiquated language, an offence committed against any person or in respect of any property in or on a carriage, cart, or vehicle employed in a journey by road or railway, or on board any vessel employed in a river, loch, canal or inland navigation may be tried by any court through whose jurisdiction the journey passes. On the wording of the subsection this will be so even though it may be possible to show that the conveyance concerned was, at the time of the offence, in some district other than that in which the case is prosecuted.

In terms of section 10 of the 1995 Act where a person is alleged to have committed crimes within the application of the section in more than one sheriff court district, he may be indicted in respect of all of them in whichever sheriff court district the Lord Advocate selects. The section applies (*a*) to a crime committed partly in one sheriff court district and partly in another (the most obvious examples of which would be a continuing offence such as reset or the *Lipsey* v *Mackintosh* type of case); (*b*) to crimes 'connected with each other' (an expression which is undefined) 'but committed in different sheriff court districts'; and (*c*) to crimes committed in different sheriff court districts in succession which, if they had all been committed in a single district could have been tried under one indictment. The precondition that they should all be capable of being tried under a single indictment excludes the operation of the section where one of the offences has already been prosecuted and the accused has been convicted, even if sentence has been deferred and the offence has not therefore been finally disposed of.

An example of the kind of situation contemplated in (*c*) is to be found in *Mackie* v *HM Advocate*.[10] The appellant was indicted in Glasgow Sheriff Court in respect of a charge of theft committed in Edinburgh. No attempt was made to argue that this was incompetent and standing the terms of the statutory predecessor of section 10 any such argument would have received short shrift. What was argued, however, was that the fact that the prosecutor had deserted (that is, dropped) the 'Glasgow' charges against the accused before the jury were empanelled, leaving only the 'Edinburgh' charge, meant that Glasgow Sheriff Court no longer had jurisdiction. The High Court held on appeal, however, that jurisdiction does not depend on what charges are remitted to the knowledge of the assize (that is, what charges are on the indictment when the jury take their oath at the start of the trial) but on whether the accused is lawfully indicted to the court. What happens thereafter is irrelevant.

District court jurisdiction

The district court may, in terms of section 6(2) of the 1995 Act, be constituted by a stipendiary magistrate (who is legally qualified) or by one or more justices (who need not be so qualified but occasionally are). By section 7(5) of the 1995 Act a district court which is constituted by a stipendiary magistrate has not only the jurisdiction of a district court but also the full summary criminal jurisdiction and powers of a sheriff.

[10] 1969 JC 20.

Accordingly, the remainder of what is said here about the jurisdiction of the district court relates to such courts when constituted by justices. At the time of writing, stipendiary magistrates exist only in Glasgow.

Section 7(1) of the 1995 Act provides that a district court shall continue to have all the jurisdiction and powers exercisable by it at the commencement of the Act. This means that it can continue to deal with common law offences but this is subject to section 7(8) of the 1995 Act, which precludes the district court from dealing with murder, culpable homicide, robbery, rape, wilful fireraising (or an attempt thereat), theft by housebreaking or housebreaking with intent to steal, offences of dishonesty where the value exceeds level 4 on the standard scale, provided for by section 225 of the 1995 Act (£2,500 at the time of writing), assault causing the fracture of a limb, assault with intent to ravish, assault to the danger of life, assault by stabbing, uttering forgeries or offences under the Acts relating to coinage.

So far as the offences involving violence are concerned, of course, the chances of the Crown proceeding in the district court even in the absence of this specific exclusion of jurisdiction would be quite remote.

The district court is, however, specifically empowered (by section 7(4) of the 1995 Act) to deal with theft, reset, fraud and embezzlement, provided the amount concerned does not exceed level 4.

The territorial jurisdiction of the district court is, by section 6 of the 1995 Act fixed by reference to its 'commission area', an expression which is defined as meaning the area of a local authority.

Section 7(2) of the 1995 Act is a direct equivalent to section 9(4) of that Act (which applies to the sheriff court). Accordingly, offences committed in multiple commission areas, which if they had all been committed in a single commission area could have been tried under one complaint, can be tried in any one of the relevant commission areas.

3 : THE PROSECUTION OF CRIME

Although centuries ago the Scottish criminal justice system had an inquisitorial aspect (which explains some of its present features) the system is now firmly adversarial, with the initiative being taken by the prosecution. Very considerable reliance is placed on the integrity and judgment of the public prosecutor, especially in the early stages of a prosecution. We must, therefore, understand the prosecution system if we are to understand the criminal justice system as a whole.

The overwhelming majority of prosecutions in Scotland are public prosecutions at the instance of either the Lord Advocate or the procurator fiscal. Cases under solemn procedure are prosecuted in the name of the Lord Advocate himself and those under summary procedure in the name of the procurator fiscal. By section 133(5) of the 1955 Act all summary prosecutions are to be brought at the instance of the procurator fiscal unless statute expressly provides to the contrary. Section 5(3) of the 1995 Act provides, without qualification, that all district court prosecutions are to be at the instance of the procurator fiscal.

Although it is possible for an individual who has suffered a personal wrong to apply to the court for authority to institute a prosecution, this procedure (known as a bill from criminal letters) is rarely invoked and hardly ever succeeds. Accordingly, the proportion of Scottish criminal cases which do not involve either the procurator fiscal or the Lord Advocate as prosecutor is so small that, in an introductory text such as this, they can safely be ignored. Even in summary prosecutions for offences under the Customs and Excise Management Act 1979, which are undertaken in the name of a customs officer and with the authority of the commissioners of Customs and Excise, the actual prosecution work is undertaken by the procurator fiscal.

The Lord Advocate

The principal prosecutor in Scotland is the Lord Advocate. He and the Solicitor-General for Scotland are the two Scottish law officers, ministers of the government equivalent to the Attorney-General and Solicitor-General in England and Wales (though the influence of the Lord Advocate on the Scottish prosecution process is far more pervasive than that of the Attorney-General south of the border). All indictments (the indictment is the document containing the charge in a serious case, prosecuted under solemn procedure) run in the name of the Lord Advocate whether they are tried in the High Court of Justiciary (the senior Scottish criminal court) or in the sheriff court. The only exception to this arises, in terms of section 287(2) of the 1995 Act, when the Lord Advocate's office is vacant. During such a vacancy, indictments are in the name of the Solicitor-General.

The Lord Advocate's office is an ancient one and in 1587 he was empowered by an Act of Parliament to instigate criminal proceedings notwithstanding the wishes of the parties.

Advocate-deputes

The Lord Advocate and the Solicitor-General are assisted in prosecution matters by the Advocate-deputes (of whom there are usually a dozen or so), who prosecute cases in the High Court and who give instructions on behalf of the Lord Advocate to procurators fiscal in connection with criminal cases. The Lord Advocate, the Solicitor-General and the Advocate-deputes are known collectively as Crown counsel.

Procurators fiscal

Brief history and functions

The procurator fiscal is a civil servant qualified as a solicitor, solicitor advocate or advocate. He or she is

> 'an independent public prosecutor, who receives and considers reports of crimes and offences from the police and over 40 other agencies and decides whether or not to take criminal proceedings in the public interest. He or she investigates the more serious cases and prosecutes all cases in court except the High Court'.[1]

The office of procurator fiscal has been recorded since 1584 but it certainly existed even before that date.

Originally, the sheriff combined both investigative and judicial functions, much like a continental examining magistrate. The procurator fiscal was originally an agent (procurator) employed by the sheriff to collect fines and pay them into the sheriff's treasury (the 'fisc'). However, the sheriff's investigative functions were gradually delegated to the procurator fiscal and his status as public prosecutor in the sheriff court was recognised by the Criminal Procedure Act 1701. His appointment was vested in the Lord Advocate by the Sheriff Courts and Legal Officers (Scotland) Act 1927.

Relationship with police and other investigators

Chief constables, and hence the police as a whole, must, by statute, obey the instructions they receive from the prosecutor in relation to the investigation of crime and cannot at their own hand commence a prosecution. Section 17(3) of the Police (Scotland) Act 1967 provides:

> '[I]n relation to the investigation of offences the chief constable shall comply with such lawful instructions as he may receive from the appropriate prosecutor.'

In similar vein, section 12 of the 1995 Act provides:

> 'The Lord Advocate may, from time to time, issue instructions to a chief constable with regard to the reporting, for consideration of the question of prosecution, of offences alleged to have been committed within the area of such chief constable, and it shall be the duty of a chief constable to whom any such instruction is issued to secure compliance therewith.'

Instructions from the Lord Advocate to chief constables tend to be in relation to classes of offence, while those from procurators fiscal tend to relate to particular cases. It is rare for the statutory provisions to be invoked explicitly but their existence underlies the whole relationship between Scottish prosecutors and the police.

[1] Crown Office and Procurator Fiscal Service Annual Report 1991/92, p 1.

The responsibility of the police as to reporting to the fiscal was considered in *Smith* v *HM Advocate*,[2] a murder by stabbing in which the police omitted to tell the fiscal that they had found not only the murder weapon but also a second knife at the locus. They reasoned that the second knife was irrelevant, as indeed it probably was. On appeal Lord Justice-Clerk Thomson had this to say about the duties of the police:

> '[I]t is their duty to put before the Procurator Fiscal everything which may be relevant and material to the issue of whether the suspected party is innocent or guilty ... a cautious officer will remember that he is not the judge of what is relevant and material and will tend to err on the safe side.'

There are no equivalent provisions with regard to non-police reporting agencies such as environmental health departments. To such agencies, the procurator fiscal can only offer advice. However, bearing in mind that such agencies have no right to initiate criminal proceedings but must depend upon the procurator fiscal to do so, one can usually expect that compliance with such advice will be prudent.

A report is submitted to the procurator fiscal whenever anyone aged sixteen or over is charged by the police, whenever the police have evidence which they think justifies charging a person they cannot find and whenever another investigating agency considers it appropriate to commence a prosecution. So far as the police are concerned, this follows from section 17(1)(b) of the Police (Scotland) Act 1967, which provides:

> '[I]t shall be the duty of the constables of a police force . . . (b) where an offence has been committed . . . to take all such lawful measures, and make such reports to the appropriate prosecutor, as may be necessary for the purpose of bringing the offender with all due speed to justice.'

The decision to prosecute

So far as other investigating agencies are concerned, the need to report to the procurator fiscal arises from the fact that there is no other way to commence criminal proceedings.

When the procurator fiscal receives a report of a crime it is his or her duty to consider it and decide whether or not to prosecute. This decision is taken under reference to such guidance and instructions as the Lord Advocate may have given either in general or, through Crown counsel, in relation to the particular case. The Lord Advocate's general guidance to procurators fiscal is not published and, although the effect of particular instructions will become apparent to the accused and his representatives from the course which the prosecution takes, those instructions will be treated as confidential.

The most fundamental assessment which the procurator fiscal will make as part of this decision-making process is whether or not there is sufficient evidence to prove a crime. This need not be the same crime with which the accused has been charged by the police. The procurator fiscal is in no sense bound by the assessment made of the case by the reporting agency and, by contrast with the position south of the border, the charging of a person by the police or other agency does not commence proceedings against that

---

[2] 1952 JC 66.

person. The concept of charging has, therefore, a very different significance in Scots law to that which it has in English law.

If the procurator fiscal is not satisfied, even after calling for such further information as may be helpful, that there is sufficient evidence to prove a crime, it is improper for him to commence proceedings or to take any other steps. His only option is to mark the report 'no proceedings'.

Once satisfied that there is sufficient evidence to proceed, the procurator fiscal's discretion comes into play. That discretion is considerable. By contrast with certain continental European jurisdictions, he is under no obligation to prosecute in every case in which a crime can be proved. There are alternatives to prosecution. However, his exercise of that discretion is something for which he is answerable only to the Lord Advocate and procurators fiscal decline to explain their decisions to anyone else. This is on the basis that

> 'the question of the guilt or innocence of the accused person falls to be determined by the court. So, when a decision is taken not to proceed against an individual, the reasons for that decision must be kept confidential, because it would be wrong for them to be discussed publicly in a way which would amount to a trial without the protection of the court. Similarly, when a trial is to follow, the evidence should not be paraded before the public until the trial'.[3]

Alternatives to prosecution

In some cases, the fiscal will decide that although there is sufficient evidence to proceed, the case is so trivial that further action is not needed. In other cases, a warning letter may be sent but that letter simply says that there is sufficient evidence to prosecute. It does not say that the fiscal has decided that the accused is guilty and it does not depend on an admission of guilt (Scottish police officers are not empowered to administer cautions in any formal sense). In some cases, diversion to the social work department or another similar agency might be a constructive way forward; the details of such schemes vary from place to place and from time to time. These are all informal options.

There is a formal option short of prosecution and that is the conditional offer, either by the police under section 75 of the Road Traffic Offenders Act 1988 or by the procurator fiscal under sections 302 and 303 of the 1995 Act.

Under those sections, where a procurator fiscal receives a report that a 'relevant offence' has been committed, he may send the alleged offender a notice giving particulars of the alleged offence and stating the amount of the appropriate fixed penalty for that offence and the arrangements for payment by instalments. If the alleged offender accepts the conditional offer by paying the first instalment of the fixed penalty he cannot then be prosecuted for the offence and the clerk to the district court will proceed to collect the remaining instalments. If the conditional offer is not accepted, the procurator can (and probably will) commence a prosecution.

Relevant offences are (by section 302(9)) those which can be tried in the district court. The appropriate fixed penalty is selected by the procurator fiscal from a sliding scale laid down in the Criminal Procedure (Scotland)

[3] Crown Office and Procurator Fiscal Service Annual Report 1991/92, p iii.

Act 1995 Fixed Penalty Order 1996. That Order sets the amount of penalties at £25, £50, £75 and £100.

Choice of procedure

Once the decision is made that the case should be prosecuted, the procurator fiscal must decide whether the case requires solemn procedure or summary and, if summary, whether the sheriff court or the district court. Once that decision has been taken he will commence proceedings.

The prosecutor as 'master of the instance'

Throughout the proceedings, until the accused is convicted (or acquitted), the prosecutor is in charge of his own case and is not subject to the directions of the court in its handling. So, in *Howdle* v *Beattie*[4] where a sheriff refused to allow a case to be called in Dumfries Sheriff Court because he thought that it would have been administratively preferable for it to be prosecuted in Kirkcudbright Sheriff Court it was held that a prosecutor has the right to decide whether a case will call in court on a given day and the sheriff cannot stop from calling the case. Moreover, it was decided in *Strathearn* v *Sloan*[5] that the prosecutor is not bound to accept a plea of guilty even to the whole indictment or complaint but may insist on proceeding to trial. In *Kirkwood* v *Coalburn District Co-operative Society*[6] it was held that a prosecutor is not bound to accept a plea to the minor of two alternative charges but is entitled to insist on leading evidence with a view to obtaining a conviction on the major alternative. According to *Clark* v *Donald*[7] the prosecutor is even entitled to substitute a new complaint for one which is still current.

The limits on the prosecutor's rights as master of the instance were set out in *HM Advocate* v *O'Neill*,[8] in which it was alleged to be oppressive for the Crown to proceed to trial against two accused and then indict the third separately. Lord Justice-General Hope said, in deciding the case:

> 'As Lord Justice Clerk Aitchison pointed out in *Clark*[9] . . . there is no doubt that in the ordinary case the court will only with the greatest reluctance interfere with the discretion of the Crown. But its power to do so is beyond question, and in all these cases where oppression is alleged, or where it is suggested that there is a material risk of grave prejudice to the accused, the ultimate decision must rest with the court.'

In *O'Neill* the court decided that there was no oppression, by contrast with *Normand* v *McQuillan*[10] in which a sheriff held that where the accused pled not guilty to complaint and was remanded in custody it was oppressive to substitute a petition two weeks later containing no new charges. The petition is the document which commences a prosecution under solemn procedure under which, as we shall see, the period during which the accused can be kept in custody before trial is longer than that under summary procedure.

[4] 1995 SCCR 349.
[5] 1937 JC 76.
[6] 1930 JC 38.
[7] 1962 JC 1.
[8] 1992 SCCR 130.
[9] 1935 JC 51.
[10] 1987 SCCR 440 (Sh Ct).

4 : INVESTIGATION OF CRIME

The first contact which a victim or offender will have with the criminal justice system will almost certainly be with the police or another investigating agency. In the course of their investigations, such agencies frequently require to use powers, granted to them by the law, which are not available to private citizens. These include powers of entry to premises, of search and seizure and of detention and arrest. Plainly, such powers require to be regulated, because they affect the liberty of the individual and his right to the enjoyment of his property and liberty without undue interference by the state. That regulation takes the form in part of detailed provision as to the extent of such investigative powers (especially in Part II of the 1995 Act) and in part of a tendency to refuse to admit in evidence material which has been obtained by means which violate those provisions or which are regarded as unfair in the circumstances of the case. Our consideration of police functions therefore incorporates elements of both procedure and evidence.

The police have the right to use their powers to investigate any crime. The powers granted to other investigating agencies are so granted only in relation to a limited range of crimes and can only properly be exercised in relation to those crimes. So the competence of HM Customs and Excise is limited to what are called 'assigned matters'. 'Assigned matter' is defined, in a somewhat circular way, by section 1 of the Customs and Excise Management Act 1979 as 'any matter in relation to which the commissioners [of Customs and Excise] are for the time being required in pursuance of any enactment to perform any duties'. As regards those matters customs officers have powers which are at least as significant as those of the police and customs officers must be regarded as the most important investigators after the police. However, there are several dozen other agencies with powers of investigation, which include the Health and Safety Executive, Environmental Health Departments and Departments of Trading Standards and Consumer Protection. The powers which they exercise vary and in each case it is necessary to look to the statute under which they operate to determine the extent of those powers.

Whatever the basis and extent of the powers which are exercised by particular investigators, the principles which the law will apply to the exercise of those powers are common. Perhaps the most fundamental principle is that, since powers of this sort tend to infringe the liberty of the subject, they will be construed strictly and powers which Parliament has not given expressly are unlikely to be implied by the courts.

It would be a mistake to assume that the fact that an investigator has exceeded his or her powers will automatically mean that the evidence which he or she has obtained thereby will be inadmissible. As we shall see, the courts are prepared, in deciding questions relating to admissibility of evidence, to excuse some excesses of zeal, especially where the investigator has acted in good faith but has made an honest mistake. On this point it is worth contrasting two cases. The first is *Lawrie* v *Muir*[1] in which a Milk Marketing Board inspector obtained entry to premises by a mis-representation and the subsequent conviction was quashed. The court pointed out that an irregularity in the method by which evidence has been obtained does not necessarily make that evidence inadmissible and that whether a given irregularity should be excused depends on its nature and the circumstances, an important consideration being fairness to the accused. It declined to make any distinction in this between statute and common law offences.

That principle was applied to the benefit of the prosecution in *Fairley* v *Fishmongers of London*[2] in which the appellant had been charged with possession of salmon contrary to a particular regulation. Essential evidence was the result of a search by an inspector charged with the enforcement of that regulation, accompanied by an officer charged with the enforcement of other regulations. The inspector had not obtained a warrant (though he could have done). The officer had obtained a warrant, but not under the regulations relating to salmon. It was held, applying *Lawrie*, that the evidence, although obtained irregularly was admissible. Lord Justice-General Cooper said, in the course of his judgment:

> 'I can find nothing to suggest that any departure from the strict procedure was deliberately adopted with a view to securing the admission of evidence obtained by an unfair trick, and in the circumstances of this case the appellant's assumption of the guise of a champion of the liberties of the subject failed to elicit my sympathies.'

The correct approach, therefore, is to examine the exercise of a power to see, first, whether it has been exercised in accordance with the law or irregularly and, second, if there has been irregularity whether that irregularity is one which may be excused or whether it is fatal to the admissibility of the evidence.

Detention and arrest

We begin with detention and arrest, because changes in the other types of powers exercised by the police and customs officers tend to flow from changes in the status of the suspect. It is worth remembering, however, that considerable investigative work may have been done before detention or arrest takes place. In particular, there may already have been searches carried out.

Detention
Section 14 of the 1995 Act reproduces what was originally contained in section 2 of the Criminal Justice (Scotland) Act 1980, under reference to which the case-law has developed. Section 14(1) provides as follows.

> 'Where a constable has reasonable grounds for suspecting that a person has committed or is committing an offence punishable by imprisonment, the constable may, for the purpose of facilitating the carrying out of investigations—
> (a) into the offence; and
> (b) as to whether criminal proceedings should be instigated against the person,

[1] 1950 JC 19.
[2] 1951 JC 14.

22

detain that person and take him as quickly as is reasonably practicable to a police station or other premises and may thereafter for that purpose take him to any other place and, subject to the following provisions of this section, the detention may continue at the police station or, as the case may be, the other premises or place.'

Customs officers have an identical power in terms of section 24 of the Criminal Law (Consolidation) (Scotland) Act 1995 and the cases on detention by police officers apply equally to that power.

No other investigators have such a power to detain. It should be noted, however, that 'constable' is not confined to officers of ordinary police forces. *Smith* v *Dudgeon*[3] decided that officers of the British Transport Police were also constables for the purposes of the section and officers of other special police forces, such as the Ministry of Defence Police, would also be included on the same reasoning.

Reasonable grounds for suspicion

The constable must have 'reasonable grounds for suspecting' that the person to be detained has committed or is committing an offence. What will amount to such reasonable grounds will vary infinitely with the circumstances of the case but the phrase is one which appears commonly in legislation which grants the police particular powers and is quite well understood in practice.

The phrase was considered by the High Court on appeal in *Wilson* v *Robertson*[4] in which it was argued that in the particular circumstances the constables concerned could not have had such grounds.

The facts were that police officers saw that the fire door of a club had been interfered with by someone from the inside some time before a theft in the club. The accused had been the only strangers in the club at the relevant time and had been the last to leave. Moreover, they were in the vicinity of the club car park when the club was locked for the night. The sheriff considered that these facts provided reasonable grounds for the relevant suspicion and the High Court agreed. Lord Justice-General Emslie said:

> 'We are concerned here not with evidence as to guilt. We are concerned here simply to know whether there were reasonable grounds on which a police officer might entertain a suspicion that the appellants had committed the offence.'

The standard required seems, therefore, to be quite low. That receives some confirmation from cases like *Dryburgh* v *Galt*,[5] in which an anonymous telephone call was held to be a sufficiently reasonable ground for police officers to suspect that a man had been drinking and driving and to operate the power under the Road Traffic Acts to require the provision of a specimen of breath for a breath test. In that case, the court followed *McNichol* v *Peters*,[6] *Copeland* v *McPherson*[7] and *Allan* v *Douglas*,[8] and Lord Justice-Clerk Wheatley summarised the effect of these cases thus:

[3] 1983 SLT 324.
[4] 1986 SCCR 700.
[5] 1981 SCCR 26.
[6] 1969 SLT 261.
[7] 1970 SLT 87.
[8] 1978 JC 7.

'[T]he fact that the information on which the police officer formed his suspicion turns out to be ill-founded does not in itself necessarily establish that the police officer's suspicion was unfounded. The circumstances known to the police officer at the time he formed his suspicion constitute the criterion, not the facts as subsequently ascertained. The circumstances may be either what the police officer has himself observed or the information which he has received.'

It seems clear, then, that it is incorrect to judge the adequacy of the grounds according to the ordinary rules of evidence and equally incorrect to judge with hindsight. What matters is the honest, subjective suspicion at the time.

The suspicion must relate to the commission of an offence which is punishable by imprisonment. This includes all common law offences. Where the offence suspected is a statutory offence, the potential penalty will be set out or referred to in the statute.

Right to enter property

Where the criteria are satisfied, a constable may 'detain' the person and *Turnbull* v *Scott*[9] is authority for the proposition that, in some cases at least, the police may enter a private house in order to do so. In that case, they saw the accused in the house but he would not come to the door. Finding a door ajar, they went in, where he attacked them. It was held that they were in the execution of their duty and, it follows, acting properly.

Information to be given to suspect

At the time when a constable detains someone he is required, by section 14(6) of the 1995 Act, to inform that person of his suspicion, of the general nature of the offence suspected and of the reason for the detention. The person detained is not obliged to answer any question other than to give his name and address and must be told so.

Taking of suspect to police station

A person who has been detained must be taken as quickly as is reasonably practicable to the police station or other premises.

The meaning of the phrase 'as quickly as is reasonably practicable' was considered in *Menzies* v *HM Advocate*.[10] In that case the appellant had been detained outside Airdrie Police Station by police officers from Dunfermline. They did not take him into Airdrie Police Station but took him instead to Dunfermline Police Station, where he made an incriminating statement. It was objected that the statement should not have been admitted and argued that the requirement to take the suspect to a police station as quickly as is reasonably practicable meant that the police had to take him to the nearest police station.

On appeal, the High Court did not agree. It considered that the phrase 'as quickly as is reasonably practicable' 'is conditioned by what is reasonably practicable, according to the circumstances as they present themselves at the time to the constable by whom the person is detained'. In *Menzies* there was evidence that there was substantial documentation

---

[9] 1990 SCCR 614.
[10] High Court, 25th May 1995; unreported.

relevant to the case at Dunfermline and also that the interviewing facilities in Airdrie Police Station were under considerable pressure at the relevant time. The High Court characterised these as 'understandable operational reasons' and held that there was no breach of the requirements of the section.

'Other premises' is not defined and has not been judicially considered.

After the detainee has been taken to the police station or other premises he may then be taken 'to another place' where the detention may continue. The purpose of this is to allow for him to be taken to hospital, for example, if he requires treatment or to a place where he has offered to point out evidence to the police.

Questioning

On arrival at the police station the detainee is entitled in terms of section 15 of the 1995 Act to be told that he has a right to have a third party and solicitor informed of the detention and where he is being held. While he is there certain matters, such as his time of arrival and the nature of the offence, must, by virtue of section 14(6) of the 1995 Act, be recorded. There are forms available to the police for making that record but it was held in *Cummings* v *HM Advocate*[11] that it is enough if the record is made in the officer's notebook. In that case the High Court was disparaging about the proposition that failure to make the record renders inadmissible any evidence obtained during the detention but did not require to decide the point.

The purpose of detention is to allow the constable to put questions to the detainee and to exercise the same powers of search which could be exercised following arrest. Section 14(7) of the 1995 Act empowers the police to do both these things.

The right to question is expressed to be without prejudice to existing rules of law as regards the admissibility in evidence of any answer given. Lord Cameron gave effect to this in *HM Advocate* v *Bell*,[12] holding that the legislation did not rule out the admissibility of a comment made by a suspect or an accused person when that comment related to something said by a police officer in answer to a question asked by the suspect himself.

Section 14(9) of the 1995 Act requires that the suspect is told upon being detained that he is not obliged to answer any question other than to give his name and address and the relationship between this and subsection (7) has required comment by the courts.

The most important case is *Tonge* v *HM Advocate*.[13] The facts of that case were somewhat complex but for present purposes it is enough to note that the police relied on the forerunner of subsection (9) rather than giving a full caution. This was a significant factor in the High Court's decision that the answers obtained were inadmissible. Lord Justice-General Emslie finished his judgment with the words

'I would strongly urge police officers throughout Scotland who proceed to accuse a detainee or to question him or to take from him a voluntary statement to rely not at all on the effect of the warning described in [the legislation].'

[11] 1982 SCCR 108.
[12] High Court, Glasgow, 10th September 1981; unreported.
[13] 1982 SLT 506.

At an earlier stage of his judgment he had referred to the provision that the right to question is without prejudice to any relevant rule of law regarding the admissibility in evidence of any answer given and said:

> 'The position is, accordingly, that the admissibility in evidence of anything said by a detainee falls to be determined by the common law and where the common law and proper practice would require, in the interests of fairness and fair dealing, that a full common law caution be given, the omission to give it before questioning a suspect who has received no more than the limited warning prescribed by [the Act] will, at the very least, on that account alone, place admissibility of any evidence elicited from the suspect in peril.'

The converse situation, in which the statutory warning was not given but a common law caution was, arose in *Scott v Howie*.[14] Lord Justice-General Hope treated the omission of the statutory warning as being of no significance and, on the basis that the common law caution had been given, held that the evidence of the statement made was not open to objection. Commenting on this decision, Sheriff Gordon said:

> 'The court do not specifically indicate whether a failure to give a . . . warning renders the detention unlawful and/or deprives the police of their right to hold the detainee for questioning, but their decision suggests that it does not.'[15]

Termination of detention

By section 14(2) of the 1995 Act detention cannot be continued beyond six hours and must in any event cease if the grounds for it cease. At the end of that time the accused must be arrested or released unless some other statutory power to detain (as for terrorism) supervenes. It does not follow, however, that failure to follow this procedure precisely will inevitably render evidence obtained inadmissible. *Grant v HM Advocate*[16] was a case in which an appeal was taken against the admissibility of evidence of a reply made by the appellant while he was detained under the section during the statutory six-hour period. It was said that he had not been arrested on the charge until some twenty minutes after the expiry of the statutory period and that this rendered his reply inadmissible in evidence. The High Court held that there was no express provision in the section which retrospectively invalidated processes carried out within the statutory period if that period was by chance exceeded and that no such consequence could be implied.

Arrest

Arrest goes beyond detention. It is much less temporary and has more far-reaching consequences. Lord Cameron considered the concept in *Swankie v Milne*[17] and, although the words he used have been rendered more liable to confusion by the introduction of a specific statutory power of detention, read with care they are still of considerable value. The 'detention' to which Lord Cameron referred was a thoroughly informal affair. He said:

> 'An arrest is something which in law differs from a detention by the police at their invitation or suggestion. In the latter case a person detained or invited to accompany police officers is, at that stage, under no legal compulsion to accept

[14] 1993 SCCR 81.
[15] 1993 SCCR 81 at 86, Commentary.
[16] 1989 SCCR 618.
[17] 1973 JC 1.

the detention or invitation. . . . I think it is important always to keep clear the distinction between arrest, which is a legal act taken by officers of law duly authorised to do so and while acting in the course of their duty, carrying with it certain important legal consequences, and the mere detention of a person by a police officer. . . . Once arrested not only is the freedom of action of the person arrested circumscribed but he is also placed in the protection of the law in respect eg of questioning by a police officer.'

The arrest of a person is a serious step, and one which, if challenged, requires to be justified; though this is by no means the same as saying that an invalid arrest will operate as a bar to prosecution.

Where a warrant has been granted by a court for the arrest of a person a police officer is unlikely to have much difficulty in justifying that course.

Arrest without warrant

In terms of section 21 of the 1995 Act any constable may take into custody without warrant any person whom he sees committing or has reason to believe has committed any of the offences mentioned in Schedule 1 to the Act, if the constable does not know and cannot ascertain his name and address or if there is reasonable ground to believe he will abscond. The offences mentioned in Schedule 1 are various sexual offences and offences involving bodily injury to a child under the age of seventeen.

There are wide powers of arrest at common law but their limits have never been defined clearly. The case-law tends to be concerned with civil actions for damages in respect of wrongful arrest and contains no fully satisfactory statement of the law for criminal purposes. This is partly because a wrongful arrest does not render subsequent proceedings void (since the procurator fiscal is not bound by the actions of the police) and does not inevitably render evidence obtained as a result of the arrest inadmissible. As always, the question is one of fairness and, although it would be possible to make a strong case for the proposition that but for the wrongful arrest the accused would never have made a statement or a search would never have taken place, the courts are likely to balance that with the interests of the public in the effective investigation of crime. Much will depend on the good faith, or otherwise, of the officers concerned.

It may be said that a constable may arrest in safety without a warrant if he witnesses a crime or breach of the peace being committed or attempted or violence being threatened or if he sees the offender in flight from the crime. He may also arrest on credible information that a serious crime has recently been committed or attempted, at any rate if there is a probability that the offender will abscond.

Telling the suspect he has been arrested

An arrested person is entitled to know that he has been arrested and to be told the nature of the charge, at least in general terms. In *Forbes v HM Advocate*[18] the accused had been taken into custody under the Prevention of Terrorism (Temporary Provisions) Act 1984 but since that legislation referred to the 'detention' of a person the word 'arrest' was not used. Nor

[18] 1990 SCCR 69.

was he told in words what the nature of the charge was but he was allowed to read a search warrant which contained that information.

Lord Justice-General Hope gave the judgment of the court and dealt first with the issue of telling the accused that he been arrested. He said that the word 'arrest' need not itself be used though it is desirable that it should be made clear to the person concerned that he is under legal compulsion and that his freedom of action is being curtailed'. He desiderated the use of clear and simple language for this purpose but, citing *Alderson* v *Booth*,[19] said that any form of words will do if they bring to the notice of the person concerned that he is under compulsion and he submits to that compulsion. The actions of the police officer, he said, may themselves be enough to convey the nature of what he is doing.

So far as information about the nature of the charge was concerned, Lord Hope said that a mere statement that the appellant had been detained under section 12 of the 1984 Act would not have been enough but that allowing him to read the search warrant was 'sufficient', when taken together with the words used by the police officers, to provide the appellant with the information which he was entitled to have as to the general nature and true ground of his arrest'.

Interview with solicitor

In terms of section 17 of the 1995 Act, an arrested person is entitled to have a solicitor told of the arrest; but there is no entitlement to an interview while in police hands. Such an entitlement only arises, as a result of subsection (2), before the accused appears in court. In practice, however, an interview while in police hands will usually be granted because refusal of an interview with a solicitor will be a significant factor in deciding whether any admission subsequently made was obtained fairly and thus admissible in evidence, as Lord Moncrieff made clear in *HM Advocate* v *Cunningham*[20] and in *HM Advocate* v *Fox*.[21]

Action following arrest

Following arrest, in terms of section 21(2) of the 1995 Act, one of three things may be done with the person who has been arrested. He may be liberated on a signed, written undertaking to present himself at a specified court at a specified time (failure to answer such an undertaking is an offence); or he may simply be liberated; or he may be kept in custody, in which event he must be placed before the court on the first lawful day after he has been taken into custody (except in terrorist cases where the period allowed is forty-eight hours or five days with the authority of the Secretary of State). The next lawful day is simply the next day on which the court sits and the practice is to convene a court in the middle of an extended public holiday (such as at Christmas) in order to deal with persons arrested and kept in custody. There is, of course, nothing to prevent the fiscal simply ordering the release of an accused person—it is consistent with the general rule that the police cannot oblige him to proceed in court against anyone.

[19] [1969] 2 QB 216.
[20] 1939 JC 61.
[21] 1947 JC 30.

Questioning of suspects and others

Initial investigation

When investigators begin their inquiries into a crime it may well be that all they know is that a crime has been committed. Their information may be sparse and, in particular, they might have no idea who committed the crime. Accordingly, Lord Justice-General Cooper said in *Chalmers* v *HM Advocate*:[22]

> '[A]t the stage of initial investigation the police may question anyone with a view to acquiring information which may lead to the detection of the criminal.'

Inevitably, those whom the police question will sometimes include the person whom they come to suspect of being the perpetrator of the crime. Sometimes, indeed, it will be that person's replies to their questions during initial investigation which focus their attention upon him. Thus in *Milne* v *Cullen*[23] the accused had been pointed out to police officers as the person who had been driving a car which had been involved in an accident. They asked him, without cautioning him, whether that was so and his reply that it was was held admissible. And in *Wingate* v *McGlennon*[24] police officers saw the accused carrying a pickaxe handle. They asked him why, without cautioning him first, and he told them he had been assaulted and was looking for those responsible. He was arrested, charged, prosecuted and convicted of possession of an offensive weapon. It was held that the reply was admissible.

Particular suspicion

There comes a point, however, at which the investigators begin to have suspicions about a particular person. This progression was recognised in *Chalmers* v *HM Advocate* and, immediately after the passage quoted above, the Lord Justice-General went on to say:

> '[W]hen the stage has been reached at which suspicion, or more than suspicion, has in their view centred upon some person as the likely perpetrator of the crime, further interrogation of that person becomes very dangerous and if carried too far, eg to the point of extracting a confession by what amounts to cross examination, the evidence of that confession will almost certainly be excluded.'

Chalmers has been the subject of considerable critical comment over the years but Lord Cooper's remarks nevertheless provide a convenient basis for consideration of the essentials of the law. As he made clear, once suspicion has centred upon a person investigators are more constrained but neither Lord Cooper nor any succeeding judge has said that the answers to questions at that stage will certainly be excluded. Such exclusion depends upon questioning being taken too far, such as into cross-examination. It was on this that Lord Avonside was commenting in *Hartley* v *HM Advocate*[25] when he said:

> 'Firstly, police officers may question a suspect so long as they do not stray into the field of interrogation. Secondly, and most importantly, cross examination is just what it means. It consists in questioning an adverse witness in an effort to

[22] 1954 SLT 177.
[23] 1967 JC 31.
[24] 1991 SCCR 133.
[25] 1979 SLT 26.

break down his evidence, to weaken or prejudice his evidence, or to elicit statements damaging to him and aiding the case of the cross examiner.'

In similar vein, in *Jones* v *Milne*[26] Lord Justice-General Emslie said:

'The mere fact that a suspected person is asked a question or questions by a police officer before or after being cautioned is not in itself unfairness and if answers are to be excluded they must be seen to have been extracted by unfair means which place cross examination, pressure and deceit in close company.'

The fairness test

The courts now consistently emphasise that the test is one of fairness. One of the clearest expressions of this came in *Brown* v *HM Advocate*[27] in which Lord Justice-General Clyde said:

'It is not possible to lay down *ab ante* the precise circumstances in which answers given to the police prior to a charge being made are admissible in evidence at the ultimate trial or where they are inadmissible. This is so much a question of the particular circumstances of each case and those circumstances vary infinitely from one another. But *the test in all of them is the simple and intelligible test which has worked well in practice—has what has taken place been fair or not?* Just for this reason, because the circumstances in each case vary so much from one another, I do not consider that it is helpful to examine in detail the circumstances leading up to the confession in this case. A meticulous examination of these circumstances only leads in future cases to the creation of subtle distinctions between one decision and another on a matter where the true criterion is neither subtle nor complicated, but is the broad principle of fair play to the accused' (emphasis added).

The courts also stress the issue of fairness to the public interest and we may remind ourselves of Lord Wheatley's remarks in *Milne* v *Cullen*:[28]

'[I]t is the function of the court to seek to provide a proper balance to secure that the rights of individuals are properly preserved, while not hamstringing the police in their investigation of crime with a series of academic vetoes which ignore the realities and practicalities of the situation and discount completely the public interest.'

Griffiths has commented that 'The modern fairness test virtually defies analysis.'[29] This might well be because it is inherently subjective and whether something is fair or not is not a question of law. It is regarded as a question of fact, for determination by the jury and not by the judge. In support of this proposition it is usual to quote the words of Lord Cameron in *HM Advocate* v *Whitelaw*,[30] approved by the High Court in *Tonge* v *HM Advocate*.[31]

'Evidence as to statements of a possibly incriminating character alleged to have been made by an accused person is prima facie of the highest relevance and the jury's function should not be in fact usurped and unless it is abundantly clear that the rules of fairness and fair dealing have been flagrantly transgressed it would be better for a jury seized of the whole evidence in the case and of all the

[26] 1975 SLT 2.
[27] 1966 SLT 105.
[28] 1967 JC 21.
[29] D B Griffiths, *Confessions* (1994) p 49.
[30] 1980 SLT (Notes) 25.
[31] 1982 SLT 506.

circumstances, under such guidance as they should receive from the presiding judge, themselves to take that decision as to the extent to which, if at all, they will take into account evidence of statements or given by a suspect after due caution.'

This fits in well with Lord Clyde's rejection, in *Brown*, of an approach which involved comparison and distinction of cases. That is appropriate where the question at issue is one of law but where what is to be decided is fairness in the circumstances of a particular case, what another tribunal has made of other circumstances cannot help and might well cause a jury to feel unduly constrained in their decision.

Cautioning
Many considerations will be relevant to what is fair but, as we have already noted, the High Court in *Tonge* v *HM Advocate*[32] laid particular stress on the matter of the giving of a caution. Lord Emslie's words will be re-called.

'[W]here the common law and proper practice would require, in the interests of fairness and fair dealing, that a full common law caution be given, the omission to give it before questioning a suspect . . . will, at the very least, on that account alone, place, the admissibility of any evidence elicited from the suspect in peril.'

Tonge came a few years after *HM Advocate* v *Von*,[33] a case in which Lord Ross had to deal in the course of a trial with an objection to the admissibility of a confession. The objection was based on the fact that no caution had been given and, in sustaining that objection, Lord Ross said:

'I do not consider that a statement can be regarded as being fairly obtained if the accused was never advised of the fact that under our law no person is required to incriminate himself.'

These cases are somewhat difficult to reconcile with the 1992 case of *Pennycook* v *Lees*.[34] In that case the appellant had been convicted of a contravention of section 65 of the Social Security Act 1986 in respect that he had made false statements that he had not worked because of incapacity in order to get benefits. Such matters are investigated by DSS officers.

Pennycook was interviewed twice without caution. On the first occasion he was under investigation and the officers wished to satisfy themselves that the man they had been following was indeed James Pennycook who was receiving sickness benefit. He said he was and signed a withdrawal of his claims for sickness benefit and income support.

Some months later he was seen again by the same officers and told that he was being interviewed in relation to an overpayment; he admitted signing the claim forms and only then was he cautioned. The evidence in relation to both interviews was objected to but the sheriff repelled the objection and the High Court sustained the conviction. The High Court took the view that in the first interview the officers were trying to determine whether there was any offence to investigate and that in the second interview, although the officers knew there had been an offence committed by the appellant, since there was an absence of pressure or deception and the

---

[32] *Ibid.*
[33] 1979 SLT (Notes) 62.
[34] 1992 SCCR 160.

appellant knew what was going on the sheriff had been entitled to conclude that there was no unfairness and allow the evidence.

There can be no doubt that a person who is being questioned in a police station knows perfectly well what is going on, and this is especially so in cases such as *Tonge* where the accused has received a statutory warning that he need not say anything. Yet the evidence in *Tonge* and in *Von* was held to be inadmissible. The investigators in *Pennycook* were not exercising any special powers which enabled them to dispense with the caution. There must be a suspicion that the High Court demands a higher standard from the police than from others but it remains to be seen whether future decisions will make the position clearer.

There are, in fact, a number of statutes which empower investigators to ask questions which must be answered. In some cases the answers are excluded from evidence and an example of this is to be found in section 20(2)(j) and (7) of the Health and Safety at Work etc Act 1974. In other cases, however, the answers are admissible. The most common example of this is probably section 172 of the Road Traffic Act 1988, which empowers police officers to require certain persons to tell them who was driving a motor-car at the time of an alleged offence and which makes it an offence to fail to do so. In considering the statutory predecessors of section 172 the High Court held in both *Foster* v *Farrell*[35] and *Tudhope* v *Dalgleish*[36] that in such cases a caution is not only inappropriate, but positively wrong. It would, of course, be a nonsense to tell someone that he is not obliged to answer a question when the law prescribes a criminal penalty for declining to do so.

A similar point arose in *Styr* v *HM Advocate*.[37] That was an insider dealing case in which inspectors were appointed under section 177 of the Financial Services Act 1986, which provides that such inspectors may require 'all assistance' and examine persons on oath. Subsection (6) provides explicitly that a statement made by a person in compliance with the section may be used in evidence against him. It was argued by the defence that a caution should have been administered. In giving the judgment, Lord Justice-Clerk Ross said:

> 'When an inspector appointed under section 177 is carrying out an investigation [into insider dealing] he is fully entitled to put any questions which he thinks appropriate to the person whom he is examining on oath . . . there was no need to administer a caution in the present case. We would stress that the investigation which the inspectors were carrying out was quite different from police enquiries. In police enquiries the person being questioned is not placed on oath, he cannot be compelled to answer, and he commits no offence if he refuses to answer.'

Section 177 inspections are rare creatures; but there are an increasing number of statues dealing with what might be called 'regulatory' matters which establish similar powers to require information, though not always on oath. The reasoning in *Styr* is likely to apply in such cases. It seems that in any case where statute empowers an investigator to ask questions the sections surrounding that power should be checked for an indication as to Parliament's intentions as to admissibility, bearing in mind other words of Lord Ross in *Von*:[38]

[35] 1963 SLT 182.
[36] 1986 SCCR 559.
[37] 1993 SCCR 278.
[38] 1979 SLT (Notes) 62.

'I cannot believe that Parliament intended to alter the well-established principle of our law that no man can be compelled to incriminate himself. If Parliament had intended to do so I would have expected it to be made clear.'

It is clear from *HM Advocate* v *Friel*[39] that a caution will not be a universal panacea for otherwise unfair practice. In that case, customs officers subjected the accused to a sixteen-hour interview, during the latter part of which they conducted what amounted to a cross-examination of him. That, it will be recalled, was one of the practices which was to be deprecated in *Hartley*. The evidence was held to be inadmissible. Nevertheless, a caution having been given, it may be difficult for the defence to argue successfully that the evidence should not be allowed. In *Heywood* v *Smith*[40] a person was detained because she smelled of cannabis. One officer searched her and found a suspicious substance, which the suspect promptly swallowed. In the presence of another officer the first officer cautioned and charged the suspect with attempt to pervert the course of justice to which she made an incriminating reply which was held admissible. The fact that, without the reply there would have been insufficient evidence against her availed her nothing.

Not only that, but a reply to a charge of committing one crime will be admissible at trial in relation to a different crime of the same category (violence, dishonesty, etc) arising out of the same *species facti*, at least if the crime actually prosecuted is less serious than that originally charged. Thus in *Willis* v *HM Advocate*[41] a reply made to a charge of murder was allowed in a trial for culpable homicide; and in *McAdam* v *HM Advocate*[42] a reply to a charge of assault to severe injury was allowed at a trial for attempted murder.

Questioning after charge

Once the police have charged the accused person, replies to further questions which they ask about that charge will be inadmissible. In *Stark & Smith* v *HM Advocate*[43] two men who had been charged with theft were questioned about that charge while in the police cells and the evidence of the reply one of them made was held to be inadmissible. This was followed in *Wade* v *Robertson*[44] in which a man was in custody charged with the theft of whisky. While he was incarcerated his lodging were searched and a stolen bottle was found. He was confronted with this and cautioned whereupon he made an incriminating statement. This too was held inadmissible.

It should be noted, however, that *Johnston* v *HM Advocate*[45] is authority for a (short) delay in charging after arrest during which there may be questioning. The accused in a murder case was at first interviewed, without caution, as a prospective witness. What he said was suspicious and he was at that point cautioned. He made a highly incriminating statement and was arrested. After arrest but before charge he was interviewed, having been reminded of the caution. He was asked specific questions about the weapon and damage to his own clothing and made certain admissions.

[39] 1978 SLT (Notes) 21.
[40] 1989 SCCR 391.
[41] 1941 JC 1.
[42] 1960 JC 1.
[43] 1938 JC 170.
[44] 1948 JC 117.
[45] 1993 SCCR 693.

The court found it hard to understand why the police had arrested the accused rather than detaining him but was not persuaded by a defence argument that a person who has been arrested cannot then be questioned. The heart of the decision seems to be a passage in Lord Justice-Clerk Ross's judgment:

> '[A]rrest may be justified on less material than is required for charge and . . . there is no justification for a general rule of law that arresting a person would debar the police from ordinary questioning provided that the questioning was not unfair. In the present case the appellant was arrested and told the general nature of the charge on which the arrest was made. Thereafter in my opinion the police were entitled to question the appellant provided that the ordinary rules of fairness were observed . . . the trial judge left the issue of fairness to the jury and in my judgment he was entirely correct to do so.'

None of this prevents the police from asking questions about other matters. In *MacDonald* v *HM Advocate*[46] the accused had been charged with conspiracy to commit robberies and with committing a particular robbery. His answers to questions about other robberies were allowed.

Tape-recorded interviews
A related question is that of the tape recording of interviews with accused persons. This practice began experimentally in May 1980 in Dundee and Falkirk and the experiment was extended in 1982 to Aberdeen and part of Glasgow. The research concluded that there were benefits to be gained from national implementation of the scheme and it is now the position that tape recording should take place in all CID interviews of those over the age of sixteen likely to be prosecuted in the sheriff court or the High Court. It should be understood that the practice of tape recording and its extent are not governed by legislation but rather by guidance issued to the police by the Secretary of State. That guidance has no legal significance and in particular it is not an enforceable code.

The practice was first noted in a reported case in *Lord Advocate's Reference (No 1 of 1983)*.[47] That case proceeded upon the basis that admissibility was to be determined according to the ordinary test of fairness, described above.

Once proceedings have been commenced, the tapes are transcribed by the Procurator Fiscal's Office and the transcript is served on the accused at least fourteen days before the trial. Where this is done, a certified transcript is to be received in evidence and is sufficient evidence of the making of the transcript and of its accuracy, all in terms of section 277 of the 1995 Act unless the accused serves notice under section 277(2) that he challenges the making of the transcript or its accuracy.

Where such a notice is served, the evidence of the person who made it is sufficient evidence of its making and accuracy in terms of section 277(4). This provision is rarely invoked in practice, however. The real issue tends to be that of fairness, which can often be resolved by the lodging of the tape as a production and the playing of the tape to the sheriff or jury. Where this is done, it is desirable for one of the police officers involved to speak to the contents of the tape, but in *Hudson* v *Hamilton*[48] the proposition that it

[46] 1987 SCCR 581.
[47] 1984 SCCR 62.
[48] 1992 SCCR 541.

should be played during the evidence of the second interviewing officer also was described by the High Court as a pure formality and a waste of the court's time.

It sometimes happens that a recording includes prejudicial material, such as the disclosure of previous convictions. In such a case, *Tunnicliffe* v *HM Advocate*[49] is authority for the proposition that the recording should be edited and that the playing of the unedited tape cannot be cured by directions. The same principle presumably applies to transcripts. Editing is, of course, done on copies so that the original and best evidence is preserved.

Search

The other investigative tool enjoyed by the police and other agencies is search of persons and of premises.

Is it a search?

Before any attempt is made to apply the law of search to the recovery of material it is as well to be sure that what has been done actually has amounted to a search. In *Devlin* v *Normand*[50] a prison officer formed the suspicion that a visitor had something in her mouth. He asked her to open her mouth and to give him the package which he saw there. She did so and it turned out to be cannabis resin. The defence argued that this was an unlawful search and that the evidence was therefore inadmissible; but the High Court held on appeal that no search took place at all within the proper meaning of that expression. Rather, the court characterised what happened as a request complied with voluntarily, basing the distinction on the absence of any element of force in what was done. Accordingly, the evidence was admissible.

The decision in *Devlin* was in line with *Davidson* v *Brown*,[51] in which police officers, for another purpose, stopped a car in which the appellant was a passenger. They saw a closed plastic bin in her possession and asked to see inside it. She handed it to them and they found it to contain stolen property. Objection was taken and repelled. On appeal the High Court held, as they were to do in Devlin, that there was no search but merely a voluntary act on the part of the accused. In this, they founded on an opinion delivered by Lord Justice-General Emslie in *Lucas* v *Lockhart*,[52] in which he said:

> '[I]f the sheriff had thought that . . . the appellant, was a volunteer in the matter of search he would not have had to waste his time or ours upon a consideration of the statutory warrant under which the search purported to be carried out.'

Baxter v *Scott*[53] is an example of another situation which was held not to be a search. Police officers arrested the accused on a drink driving charge. They took possession of his car pending him becoming fit to drive and, since they were responsible for its safekeeping, checked its contents. They found stolen property. The High Court held on appeal that the police were entitled to check the car routinely, that there had been no search as such and that the evidence that particular property had been found in the course

---

[49] 1991 SCCR 623.
[50] 1992 SCCR 875.
[51] 1990 SCCR 304.
[52] (1980) SCCR Supp 256.
[53] 1992 SCCR 342.

of the checking of the vehicle was admissible. The court did not adopt the approach urged by the Crown, which was to treat what happened as a search which was lawful because the accused had been arrested under the Road Traffic Act.

We have to contrast *Baxter* with *Graham v Orr*.[54] In that case, as in *Baxter*, the appellant had been arrested for a drink driving offence. However, by contrast with *Baxter*, the police did not check the contents of the car as a matter of routine but only when the accused became agitated on learning that he could not have his car back until he provided a clear breath test. This aroused the suspicions of the police who looked inside the car and found a bag of cannabis resin.

Lord Justice-General Hope started from the proposition that the police did not have a power at common law to search the car. He regarded it as being significant that the suspicions aroused were general ones and did not focus on any particular offence. He was clear that what the police had done amounted to a search. The Crown had conceded, as it was bound to do, that section 23(2) of the Misuse of Drugs Act 1971, which gives power to search persons and vehicles where a drug offence is suspected, could not justify the search, because the suspicions did not relate to drugs in particular. It followed that, since what was done was to conduct a search of the car in the absence of any power to do so, the evidence of what was found inside was inadmissible.

Was the search lawful?
Once it has been established that what has happened in a given case is in fact a search properly so called, the question will be whether that search was lawful.

Search of premises without warrant
In the absence of a warrant, search of premises is likely to be irregular and evidence obtained is at risk of being held to be inadmissible. Renton and Brown[55] suggests that 'where a person is arrested with or without warrant in his house it may be competent to search the house for stolen property or any evidence of guilt', but cites only English authority in support of this proposition, the validity of which must be regarded as unconfirmed, especially since English law on this subject is founded on the provisions of the Police and Criminal Evidence Act 1984, which does not apply to Scotland.

Many statutes allow particular types of investigator a right of entry to premises and a right to require the production of articles (often documents) of a particular description. Such rights of entry tend not to be made available to the police but rather to agencies with a function which is primarily regulatory. It is always for consideration in the case of the exercise of such a power whether Parliament intended the results to be available for use in a criminal trial or intended them to be confined to administrative regulation. The principle would be that since these provisions interfere with the liberty of the subject and no one can be required to provide evidence against himself without clear parliamentary sanction, in case of doubt the recovered material will not be admissible in evidence.

[54] 1995 SCCR 30.
[55] R W Renton and H H Brown, *Criminal Procedure According to the Law of Scotland* (5th edn, 1983) para 5-34.

Many statutes make specific provision for search warrants. The most commonly encountered statutory search warrant is probably that provided for by section 23(3) of the Misuse of Drugs Act 1971. We examine it briefly here not only for its own importance but also as an example of a type.

Section 23(3) permits the granting of a warrant by a justice of the peace, a magistrate or a sheriff, who is satisfied by information on oath that there is reasonable ground for suspecting either (*a*) that there are controlled drugs in the possession of a person on the premises in contravention of the Act or regulations made under it, or (*b*) that a document relating to a drugs offence is in the possession of a person on the premises. The warrant may be executed within one month of the date of its grant and allow a constable to enter the premises, if need be by force, to search the premises and anyone found thereon and to seize and detain drugs or any document fitting the description in the application.

Like all Scottish search warrants, the section 23(3) warrant takes the form of an application which narrates the essential facts and is followed by a docquet signed by the grantor to the effect that he or she 'grants warrant as craved'. The section 23(3) warrant can only be granted if the grantor is satisfied by evidence on oath that the criteria are fulfilled and that oath and satisfaction are narrated on the face of the application and warrant.

Even if there is no statutory provision for a warrant, the procurator fiscal is always entitled, even in relation to a statutory offence, to seek a warrant at common law from the sheriff unless statute specifically excludes that a right in the particular circumstances. In a *Bill of Advocation for MacNeill*[56] a procurator fiscal sought such a warrant but the sheriff refused on the ground that the particular statute said to have been contravened did not provide for a search warrant. The High Court held that this was an incorrect approach. The sheriff is, of course, perfectly entitled to refuse to grant a warrant if after considering the balance to be stuck between the public interest in the detection of crime on the one hand and the interest of the citizen whose property it is intended to search on the other he or she is not satisfied that it would be appropriate to grant the warrant. Such a refusal has been reported[57] where it was apparent that the true purpose of the search was not directly proof of the offence which had been reported to the police (indecent assault during a consultation with an aromatherapist) but an attempt to recover a list of other customers in the hope that interviewing them would discover other offences, so as to enable the *Moorov* doctrine to be invoked (a matter dealt with at p 139 below).

Common law search warrants can be obtained by the procurator fiscal by *ex parte* application to the sheriff. This means that the application is made in private and usually without the application being intimated either to the holder of the material or to the suspect, neither of whom has any opportunity to make representations about whether or not it should be granted. The procedure is available both before and after the institution of proceedings in relation to any offence whatever and in relation to any type of material.

Defective warrants
The obvious question which arises in relation to a warrant is what happens when it is defective. The first point to be made about this is that the High

[56] 1984 SLT 157.
[57] 1993, *Greens Criminal Law Bulletin* 3-4.

Court has held in *Allan* v *Tant*,[58] in the context of a warrant under section 23(3) of the Misuse of Drugs Act 1971, that where a warrant is *ex facie* valid it is not permissible for the trial court to hear evidence designed to show that the procedure for obtaining the warrant was not followed properly. It appears that the only remedy available to the accused in such a case will be to take a bill of suspension before the trial in an attempt to reduce the warrant, as was done in *Stuart* v *Crowe*.[59] In *British Broadcasting Corporation* v *Jessop*,[60] interim suspension was achieved while the search was going on.

So far as patent defects are concerned, the absence of the signature of the grantor of the warrant was held to be fatal in *HM Advocate* v *Bell*.[61] Stoddart has suggested,[62] with considerable hesitation, on the basis of *Cardle* v *Wilkinson*[63] that a facsimile signature might be sufficient.

Failure to state the address of the premises to be searched led to the refusal of the High Court to hold evidence admissible in *HM Advocate* v *Cumming*.[64]

It is not clear whether it is absolutely necessary for the date of granting the warrant to appear except where there is a statutory time-limit on the execution of the warrant when it certainly is essential. Warrants under section 23(3) of the Misuse of Drugs Act 1971 are an example of this.

Other defects may be excusable and the test, as so often in relation to the admissibility of evidence, will be that of fairness. If there is no material prejudice to the accused, the defect is likely to be excused. So, for example, failure to give the name and designation of the sheriff who granted the warrant was not fatal in *HM Advocate* v *Strachan*.[65]

Was the search within the scope of the warrant?

Whatever kind of search is in contemplation and whatever the kind of warrant obtained, the question which will arise is whether the search which was carried out was within the scope of the warrant. A relatively relaxed view of this is taken by the courts and the cases of *Lawrie* v *Muir* and *Fairley* v *Fishmongers of London* will be recalled.

The general principle is that once the police are lawfully on premises with a search warrant or the permission of the occupier they may take any suspicious articles they happen to see, even if these are outwith the strict terms of the warrant (or permission) but they may not search actively for articles outwith the warrant or take away articles which might on further examination disclose other offences. Thus in *HM Advocate* v *Hepper*[66] police searched the house of a suspect without warrant but with the permission of his wife in pursuance of an investigation not connected with the subsequent charge; they saw a briefcase with someone else's name and address on it and that was plainly suspicious. It was held at the trial for theft that the removal of the briefcase had been proper and the evidence was allowed.

---

[58] 1986 SCCR 175.
[59] 1992 SCCR 181.
[60] High Court, Edinburgh, February 1987; unreported (see C N Stoddart, *Criminal Warrants* (1991) p 108).
[61] 1984 SCCR 430.
[62] Stoddart, *op cit*, p 11.
[63] 1982 SCCR 33.
[64] 1983 SCCR 15.
[65] 1990 SCCR 341.
[66] 1958 JC 39.

With *Hepper*, we must contrast *HM Advocate* v *Turnbull*[67] in which a warrant was obtained for the search of an accountant's office in relation to the affairs of a particular client. The police removed a large quantity of material relating to other clients which they subsequently trawled through, finding other offences. It was held that the removal of the documents which were not in themselves plainly suspicious was illegal and that evidence was not allowed.

Stoddart has suggested that the result of *Hepper* and *Turnbull* has been to produce a situation which is 'somewhat problematic for all parties' because the police do not know how far they can go and the citizen does not know how far they can go and the citizen does not know where his right to have his property protected against illegal searches ends.[68] He calls attention to two cases in particular, *Tierney* v *Allan*[69] and *Innes* v *Jessop*.[70] In Tierney evidence that police officers searching a house under a warrant in relation to stolen gas cylinders had found a stolen typewriter under a cot was held to be admissible. It was clear that the search had not been random. However, in *Innes* the search was under a warrant granted under the Firearms Act 1968 and the police removed a driving licence, a subcontractor's tax certificate and a number of other items which had nothing to do with anything and less to do with firearms. This was held to be a random search and the results were inadmissible.

As Stoddart says, the whole circumstances will be taken into account in decisions like this, and *Tierney* and *Innes* both make sense on their own facts. The significance of the individual circumstances of a case is carried perhaps as far as it can get by *Drummond* v *HM Advocate*.[71] Two police officers searched a house and the evidence of the first was that he had been looking deliberately for items not covered by the warrant. His evidence was held to be inadmissible. The evidence of the second officer, however, was that he had been looking for items which *were* covered by the warrant and he had happened upon other articles. His evidence of finding such other articles was held to be admissible.

Cases of urgency

In some cases, as section 18(8) of the 1995 Act recognises, there can be a substantial risk of evidence being lost during the time it takes to get a warrant. As the law has developed, urgency has become the most common ground upon which irregular searches are excused. So, for example, it was held in *Bell* v *Hogg*[72] that a police officer was entitled to take palm rubbings from men suspected of the theft of copper but who had not been cautioned or charged in view of the risk of the evidence being lost. A similar result was reached in *Edgley* v *Barbour*.[73] In that case, police officers saw the accused driving at speed. When they directed a radar gun at his car, he braked at once. They suspected that he was using a radar detection device contrary to section 5(b)(i) of the Wireless Telegraphy Act 1949 and saw what appeared

[67] 1951 JC 96.
[68] Stoddart, *op cit*, p 114.
[69] 1989 SCCR 334.
[70] 1989 SCCR 441.
[71] 1992 SCCR 290.
[72] 1967 JC 49.
[73] 1994 SCCR 789.

to be such a device on his dashboard as they stopped him. When they approached him, it had gone and he declined to open the door or step out of the vehicle. One officer opened the passenger door and opened the glove compartment where he found such a device. It was found as a fact that in view of the lateness of the hour and the remoteness of the locus it would have been impracticable for the officers to get a search warrant. The appellant could not have been detained and the time lapse would have allowed him to dispose of the device. The High Court held that the officers were entitled to act as they had and that the interest of the public outweighed the relatively minor interruption of the appellant's privacy.

It is worth noting that, on the question of urgency, Lord Justice-Clerk Aitchison in *HM Advocate* v *McGuigan*[74] placed some emphasis on the subjective view of the officers concerned as to the need to search at once. This, of course, is consistent with what we noted in the context of detention about the test of what constitutes reasonable grounds to suspect something.

Search of the person

The reference to *Bell* v *Hogg* leads us to consider search of the person and we start with section 18 of the 1995 Act, which makes provision for the taking by the police of prints and other impressions, hair and nail clippings and swabs, etc, of body fluids on external parts of the body.

By section 18 where a person has been arrested and is in custody, or has been detained under section 14, a constable is allowed to take fingerprints, palm prints and such other prints and impressions of an external part of the body as the constable reasonably considers it appropriate to take in the circumstances of the suspected offence; but the samples thus taken must, by subsection (3), be destroyed if the person is not subsequently convicted of that offence.

By section 18(6) of the 1995 Act a constable is allowed, with the authority of an officer of a rank no lower than inspector, to take from the person, from the hair of an external part of the body (other than pubic hair) a sample of hair or other material by cutting, combing or plucking; from or from under a fingernail or toenail, a sample of nail or other material; from an external part of the body, by swabbing or rubbing, a sample of blood, other body fluid, body tissue or other material; and, from inside the mouth, by means of swabbing, a sample of saliva or other material.

The meaning of the phrase 'external part of the body' was much discussed in Parliament during the passage of the Prisoners and Criminal Proceedings (Scotland) Act 1993 (in which the provision first appeared) but was never satisfactorily defined. It is thought that it means precisely what it says and that the section will permit samples from intimate parts of the body provided no degree of penetration is involved. It is to be noted that, although there is a prohibition on the taking of samples from pubic hair, the taking of a swab from the external genitalia is not excluded.

Section 18(8) of the 1995 Act provides that the provisions of that section are without prejudice to other powers of search, powers to take possession of evidence where there is imminent danger of its being lost or destroyed, or

---

[74] 1936 JC 16.

power to take prints, impressions or samples under the authority of a warrant.

Invasive search

As the contribution which forensic science can make to the proof of crimes increases, so there is an increasing need for invasive search to obtain such things as blood samples or impressions of parts of the body. If the material required is not within the categories contemplated by section 18(2) and (6) of the 1995 Act, such sampling requires either the consent of the person from whom the samples are taken or a warrant. This has resulted in a considerable body of case-law.

The starting-point is *Hay* v *HM Advocate*.[75] The appellant had been convicted of murder. Part of the evidence had been that a bite mark was found on the body of the victim. The inmates of a nearby approved school were under suspicion and, after impressions of the teeth of all the inmates, obtained with their consent, had been examined, they were all eliminated except the appellant. In order to permit the carrying out of a more detailed comparison, the procurator fiscal presented an application to the sheriff court for a warrant to take dental impressions, photographs and measurements of the appellant's mouth. The warrant was granted and the samples were obtained. The subsequent examination demonstrated that the appellant's dental configuration matched the mark precisely and that evidence was led at his trial.

It was argued on appeal that the granting of the warrant had been incompetent and that, even if the warrant had been competent, the evidence should not have been admitted.

The court, in dealing with the competence of the warrant, noted that the need in the public interest for 'promptitude and facility in the identification of accused persons and the discovery on their persons or on their premises of indicia either of guilt or innocence' was to be held in balance with the need to protect the liberty of the subject from any undue or unnecessary invasion. This is, of course, the balance which we have noticed on several occasions and which, as we shall see, is the whole theme of the area of law now under consideration.

The court went on to say that warrants of this sort, sought before the accused has been arrested, will only be granted in special circumstances and that the hearings on such applications are by no means formalities. However, after reviewing a number of early authorities, the court expressed the unequivocal view that such warrants are competent.

This decision is of high authority. It was a Full Bench decision by five judges and, indeed, the trial judge had heard argument on the point with two other judges to assist him before repelling the defence objection. In all, therefore, eight judges, including the Lord Justice-General and the Lord Justice-Clerk, were unanimous that such warrants are competent. It is no longer seriously possible to argue that they are not.

The issue next appears in the reports as *HM Advocate* v *Milford*,[76] a sheriff court decision. The allegation was rape and the procurator fiscal sought a warrant to take a sample of blood from the accused for comparison with blood on the inside of the fly of his trousers. By contrast with *Hay*, the

[75] 1968 SLT 334.
[76] 1973 SLT 12.

accused had been arrested and appears to have been committed for further examination at least. It was argued in opposition to the application that the medical process involved went beyond the mere taking of impressions and was truly invasive. This, it was said, was an unprecedented invasion of personal liberty.

The sheriff noted that the offence alleged was a very grave one and that the taking of a blood sample is comparatively innocuous. He decided that the balance was in favour of him granting the warrant, which was neither too wide nor too oppressive.

There was no appeal in *Milford* but that case was reviewed by the High Court in *Wilson* v *Milne*,[77] an assault case in which a warrant to take a sample of blood from the accused had been granted. It was argued that *Milford* had been wrongly decided but the High Court, far from disapproving *Milford*, treated it as authoritative when read along with Hay. The need for a balance was again stressed and the court pointed out that it was in fact in the interests of the accused, as well as of justice, that the blood found on his boots and the victim's clothing should either be reconciled or distinguished.

An attempt was made by the defence in *Morris* v *MacNeill*[78] to argue that the above line of authority is confined to cases where the crime is particularly serious, a proposition which was rejected by the sheriff and not insisted on before the High Court on appeal. The case was one of theft by housebreaking where blood had been found at the point of entry. It was, however, argued on appeal that the sheriff had erred in granting the warrant where the circumstances were not 'special'. The High Court, however, indicated that the high value of the property taken and the fact that the procedure would help to clear up the housebreaking and either eliminate or implicate the appellant were sufficient to make the case special. We may note, on this, Gordon's observations that

> '[T]he offence in the instant case was certainly serious, if hardly comparable to murder. It remains to be seen how far down the calendar of crimes the courts will be prepared to go in cases of this kind'

and, on the matter of the possibility of analysis exculpating the accused,

> 'with the emphasis on the result of the comparison as the focus of interest, the conclusion sounds a little disingenuous. . . . It has to be said, however, that there are not likely to be many cases in which an innocent suspect will be so attached to his constitutional rights as to object to giving blood or hair, or whatever, in order to establish his innocence'.[79]

In deciding *Morris*, the court reiterated the test in words which have come to be quoted regularly in the context of applications for warrants such as this. It said:

> 'Although it is competent to grant a warrant such as was sought in the present case to take a blood sample from an accused or a suspect, such a warrant will not be lightly granted and will only be granted where the circumstances are special and where the granting of the warrant will not disturb the delicate balance that must be maintained between the public interest on one hand and the interest of the accused on the other.'

[77] 1975 SLT 26.
[78] 1991 SCCR 722.
[79] *Ibid* at 726, 727, Commentary.

In other words, the Crown cannot expect the court to 'rubber stamp' such applications and this was made even clearer by *Hughes* v *Normand*[80] in which the High Court suspended such a warrant where it was not known whether the stain found on the suspect's shirt was blood at all and, if it was, whether it was that of the victim. The application was regarded as premature. However, a further application was made by the procurator fiscal for such a warrant against Hughes and one of his co-accused. The application for that warrant narrated that the staining had been identified as blood and that there had been certain comparisons made, the results of which were given. It was further stated that it was necessary in the interests of justice to ascertain whether the blood could have come from the accused. The warrants were granted and appealed.

On this occasion (also reported as *Hughes* v *Normand*[81]), the defence did not argue that the application was premature—patently it was not—but did contend that it was not justified since at best the results would, in the particular circumstances, be in favour of the accused or neutral. The court took the view, however, that it was desirable that the comparison process should be completed and refused to suspend the warrants.

Gordon has observed on this that:

'[T]he High Court said nothing about the circumstances being exceptional or about balancing the rights of the accused and that public interest. We have probably now reached the stage at which the Crown will be entitled to obtain warrants of this kind in any case in which they can show that they have information which indicates that the samples sought will be useful evidence.'[82]

It is not only blood samples for which the Crown has sought warrants of this type. In *Lees* v *Weston*[83] a warrant was sought to fingerprint the accused where the police had omitted to do that when he was arrested in connection with drugs offences. The sheriff refused the warrant, on the basis that the police had had their chance and that it was not appropriate to grant a warrant such as this to allow the Crown to improve its case by trying to get round a 'police blunder'. The High Court took a different view on appeal, pointing out that the taking of finger impressions involved a relatively minor invasion of bodily integrity, which was outweighed by the public interest. Again, in *Smith* v *Cardle*[84] the procurator fiscal recovered a video recording of a fatal assault; it was known that the perpetrator must be either the complainer (in this bill of suspension) or his identical twin brother. A warrant was sought to obtain precise physical measurements for comparison with the video, although by definition the complainer was not yet the suspect. The High Court held that the balance was in favour of the public interest and that there would be no bodily invasive procedures or any great inconvenience. Accordingly the sheriff was entitled to grant the warrant.

With these cases must be contrasted *McGlennan* v *Kelly*.[85] That case concerned an allegation of rape. A pubic hair, which could not have come from the victim, was found at the locus, but at the time of the offence the particular comparison of such hairs which was necessary was not known to

[80] 1992 SCCR 908.
[81] 1993 SCCR 69.
[82] *Ibid* at 74, Commentary.
[83] 1989 SCCR 177.
[84] 1993 SCCR 609.
[85] 1989 SCCR 352.

be scientifically practicable. It became so before the accused was brought to trial and an application for a warrant to take such a sample was presented almost two years after the offence.

The sheriff refused the application and it was of some importance to the decision that the accused had provided such samples at the time of the initial investigation of the offence and they had been examined within the limits of the technology then available. The sheriff took the view that the balance in these circumstances was against granting the warrant, a decision which the High Court declined to disturb. Lord Dunpark said:

> '[T]he grant or refusal of a warrant of this nature is ultimately a matter for the discretion of the sheriff and, unless it can be shown that he failed to exercise a proper balancing exercise in the public interest and in the interest of the respondent, there was no wrong exercise of the discretion.'

5 : PETITION PROCEDURE

Solemn procedure usually starts with a document called the 'petition', though it is competent to raise an indictment without any prior petition. An attempt was made to argue the contrary in *O'Reilly* v *HM Advocate*[1] but the High Court gave this short shrift. It did, however, point out the effect of a petition, saying:

> '[A] petition is required in order to obtain from the court a variety of orders, such as an order for the accused to be committed or for warrants of one kind or another to be granted. Normally the prosecutor will wish to obtain such things from the court and so it is in his interests to have a petition in the appropriate form served on the accused. This is the normal procedure, but if it is not followed and no petition is served it does not mean that the Lord Advocate cannot indict. What it does mean is that the accused cannot be committed or arrested on warrant or have his property searched, because court orders authorising such things cannot be obtained in the absence of a petition which brings an accused before the court.'

The High Court might have qualified this last sentence because, as we have seen, search warrants can be obtained other than as an ancillary to petition. Its point, however, was that a petition is a package. Petition procedure is dealt with in Part IV of the 1995 Act. To deal with it here means departing from the order of the 1995 Act, because Part III of the Act deals with the bail. However, that subject makes much better sense once petition procedure is understood.

In the petition the procurator fiscal informs the court that 'from information received' by him 'it appears, and he accordingly charges' that the accused person named committed a particular offence or offences. The petition goes on to ask the court among other things.

(*a*) to grant warrant to search for and apprehend the accused—in short, to arrest him;

(*b*) to imprison the accused either for further examination or until liberated in due course of law;

(*c*) to search the person and property of the accused;

(*d*) to grant warrant to cite witnesses for precognition.

Most of these will only be of significance if the accused is not yet in custody for the offence but the warrant to imprison the accused will be significant in all cases.

Where the accused is not in custody, the procurator fiscal will present the petition to the sheriff, obtain a signature to the warrant, and issue it to the police for execution by arresting the accused.

Where the accused has been arrested on a petition warrant, or where the procurator fiscal has decided to proceed on petition against an accused who has been arrested without warrant, the accused will appear in court on the

---

[1] 1984 SCCR 352.

next day on which it sits. This follows from section 17(1) of the Police (Scotland) Act 1967, which obliges the police to bring offenders before the court without detaining them unreasonably or unnecessarily and from section 135(3) and (4) of the 1995 Act, which provides that a person apprehended shall, wherever practicable, be brought before a court competent to deal with the case not later than in the course of the first day after he has been taken into custody, where that is not a Saturday, a Sunday or a court holiday.

The appearance will be in private, in the sheriff's chambers, or in a closed courtroom which will be regarded as chambers. A copy of the petition will have been handed to the accused in the cells. His solicitor is entitled to an interview in private with the accused before he appears before the sheriff, in terms of section 17(2) of the 1995 Act.

Procedure in relation to appearance on petition bears the marks of its history. At a time when the investigation was in the hands of the sheriff, the appearance on petition was the occasion on which the accused was examined as to his account of the events relevant to the offence and he was entitled to make a declaration. That declaration would in due course be part of the evidence at trial and, since the accused was at one time not allowed to give evidence at the trial, the declaration was his only chance to give his side of the story. Now that the accused is a competent witness at his own trial and the Crown case will have only an embryonic form when most accused persons appear on petition, it is rare, though not entirely unknown, for the accused to make a declaration.

If the accused is going to make a declaration, he must do so himself, in his own words. In *Carmichael* v *Armitage*[2] the accused's solicitor had noted his client's account of relevant events and then edited it—the word used was 'structured'—to make it 'reasonable'. The High Court held that the basic rules of evidence applied to such a declaration and that something edited by the solicitor had become a precognition (that is, a statement prepared by one engaged on behalf of one of the parties in preparing the case for trial) and so was not admissible.

After the sheriff clerk has asked the accused to confirm his identity it is usual for the accused's solicitor to say that his client makes 'no plea or declaration' and the sheriff then looks to the procurator fiscal to hear what the Crown wishes to do. The first question is whether the fiscal wishes to conduct a judicial examination. Once this has been dealt with, the fiscal may either seek the committal of the accused for further examination (in custody or on bail) or seek his full committal (in custody or on bail).

Judicial examination

The judicial examination procedure was introduced by the Criminal Justice (Scotland) Act 1980 and now finds expression in sections 35 to 39 of the 1995 Act.

Scope of questioning

In terms of section 36 of the 1995 Act the accused may be questioned by the prosecutor insofar as such questioning is directed towards eliciting any admission, denial, explanation, justification or comment which the accused

[2] 1982 SCCR 475.

may have as regards three things. The first of these (subsection (2)) is whether any account which the accused can give ostensibly discloses a defence and, if so, the nature and particulars of that defence. The second (subsection (3)) is the alleged making by the accused, to or in the hearing of an officer of police, of an extrajudicial confession (whether or not a full admission) relevant to the charge and a copy of which has been served on the accused. The third (subsection (4)) is any declaration made by the accused. Where the accused discloses an ostensible defence, section 36(10) of the 1995 Act obliges the prosecutor to secure the investigation of that defence, though it may be thought that any competent prosecutor would do so anyway and the Act provides no remedy for the situation where a prosecutor ignores this requirement.

Confessions

Questioning about statements to the police has generated some appeal business, essentially about what amounts to a confession. In *McKenzie* v *HM Advocate*,[3] following an identification parade the accused had said, 'Just my luck, I knew I'd be picked out.' The accused said that he saw his remark as an expression, not a confession. The accused sought to have those words omitted from the transcript to be read to the jury and on appeal Lord Robertson said:

> 'The wording of this particular section does not appear to be as clear as it might have been. There is no definition of "confession" in the statute and it is accordingly doubtful as to exactly what is intended. The wording "extrajudicial confession (whether or not a full admission relevant to the charge)" suggests that the confession referred to is something less than a full admission and must be susceptible of interpretation provided the statement is relevant to the charge. In the context it seems to me that the definition of "confession" must be that the statement is clearly susceptible of being regarded as an incriminating statement. . . . In the present case the statement allegedly made is perhaps not a full admission but in my view it cannot be said that the statement was not or cannot be susceptible of being regarded as an incriminating statement.'

Lord Robertson went on to say that the accused always has the opportunity at trial to challenge the admissibility of such a statement.

In some cases, of course, such as *Moran* v *HM Advocate*[4] it will only be possible to determine whether something is a confession in light of other evidence and in such cases the court will be inclined to let the matter go to the jury with an appropriate direction.

Moran concerned a statement said to contain 'special knowledge', a concept to be considered below. For now, it may be noted that there will be sufficient evidence for a conviction if an admission contains information which the accused could only have known if he was a party to the crime, and which is proved to be true by evidence from another source. Objection was taken, and repelled, to the reading to the jury of that part of the transcript which contained this material.

On appeal, Lord Brand pointed out that whether or not the passage could be said to be an extrajudicial confession could only be decided in the light of other evidence and that it had been proper to allow it to be read to the jury. It is thought that what he meant was that whether or not the knowledge was

[3] 1982 SCCR 545.
[4] 1990 SCCR 40.

'special' could only be decided by the jury and that only once they had heard other evidence to demonstrate both that the information given was accurate and that it was in restricted currency.

HM Advocate v *Cafferty*[5] is sheriff court authority that the Crown can choose which statements to put to the accused and need not put them all.

Alleged confessions made in the hearing of others, such as customs officers, are not provided for and accordingly, it is suggested, cannot form the basis of questions.

In framing his questions, the procurator fiscal is required by section 35(5) of the 1995 Act to have regard to certain principles. These are that questions should not be designed to challenge the truth of anything said by the accused, that questions which the accused has refused to answer should not be reiterated and that there should be no leading questions.

Refusal to answer

By section 36(8) of the 1995 Act the accused is always entitled to decline to answer questions at judicial examination, and many do so refuse. However, where at trial the accused (or any witness called on his behalf) says something, or calls a witness who says something, in evidence which could have been stated appropriately in answer to a question which he refused to answer at judicial examination, his refusal to answer at judicial examination may be commented on by the prosecutor, the judge presiding at the trial, or any co-accused. The intention of the Thomson Committee, which recommended the introduction of the judicial examination procedure, was that this provision would make it difficult for the accused to decline to answer[6] but the view which Lord Dunpark took in *Gilmour* v *HM Advocate*[7] was rather different. In that case, he pointed out to the jury that the accused had refused to answer questions on the advice of his solicitor and that he had the right to remain silent. He therefore advised the jury to ignore the judicial examination altogether. However, the High Court seem to have taken a different approach in the appeal in *Alexander* v *HM Advocate*[8] (though the absence of a recorded judgment is unhelpful). There, the three accused had made no reply at judicial examination beyond what has become something of a standard formula 'On the instructions of my lawyer I don't wish to say anything'. At trial, they put forward alibis. The trial judge (Lord Brand) told the jury that the failure to disclose the alleged alibis at judicial examination was a matter for them to assess in weighing the evidence. There was an appeal on the basis that this was a misdirection but the appeal was refused. Gordon comments[9] that this indicates that Lord Dunpark's approach in *Gilmour* was incorrect. However, in *McEwan* v *HM Advocate*[10] the High Court on appeal counselled restraint in the way in which trial judges should comment to juries on this sort of point.

[5] 1984 SCCR 444.
[6] Criminal Procedure in Scotland, Second Report, 1975, Cmnd 6218, para 8.19.
[7] 1982 SCCR 590.
[8] 1988 SCCR 542.
[9] *Ibid* at 545, Commentary.
[10] 1990 SCCR 401.

Role of defence solicitor

The role of the defence solicitor at a judicial examination is rather limited. Section 36(5) of the 1995 Act lays upon the sheriff the responsibility of ensuring that all questions are fairly put to, and understood by, the accused and, although the accused must be told by the sheriff that he may consult his solicitor before answering any question (section 36(6) of the 1995 Act), the solicitor is not entitled to intervene by way of objection to questions. What he can do, by section 36(7) of the 1995 Act after the completion of the procurator fiscal's questions, is ask the accused questions designed to clarify any ambiguity in an answer given by the accused to the prosecutor at the examination or to give the accused an opportunity to answer any question which he has previously refused to answer.

Transcript

Judicial examination is tape recorded and, by section 37(6) of the 1995 Act, a copy of the transcript must be served on the accused and his solicitor within fourteen days. There is provision in section 38 of the 1995 Act for application to the court for rectification of any perceived errors in the transcript.

Committal

Once the judicial examination is completed the procurator fiscal will move the court either to commit the accused for further examination or to commit him until liberated in due course of law. Committal until liberated in due course of law is usually referred to as 'full committal'.

Full committal

Full committal is committal for trial. In times past the sheriff would at this stage be shown the 'precognition', which is the volume of statements taken by the Crown. That practice fell out of use a long time ago and modern practice is that the procurator fiscal, by moving for full committal, is in effect saying to the sheriff that he is satisfied that there is a *prima facie* case, at least on paper. Provided that the petition contains a relevant charge the sheriff will almost always order full committal without further inquiry, though the sheriff does retain the jurisdiction to refuse to do so. The few occasions where this happens are cases where the sheriff considers that in the particular circumstances the motion is oppressive or frankly incompetent. So, for example, in *Normand* v *McQuillan*[11] a sheriff refused full committal in a case in which the Crown substituted a petition for a summary complaint a fortnight after the accused had been remanded in custody to await trial on that complaint. The sheriff regarded this as oppressive in the circumstances. In refusing the motion for full committal the sheriff rejected an argument by the procurator fiscal that it is incompetent for the defence to challenge the competency of a petition, observing:

> 'For present purposes I am satisfied that complaints of unfairness and oppression can be entertained by the court at any stage of the prosecution procedure. The prevention of such ills must surely be a primary justification for the presence of a judge.'

[11] 1987 SCCR 440.

An example—perhaps the only example—of refusal of a motion to commit as frankly incompetent is to be found in *Herron v A, B, C and D*[12] in which the sheriff noticed that the time-limit between committal for further examination and full committal had been exceeded. The judgment is worth reading for its description of just how far things can go wrong when all parties assume that the fact that sheriffs scarcely ever refuse full committal means that it is no more than an administrative rubber stamp.

It should be understood that refusal of a motion to commit does not prevent the Crown from subsequently serving an indictment and proceeding to trial.

Committal for further examination

Committal for further examination is used where the fiscal does not consider that he is yet in a position to take the responsibility for full committal. It may be that he is working from a summary of the evidence and wants to see the full statements which the police have taken; or he may expect that there are further charges to come; or he may consider that further inquiries are necessary to provide a sufficiency of evidence. Committal for further examination happens only once. If the accused is granted bail at committal for further examination, it operates as full committal as a result of section 23(3) of the 1995 Act. Where the accused is kept in custody he must be brought back to court for full committal. The period within which that must be done depends on an understanding of the Criminal Procedure Act 1701 which provides, *inter alia*:

> 'And farder Discharges all closs imprisonments beyond the space of Eight dayes from the commitment.'

Sheriff Macphail analysed the effect of this in *Herron v A, B, C and D* and the High Court approved his reasoning in *Dunbar, Petitioner*.[13] The effect is that no more than eight days may elapse between committal for further examination and full committal but neither of the days on which one of these committals takes place counts towards that total. Accordingly, an accused who is committed for further examination on a Monday, if he is to be fully committed must be so committed on the Wednesday of the following week at the very latest. If the Monday is the first of the month, the Wednesday on which full committal takes place will be the tenth.

[12] 1977 SLT (Sh Ct) 24.
[13] 1986 SCCR 602.

6 : BAIL

Bail applications

At committal for further examination
When the accused first appears in court one question which will be
prominent in his mind is whether he is going to get bail—that is, to be
liberated pending his trial. Part III of the 1995 Act deals with bail and the
starting-point is section 23. By subsection (1) any person accused on
petition (that is, under solemn procedure) of a crime which is by law bailable
is entitled immediately, on any occasion on which he is brought before the
sheriff prior to full committal, to apply to the sheriff for bail. The prosecutor
is entitled to be heard against that application.

By subsection (2), the sheriff is entitled in his discretion to refuse that
application.

Subsections (1) and (2), therefore, deal with the situation on committal
for further examination, at which stage a practice has become well
established by which, if the procurator fiscal states to the sheriff at committal for further examination that there are further inquiries which
would in his judgment be prejudiced by the liberation of the accused, the
accused will not get bail. The fiscal does not require to state what those
inquiries are. This is an example of the reliance which the Scottish courts
are accustomed to place on the probity and good sense of the public
prosecutor and reflects the view expressed by Lord McLaren in *AB* v
Dickson[1] where he said:

> 'It must be kept in view that in earlier stages of a criminal investigation the
> Procurator Fiscal is the person who knows most about the circumstances of the
> case . . . it is in accordance with good sense and justice that great weight should
> be given to the representations of the Procurator Fiscal on this question.'

The law on this was considered and restated by Lord McCluskey in *HM
Advocate* v *Boyle*,[2] a case in which the sheriff at committal for further
examination had said that he was not prepared to accept the bald assertion
that the Crown had further inquiries and that in the judgment of the Crown
it was necessary that the accused remain in custody to allow those inquiries
to take place. He invited the procurator fiscal to elaborate and, when the
fiscal declined to do so, granted bail.

Hearing the Crown bail appeal, Lord McCluskey said:

> 'At the stage when accused persons are first brought before the sheriff on the
> procurator fiscal's petition and the procurator fiscal makes a motion to commit
> the accused for further examination and states that the Crown are continuing to
> make enquiries and that it is necessary for the proper pursuit of these inquiries
> that the accused should remain in custody at that stage the court should not seek
> to go behind that statement . . . the sheriff . . . should accept that the procurator

[1] 1907 JC 111.
[2] 1995 SLT 162.

51

fiscal is acting in the public interest and in his role as a minister of justice. His judgment on the matter of the necessity of keeping accused persons in custody at that stage should be respected.'

Lord McCluskey went on to say that the Crown cannot be compelled to reveal the details of the inquiries to the defence.

A distinction is, however, to be drawn where the other inquiries do not relate to the charge on the petition. In *HM Advocate v Leech*,[3] decided on the same day as *Boyle*, Lord McCluskey refused a Crown bail appeal where the inquiries related not to the petition but to murders and serious assaults committed in England; in other words there seemed to be no prospect of the accused ever being prosecuted in Scotland for those matters and Lord McCluskey noted that the Crown was not saying that it expected to bring charges against him in respect of those matters.

At full committal and under summary procedure
By section 23(5) of the 1995 Act bail may be sought after full committal even if it has been refused at committal for further examination. Under summary procedure, by subsection (6), any judge having jurisdiction to try the offence (in other words, sheriffs and district court justices, as the case may be) may, at his discretion, on the application of the accused and after giving the prosecutor an opportunity to be heard, admit or refuse to admit the accused to bail. Subsection (7) requires a bail application under subsection (5) or (6) to be dealt with within twenty-four hours after its presentation to the judge, failing which the accused must be liberated forthwith. In *Gibbons, Petitioner*[4] an application lodged at 11.30 am one day was, for administrative reasons, not dealt with until 11.50 am the following day, when it was refused. It was held that the time-limit is mandatory and the release of the accused was ordered.

The law on bail other than at committal for further examination is substantially the same as between summary cases and solemn cases. At this stage it is not enough for the Crown to say that it thinks the accused should be kept in custody. More substantial grounds are required, though even here there is a tendency for the court to accord particular weight to the assessment made by the Crown.

Offences for which bail is not available
All of the subsections of section 23 of the 1995 Act which contemplate the granting of bail recognise that there are some offences for which bail cannot be granted. Murder and treason are, in subsection (5), specifically excluded from the crimes for which bail can be granted after full committal and section 24(1) and (2) of the 1995 Act provides in terms that those two offences are not bailable at all except by the Lord Advocate or the High Court. However, section 26 of the 1995 Act imposes additional restrictions on the availability of bail in cases of attempted murder, culpable homicide, rape and attempted rape. A person charged with one of these offences, or who has been convicted of one of them and has either not yet been sentenced or has appealed, cannot be granted bail if he has a previous conviction in any UK court for one of those offences

[3] High Court, 8th December 1994; unreported.
[4] 1988 SCCR 270.

or for murder or manslaughter. Where the conviction was for culpable homicide or manslaughter the restriction depends upon him having been sentenced to imprisonment or detention or made the subject of a hospital order.

Relevant considerations

In other cases, a variety of matters will be relevant to whether or not bail is granted. The starting-point has to be that bail will be granted unless there is a good reason to refuse it. As Lord Justice-General Clyde put it in *Mackintosh* v *McGlinchy*:[5]

'It is perhaps right to make ... the self evident observation that, when an accused person asks for bail or appeals for bail, bail he must get, unless a sufficient ground is brought forward requiring the court to exercise its discretion by refusing it. A good deal was said about the presumption of innocence. I prefer not to treat the matter as a question of presumption. The accused person has the right to ask for bail; he has the right to have his application considered; and unless the Court has some good reason why bail should not be granted, bail ought to be allowed.'

This, however, must be seen against the background of the paragraph which immediately precedes it. Lord Clyde emphasised that each case must be seen on its own merits, 'with the sole view to the public interest and to securing the ends of justice'. He then gave, as examples of cases in which it would be proper to refuse bail, the situation in which there is reason to believe that the accused will interfere with the evidence, where the offence is one such as incest or domestic violence where grave consequences could ensue from the accused returning home, or where the accused is alleged to have been acting in concert with others and liberation would allow him to continue that association. To these examples must be added that to which Lord Justice-Clerk Macdonald drew attention in *HM Advocate* v *Saunders*,[6] when he said:

'[W]hen the Crown does consent the application is always granted; but in cases where the Crown does not consent, and in cases where the information possessed by the prosecutor who has charged the offence points to a very serious crime, I am unable to see how it can be in accordance either with the public interest or with justice to allow bail.'

The most comprehensive statement in more recent years is probably that of Lord Justice-Clerk Wheatley in *Smith* v *McCallum*[7] in which he said that where an accused has a criminal record which with the present charges raises the question of the protection of the public, or is in some sense in a position of trust in relation to the court (for example, on probation, deferred sentence or community service), unless there are cogent reasons for deciding otherwise, bail should be refused. Other grounds of refusal are the nature of the offence, intimidation of witnesses, no fixed abode and reasonable grounds to suspect the accused will fail to appear. This approach is not in fact applied rigorously but the factors identified by Lord Wheatley do retain considerable significance.

[5] 1921 JC 75.
[6] (1913) 7 Adam 76.
[7] 1982 SLT 421.

Conditions

By section 24(4) and (5) of the 1995 Act the court in granting bail must impose conditions that the accused appears at the appointed time at every diet in the case of which he is given due notice, that he does not commit an offence while on bail, that he does not interfere with witnesses or otherwise obstruct the course of justice and that he makes himself available for interview for reports to assist the court in dealing with him for the offence. These are known as the 'standard conditions'. The court must also impose such conditions as it considers necessary to ensure that the standard conditions are observed and that the accused makes himself available for an identification parade or for prints, impressions or samples to be taken from him.

Section 27 of the 1995 Act creates offences in relation to breach of bail conditions. These are substantive offences rather than matters of evidence or procedure and are therefore not dealt with in this book.

By section 24(6) the court may impose a requirement for the lodging of money bail but only where that is appropriate to the particular circumstances of the case. The use of this power is infrequent. Section 29 provides for forfeiture of the money where there is a breach of bail conditions.

A bail order will continue in force until the disposal of the case in relation to which it was made unless it is actually recalled. In particular, if the trial is adjourned in the absence of the accused that does not cause the bail order to fall (the situation and result in *Walker v Lockhart*).[8]

Bail appeals and reviews

The High Court made it clear in *Milne v McNicol*[9] that, under solemn procedure, it is only the prosecutor who has a right to a bail appeal before full committal. In that case the court refused such an appeal by an accused before full committal as incompetent and settled a conflict between previous decisions of single judges of the High Court on the point.

Under both solemn and summary procedure, where the accused is untried, both the prosecutor and the defence have a right to appeal the grant or the refusal of bail or the particular conditions imposed. Under summary procedure, the prosecutor has a right to appeal against an order ordaining the accused to appear (which is not a bail order and has no conditions attached).

Marking and intimation

The marking of a bail appeal is not subject to any time-limit, though for obvious reasons it is usually (and, in the case of a prosecution appeal, always) done at once upon the court of first instance making the order which it is desired to review. In the case of the prosecutor, there will be a desire on the part of the authorities to get the benefit of that part of section 32(2) of the 1995 Act which provides that 'the applicant [for bail] shall not be liberated . . . until the appeal by the prosecutor is disposed of'. In the case of the accused there will be a compelling desire to secure his liberty as soon as that can be accomplished.

[8] 1993 SCCR 148.
[9] 1944 JC 151.

In either event, section 32(3) of the 1995 Act requires that written notice of appeal is to be immediately given to the opposite party by the party appealing. This is probably more critical in the case of a defence appeal, which might not be marked immediately, than in the case of a prosecution appeal, where the reason for the continued incarceration of the accused will quickly become apparent to his advisers even if they do not see the procurator fiscal physically marking the appeal. Nevertheless, the provision is mandatory and ensures that the opponent has the chance to prepare for the appeal, which, by section 32(7) of the 1995 Act must be heard within seventy-two hours (Sundays and public holidays do not count) in terms of subsection (8). If this time-limit is not met in the case of a procurator's appeal the accused is to be liberated.

Conduct of appeal

By section 32(4) of the 1995 Act a bail appeal is to be disposed of by the High Court or 'any Lord Commissioner of Justiciary in court or in chambers after such inquiry and hearing of parties as shall seem just'. The practice is that such appeals are dealt with in Parliament House in Edinburgh, by a single judge in chambers, before the start of the other business of the court. The Crown is represented by an Advocate-depute, instructed by a member of the Procurator Fiscal Service from the Crown Office. The accused, unless he represents himself, is not usually present but is represented by counsel, a solicitor advocate or (sometimes, during vacation only) a solicitor.

The appeal is usually a brief affair, decided on *ex parte* statements, and occasionally continued for twenty-four hours to allow further information to be obtained. Although the legislation allows 'inquiry', anything more than what has been described is uncommon.

If a defence bail appeal is successful, the High Court interlocutor is sent (by fax) to the clerk of court of first instance, who (again by fax) sends it to the prison in which the accused is held. The accused signs a form of acceptance of the conditions and is then released.

Bail review (defence)

At the instance of the accused, any court can review its own decision on bail in terms of section 30 of the 1995 Act. A material change in circumstances is usually necessary before there is any prospect of success, although that is not demanded by the Act. What is clear is that, where there has been a bail appeal, the court of first instance cannot review the decision taken by the High Court. In *HM Advocate* v *Jones*[10] a sheriff refused to entertain a motion to review bail where the case had been the subject of a bail appeal, holding that any review would have to proceed in the High Court. This decision was approved by Lord Cameron in *Ward* v *HM Advocate*,[11] with the proviso that the court of first instance can review other elements of the bail order, such as conditions, which were not at issue in the High Court.

Bail review (prosecution)

By section 31 of the 1995 Act the prosecutor has an equivalent right to seek review of a court's decision to grant bail but this is limited explicitly to cases

---

[10] 1964 SLT (Sh Ct) 50.
[11] 1972 SLT (Notes) 22.

where the prosecutor puts before the court 'material information' which was not available to it when it granted bail.

The procedure is by application to the court and, by subsection (2), on reciept of such an application, the court must do three things. First, it must intimate the application to the person granted bail; secondly, it must fix a diet for hearing the application and cite the person on bail to attend that diet; and thirdly, 'where it considers that the interests of justice so require', it must grant warrant to arrest that person.

On hearing an application the court may, by subsection (3), either withdraw the grant of bail and remand the person in custody or may grant bail, or continue the grant of bail, varying the conditions if it sees fit.

This is a new procedure which, at the time of writing, has not been operated. Accordingly the courts have not yet had the opportunity to comment on it or to develop practice.

The sections do not restrict the operation of the procedure to cases in which the prosecutor has unsuccessfully opposed bail. It might be argued that a prosecutor who has not opposed bail in the first place is then barred from operating this new procedure. However, such an argument would seek to place in the path of the Crown an additional obstacle to those for which Parliament has legislated and the courts might be slow to give effect to it for that reason. That said, it would be understandable if the courts were reluctant to grant such applications where the new information was in the hands of the police but by oversight or design was not communicated to the prosecutor at the time of the original bail application. Still more, they are likely to be reluctant to grant applications if the information was in the prosecutor's hands and he failed to put it before the court. Even here, however, if the information is sufficiently critical and the offence sufficiently serious, the courts may take the view that the public interest requires the granting of the application. Certainly, it will be open to them to take that view.

Although the grant of a warrant to arrest is not an inevitable part of the procedure it seems likely that it will be common. It is doubtful whether the Crown will operate the procedure except where the new information makes a very significant difference indeed to the case and where there are substantial reasons for thinking that the public interest requires that the accused be in custody pending trial. In such a case, the incentive to the accused not to obtemper the citation is obvious and the need to ensure that he is present to be remanded in custody (should the court so decide) is equally obvious.

Bail appeal after conviction

The accused who has been convicted, made the subject of a deferred sentence and remanded in custody, or on bail with conditions which he finds unacceptable, has a right of appeal in terms of section 201(4) of the 1995 Act. The prosecutor has no equivalent right to appeal against the liberation of a person on deferred sentence.

An appeal by an accused person under this provision can only be marked within twenty-four hours of the remand and is by note of appeal presented to the High Court. In *Long* v *HM Advocate*[12] the accused, upon whom

---

[12] 1984 SCCR 161.

sentence had been deferred in custody for reports had, for reasons which are not disclosed, not marked a bail appeal within the twenty-four hours allowed. An attempt was made to operate the bail review provisions instead but Lord Justice-Clerk Wheatley held that they apply only to pre-trial procedure and have no application to the accused after conviction. It is thought that this would probably also apply to the prosecutor's right to a bail review but since prosecutors traditionally do not intervene on the matter of bail during deferred sentence it is unlikely that the point will ever need to be decided.

In *McGoldrick v Normand*[13] Lord Grieve called attention to the fact that persons on deferred sentence for reports are usually given bail and said that

'In all cases, where, in the opinion of the judge concerned, reasons exist for remanding a person in custody pending the obtaining of reports, he, or she, should set them out in a brief note for the consideration of the court which has to deal with an appeal against the refusal of bail.'

[13] 1988 SCCR 83.

7 : SOLEMN PROCEEDINGS

Crown precognition

Precognition on authority of petition warrant
After full committal, the procurator fiscal will conduct such precognition as he thinks necessary. The witnesses will, upon the authority of the warrant to cite for precognition which is contained in the petition warrant, be cited to attend the Procurator Fiscal's Office and will there be interviewed in private by the procurator fiscal himself, one of his deputes or a precognition officer (who is a paralegal). It was made clear in *Carmichael* v *B*[1] that a witness is not entitled to be accompanied by a solicitor when being precognosced and it has long been recognised that witnesses should not be precognosced in one another's company.[2] Certainly the representatives of the accused have no right to be present.[3]

Precognition on oath
The High Court said in *HM Advocate* v *Monson*[4] that it is every citizen's duty to co-operate with the Crown in this process. That, however, is a duty which is not attended by a sanction and it quite often happens that a witness fails to attend for precognition. In that event the procurator fiscal may petition the court for warrant to cite the witness to attend for precognition on oath. Where such a warrant is granted, the witness will be interrogated in the presence of a sheriff and the precognition will be taken down by shorthand writer, transcribed and subsequently signed by the witness and the sheriff.

A person who is precognosced on oath cannot thereafter be prosecuted for the offence.[5] Indeed *Mowbray* v *Crowe*[6] seems to establish that it will be oppressive for the Crown to commence proceedings against a person who has been interviewed by the procurator fiscal at all in connection with a case. In that case the fiscal was considering a report against the appellant and wrote inviting her to attend for a discussion about the case. During the discussion which took place the appellant disclosed her version of events. The fiscal decided to prosecute.

It seems that what the fiscal had in mind was to give a warning if the appellant admitted the offence. However, as the court pointed out, discussions with the accused are not normally undertaken when a warning is contemplated and, in a criminal justice system which is adversarial, the prosecutor and the accused are to be at arm's length. The appellant had not been told that she could bring a solicitor to the interview. As one who had

[1] 1992 SLT 101.
[2] Baron Hume, *Commentaries on the Law of Scotland Respecting Crimes* (4th edn, 1844) ii, 82; *Reid* v *Duff* (1843) 5 D 656.
[3] Hume, ii, 82.
[4] (1893) 1 Adam 114 at 135.
[5] A J Alison, *Practice of the Criminal Law of Scotland* (1833) ii, 138.
[6] 1993 SCCR 730.

been cautioned and charged she could not have been interviewed by the police and it was equally wrong that she should have been interviewed by the procurator fiscal. The court took the view that there had been oppression and directed the district court to sustain a plea in bar of trial.

Defence precognition and identification parade

If the defence are aware of the identities of the Crown witnesses, they too can proceed to precognosce. They will certainly wish to precognosce witnesses whom they expect to call, whether or not those witnesses are on the Crown list.

Occasionally, the defence will wish to operate section 291 of the 1995 Act. That section permits a sheriff, on the application of the accused, to grant warrant to cite for precognition on oath any person who is alleged to be a witness in relation to any offence of which the accused has been charged. The test which the sheriff must apply is whether it is 'reasonable' to require such precognition on oath in the circumstances and it was held by the sheriff in *Low* v *MacNeill*[7] and *Cirignaco* v *Lockhart*[8] that the reasonableness test applies not only to the requirement for a precognition—which could be satisfied in almost every case—but also to the requirement that it be given on oath. The reasoning was that the defence need to find out what Crown witnesses are going to say in evidence is catered for adequately by other existing law and practice, leaving the possibility of defence precognition on oath for 'unusual and exceptional circumstances'. The High Court has not had an opportunity to consider this issue.

The defence might also wish to invoke section 290 of the 1995 Act which provides that, on the application of the accused, the sheriff may order that the prosecutor shall hold an identification parade. Three criteria must be satisfied, these being that the prosecutor has not already held such a parade, that the accused has requested him to do so but that the prosecutor has refused or unreasonably delayed and that the sheriff considers the application to be reasonable.

Plea of guilty before service of indictment

At any time after he has appeared on petition, the accused can intimate in terms of section 76 of the 1995 Act that he intends to plead guilty, in which case he will be served with an abbreviated form of indictment (unless an indictment has already been served) and a notice to appear at a diet of the appropriate court not less than four clear days after the date of the notice. A section 76 indictment does not contain any list of witnesses or productions. The 'appropriate court' means either the High Court or the sheriff court where no indictment has been served or the court in which the case has been indicted if an indictment has already been served.

At the section 76 diet if the accused does in fact plead guilty, he will be sentenced on that basis. Submission of such a section 76 letter does not, however, bind him and if he does not plead guilty, or pleads guilty only to a part of the indictment and the prosecutor is not prepared to accept a restricted plea, the section 76 indictment must be deserted *pro loco et*

[7] 1981 SCCR 243.
[8] 1985 SCCR 157.

tempore—that is to say, the court, on the motion of the prosecutor, dismisses the case but with the possibility of reindicting.

The decision to indict

Once his precognition is complete, the procurator fiscal will submit the papers to Crown counsel who decide the future course of the case. It may be marked 'no further proceedings', reduced to summary procedure, indicted in the sheriff court for jury trial there or indicted in the High Court.

Prevention of delay in trials

It has for centuries been a feature of solemn procedure in Scots law that the procurator does not have unlimited time to serve the indictment and bring the case to trial. Sections 65 and 66 of the 1995 Act set out strict time-limits, though some of them are capable of being extended. The purpose of those time-limits is, according to Lord McCluskey (speaking in *Gardner* v *Lees*[9]) 'to require the Crown to proceed with deliberate expedition in cases where the circumstances are serious enough to warrant procedure on indictment and/or the detention of the accused in custody awaiting trial'. These time-limits provide a framework within which the Crown must work.

The time-limits are as follows.

Service of indictment

Accused in custody—time allowed after full committal
By section 65(4) of the 1995 Act an accused who is in custody must be served with the indictment within eighty days of full committal, which failing he must be liberated forthwith. This provision does not, however, affect the validity of the indictment. In *McCluskey* v *HM Advocate*[10] an attempt was made to argue the contrary but the High Court rejected that argument, observing that if the appellant had been unlawfully detained he might have a civil remedy, but that nothing in the legislation provided him with protection from prosecution.

As well as being significant for the situation with which it dealt, *McCluskey* also highlights the fact that acquittal on the substantive charge is not the inevitable remedy for every procedural defect.

A single judge of the High Court (but not a sheriff) may for what section 65(5) of the 1995 Act calls 'any sufficient cause' extend the eighty-day period. Section 65(6) of the 1995 Act bars such extension where the failure to serve the indictment within the eighty-day period is the fault of the prosecutor.

In *Farrell* v *HM Advocate*[11] it was held that it is competent to grant such an extension retrospectively, that is even after the accused should have been liberated. The court did, however, say:

'It may be thought that retrospective extension of the time limit does nothing for the protection of accused persons but the answer to that supposition lies in this, that when a court is faced with a retrospective application for extension, it may well look for very powerful reasons in support of the application which is made before deciding to grant it.'

[9] 1996 SCCR 168.
[10] 1992 SCCR 920.
[11] 1985 SLT 58.

In *Farrell,* the reason was that a witness had become ill and the sheriff was obliged to desert the indictment *pro loco et tempore.*

All cases—induciae

By section 66(6) of the 1995 Act the indictment must in all cases be served on the accused not less that twenty-nine clear days before the trial diet. This is to allow the accused time to prepare his defence. The reference to 'clear days' means that neither the day the trial starts nor the day the indictment is served counts towards the computation of the twenty-nine days. Moreover, in a case to be tried in the sheriff court, there must be at least fifteen clear days between service of the indictment and the first diet (the purpose of which is discussed below at p 72). A Full Bench held in *HM Advocate* v *McDonald*[12] that failure to meet the twenty-nine-day time-limit does not render the indictment fundamentally null and also that is it open to the defence to waive the twenty-nine-day *induciae.* The court also held that the failure of the defence to object to the failure to meet the time-limit in that case by the procedure provided by the predecessor of section 72 of the 1995 Act (which is considered below at p 73) meant that it ws incompetent for them to take objection at the trial diet. This was on the ground that it was (and, by sections 72 and 79 of the 1995 Act, still is) provided that matters which can be dealt with by preliminary plea under section 72 cannot thereafter be raised except by leave of the court on cause shown.

What the court in *McDonald* did not do is say what would happen if the defence do not waive their objection to the failure to provide twenty-nine clear days. Presumably the accused's remedy is a postponement of the trial. However, the Crown might be presented with an acute difficulty if such a postponement would take the case beyond one of the other time-limits, as we shall see under reference to *HM Advocate* v *Swift* (discussed at p 62 below).

Commencement of trial—accused on bail

By section 65(1) of the 1995 Act an accused cannot be tried on indictment for any offence unless the trial is commenced within a period of twelve months of the first appearance of that accused on petition in respect of that offence. If the trial does not commence within that period, the accused must be discharged forthwith and 'thereafter he shall be for ever free from all question or process for that offence'. There is, of course, an exception to this (in terms of section 65(2)) in the case of an accused for whose arrest a warrant has been granted for failure to appear at a diet in the case. Parliament did not intend to provide an encouragement for accused persons to abscond in the hope that, if they could stay at large for over a year they could thus obtain immunity from prosecution.

The High Court made it clear in *McCulloch* v *HM Advocate*[13] that the date on which the accused appeared on petition is to be discounted in calculation of the twelve-month period. In that case, the first appearance was on 6th October 1993 and the twelve months was, accordingly, due to expire on 6th October 1994 (and not on 5th October). This follows the

[12] 1984 SCCR 229.
[13] High Court, 2nd November 1994; unreported.

decision in *Keenan* v *Carmichael*,[14] which established that this is the correct approach to take to the computation of any period of time in a Scottish criminal context.

By section 65(3) of the 1995 Act upon application being made, the sheriff or (where an indictment has been served on the accused for trial in the High Court) a single judge of the High Court may on cause shown extend the period of twelve months.

Such extensions are essentially a matter for the discretion of the court, no definitive test being laid down in the Act. However, some assistance may be gained from the cases.

In *Watson* v *HM Advocate*[15] it was learned that the accused had decamped from his domicile of citation, possibly to the Republic of Ireland. A further petition warrant was granted and issued to the police for enforcement in relation to other charges. Efforts to trace him were unsuccessful and it was learned that he had failed to comply with bail conditions in England. The Crown, instead of serving an indictment at the domicile of citation which it knew to have been abandoned, sought and obtained an extension of the twelve-month period. The accused appealed against the grant of that extension (though since it appears from the report that at the time of the appeal hearing he was still untraced it is not clear how he managed to do so).

The ground of appeal was that the extension was unreasonable since the indictment could have been served timeously at the domicile of citation. In support of this it was argued that, if the accused had failed to appear for trial having been so cited a warrant could have been obtained for his arrest and the extension was therefore not necessary. The High Court, however, was persuaded by the Crown's argument that it is not in the public interest to require jurors and witnesses to come to court for a trial diet which is almost certain not to proceed because of the absence of the accused. The appeal was refused.

With some hesitation, the court supported the Crown's position in *McGinty* v *HM Advocate*[16] where the indictment was not served timeously because of the unforeseen illness of the police officer tasked with effecting service and an extension had to be sought. The court did point out in that case that mere pressure of business will not justify an extension. However, although it is one thing for the Crown to take a considered decision not to serve the indictment at the domicile of citation (as in *Watson*) or to be caught out by something unforeseen (as in *McGinty*), it is quite another for the Crown to seek an extension where it has itself made what Lord Justice-General Emslie was to call 'repeated inexcusable and major errors'—the situation in *HM Advocate* v *Swift*.[17]

In that case, the Crown twice made a mistake as to the accused's domicile of citation and left service copy indictments at an address which the accused had long since left and which had never been his domicile of citation. These indictments were, accordingly, never served and the Crown, when it discovered its error, had to attempt to serve a new indictment for yet another trial diet. However, there was less than twenty-nine clear days available

[14] 1991 JC 169.
[15] 1983 SCCR 115.
[16] 1985 SLT 25.
[17] 1984 SCCR 216.

before the expiry of the twelve-month period and so it could not comply with the requirement to give a clear twenty-nine day *induciae*. An application was made for an extension but the sheriff refused it and the Crown appealed.

The appeal was refused. The High Court did not exclude the possibility of an extension even though the Crown may have been at fault, but Lord Justice-General Emslie did say that 'any particular fault on the part of the prosecutor and its nature and degree will be relevant considerations'. In this case there was considerable and inexcusable fault and the court did not consider that the seriousness of the charges was enough to override that.

A similar conclusion was reached in *Lyle* v *HM Advocate*[18] in which the Crown made an error in the calculation of the expiry of the twelve-month period and applied for an extension which was granted. On appeal the court held that in the circumstances of the case the error was inexcusable and, in respect that the charges were not of an unusual or exceptional gravity, that the wider public interest lay in favouring the observance of the statutory time-limit. The appeal was allowed.

With *Swift* and *Lyle* must be contrasted *Black* v *HM Advocate*[19] in which the failure of the Crown to serve at the correct domicile of citation was attributable not to the fault of the Crown but to the fact that the change in domicile had not been intimated to the Crown. In that case the extension was granted.

The Crown is, of course, quite likely to get an extension if the delay in bringing the case to trial is attributable to the defence. In *HM Advocate* v *Brown*[20] the sheriff granted a defence motion for an adjournment of the trial but refused to grant an unopposed application by the Crown to extend the twelve-month period. Her reasoning was that the Crown still had time to proceed within the twelve-month period and that pressure of court business occasioning difficulty in finding court time to do so was not a sufficient reason for an extension. Lord Justice-General Emslie characterised this as 'wholly unreasonable' and the Crown appeal was granted. Similarly, in *Duffy* v *HM Advocate*[21] the appeal court upheld a decision by the trial judge to extend the twelve-month period in the absence of the appellant at the diet. The appellant was legally detained in England and the appeal court held that the delay in trying the case in Scotland was attributable to the appellant, not to the Crown.

In *HM Advocate* v *M*[22] the High Court held that it is competent to extend the twelve-month period retrospectively.

Commencement of trial—accused in custody

Additional limits apply in the case of the accused who is in custody. By section 65(4) of the 1995 Act the trial of the accused who is in custody must be commenced within 110 days, failing which he is to be liberated forthwith and thereafter 'he shall be for ever free from all question or process for that offence'. In *JTAK* v *HM Advocate*[23] the 110-day rule was held to apply to two children who were committed for trial and sent initially to prison on

[18] 1991 SCCR 599.
[19] 1990 SCCR 609.
[20] 1994 SCCR 347.
[21] 1991 SCCR 685.
[22] 1986 SCCR 624.
[23] 1991 SCCR 343.

unruly certificates but afterwards were granted bail on condition that they resided in a List D school, it being held that the bail order was in that case merely a procedural device for locking them up in the List D school.

HM Advocate v *Meechan*[24] decided that any period during which the accused is serving a substantive sentence for another offence does not count towards the 110 days; nor, in terms of *Bickerstaff* v *HM Advocate*,[25] does any period during which the accused is confined in a mental hospital as being insane in bar of trial. So, in *Wallace* v *HM Advocate*[26] where an accused was, after full committal, sentenced to two years' imprisonment on another charge, it was held that the running of the 110 days was interrupted when the accused began his sentence of two years' imprisonment, as his detention after that date was not referable to the committal order.

HM Advocate v *McCann*[27] established that the release of the accused from custody, on the authority of the prosecutor, at any point during his incarceration interrupts the running of the 110 days.

Section 65(7) of the 1995 Act permits a single judge of the High Court to extend the 110-day period if he is satisfied that delay in the commencement of the trial is due to the illness of the accused or of a judge, the absence or illness of any necessary witness or 'any other sufficient cause which is not attributable to any fault on the part of the prosecutor'. *Young* v *HM Advocate*[28] provided an example of the extension of the 110-day period because of the illness of the judge and the illness of the two co-accused.

Such applications are considered with great care, especially where the 'any other sufficient cause' ground is in issue and the court will usually be reluctant to grant them. As Lord Justice-Clerk Wheatley said in *HM Advocate* v *McTavish*:[29]

> 'That section was designed to give protection to the lieges, to ensure that they were not held in custody for an undue period of time before the case was finally disposed of. That is a very important right, and it can only be departed from when sufficient cause is shown to the court to justify that departure. Whatever the other conditions may be, it is certainly a positive condition that the delay in respect of which the case is said not to be able to go on within 110 day is not a delay for which the prosecutor is himself responsible.'

However, this is not to say that the possibility of criticising the approach taken by the prosecutor will be an absolute bar to an extension. In *Gildea* v *HM Advocate*[30] the Crown took a calculated risk with the timing of cases at an assize but one case took longer than expected. An extension was sought, granted and upheld.

The indictment

The indictment which is served on the accused must be accompanied by a list of the names and addresses of the prosecution witnesses (as provided for by section 66(4) of the 1995 Act). Section 66(5) requires the Crown to

[24] 1967 SLT (Notes) 75.
[25] 1926 JC 65.
[26] 1959 JC 71.
[27] 1977 SLT (Notes) 19.
[28] 1990 SCCR 315.
[29] 1974 SLT 246.
[30] 1983 SCCR 144.

provide the clerk of court with a record copy of the indictment, a copy of the list of witnesses and a copy of the list of productions. The practice is to provide the accused with a copy indictment containing not only the charge but also the list of witnesses and the list of productions.

The list of witnesses is governed by section 67 of the 1995 Act. By that section the list must provide the names of the witnesses together with an address at which they can be contacted for precognition. It is in general not open to the Crown to call any witness whose name does not appear on the list or refer to any production not included in the list of productions. However, by section 67(5) of the 1995 Act it is competent, with leave of court, for the prosecutor to examine such witnesses or refer to such productions, provided that written notice has been given to the accused not less than two clear days before the jury is sworn to try the case. Notices of this sort are a feature of the overwhelming majority of prosecutions on indictment.

Productions

It is sometimes argued that the law requires that absolutely any object mentioned in the course of evidence should be produced in court. There is a battery of cases about this question and they demonstrate that the law makes no such requirement; rather, it discriminates between those things which truly add to the reliability of the evidence and those which do not.

The best starting-point is *MacIver* v *Mackenzie*,[31] in which a man was charged with taking wreck (pit props, battens and logs) without delivering it to the receiver of wreck. The wreck was not produced at trial. Lord Justice-General Normand said in the course of the judgment:

> 'The learned counsel for the appellant asserted that there was an obligation on the prosecutor to produce any article which was referred to in an indictment or complaint unless it was beyond his power to do so. There is certainly no such rule. It is no doubt the proper practice to produce any article referred to in the indictment or complaint where there is no practical difficulty in doing so. There are, however, many cases where it is inconvenient, though not wholly impossible, to make articles productions in the case because of the size of the articles. Livestock cannot conveniently be made productions in all cases. Perishable goods cannot be made productions and there are other examples. *The question in each case is whether the real evidence is essential for proving the case against the accused*' (emphasis added).

The final sentence is the key to this whole area of law. If the article—what Lord Normand referred to as 'the real evidence'—is essential to proof of the case, it should be produced unless that is impracticable.

This must now be seen in the light of section 276 of the 1995 Act. Although in general it could be argued that the production in court of biological material, such as blood, is undesirable on health grounds and not necessary to proof (since no one ever analyses a blood sample in the courtroom), section 276(1) puts the matter beyond doubt by providing that evidence as to the characteristics and composition of such a sample is admissible, notwithstanding the fact that neither the material nor a sample of it is lodged as a production.

[31] 1942 JC 51.

The position reached in *McIver* was reaffirmed in *McKellar* v *Normand*[32] in which the appellant had been charged with reset of a bed and blanket which were not produced and it was held that, although it is good practice for items which are the subject of this sort of charge to be produced if it is convenient to do so or, failing production, for labels relating to them to be produced in their place, the question is always whether injustice is likely to result from failure to produce them. In *McKellar* the court took the view that it was not and upheld the conviction.

In *Hughes* v *Skeen*[33] a man was convicted of the theft of seventy-eight newspapers which were not produced at the trial. In upholding the conviction the High Court observed that it was not explained what purpose in the interests of justice would have been served by the production of the newspapers and that such production was neither necessary, convenient nor practicable.

We may contrast *Anderson* v *Laverock*,[34] a poaching case in which the manner in which fish had been taken was essential to the charge and was proved by distinctive marks on the fish. As fish are perishable, the prosecution did not produce them at trial and for that the court did not make any criticism. However, the prosecution went further and destroyed the fish without giving the defence any opportunity to have them examined. This, it was held, was prejudicial and the conviction was quashed. *Milne* v *Maher*[35] was for practical purposes an identical case concerning deer carcasses.

Where, however, the original material is made available, it is open to the Crown to use derivatives of that material to produce the evidence. In *Hamilton* v *Grant*,[36] for example, fingerprint lifts were made on vinyl sheets at the locus but photographs of those lifts were used by forensic scientists for comparison with the fingerprints of the accused. The vinyl sheets were lodged as productions at the trial but the sheriff upheld the 'no case to answer' submission on the basis that the best evidence rule required that vinyl lifts should have been used for comparison. The Crown appeal against the sheriff's decision was allowed, though the court did not issue an opinion and we cannot therefore know the reasoning. We do know that in *HM Advocate* v *Dennison*[37] a trial judge allowed evidence to be led of Sellotape lifts from prints on a cigarette packet, on the ground that there was nothing distinctive about the packet itself, though he regretted the absence of the packet.

It may be said, then, that the other party is entitled to an opportunity to test the accuracy of any assertion made about an article. Usually that opportunity will be given by producing the article at court; but if that is impracticable the party making the assertion imperils his case if he voluntarily does or acquiesces in anything which deprives his opponent of that chance. It does not, however, appear to be necessary to allow an opponent to test the proposition that an article exists (for example, the newspapers in *Hughes*). This principle is preserved for biological material by section 276(2) of the 1995 Act, which requires that a party wishing to lead evidence of the characteristics or composition of such material but

---

[32] 1992 SCCR 393.
[33] 1980 SLT (Notes) 13.
[34] 1976 SLT 62.
[35] 1979 JC 58.
[36] 1984 SCCR 263.
[37] 1978 SLT (Notes) 79.

not lodging it as a production must make it available for inspection by the other party, unless the material constitutes a hazard to health or has been destroyed in the process of analysis.

The point has sometimes been taken that the party wishing to lead evidence about the results of the examination of an article needs to have that article in court to have it identified not only by the person who speaks to the circumstances in which it was found but also by the person who made the examination. The argument is that it is only in this way that it can be proved that the article examined is that which was found in circumstances of significance to the case.

Such was the argument made in *Williamson* v *Aitchison*,[38] a drink driving case in which the evidence related to a blood sample which was not produced at court. The appellant argued that this made it impossible for a constable to give evidence that the blood referred to in the analyst's certificate was that taken by the doctor from the accused, thereby breaking the link between the blood taken and that analysed. The court observed that although it would be usual to produce the sample it was not the only way to make the link. It held that the analyst's and doctor's certificates taken with the evidence of the police that one part of the sample taken by the doctor had been sent to the analyst were enough to make the link. The conviction was upheld.

It must be noted, however, that it does not follow from any of this that the defence are entitled to access to everything which the prosecution hold which is potentially of relevance to the case. The law just described relates to admissibility of evidence and no more. In this the law of Scotland differs very significantly from that of England. Scots law is summarised in the following passage from the judgment of the High Court in *Higgins* v *HM Advocate*.[39]

'It was said by the appellants today that, having regard to the exclusive powers given to the police and the procurator fiscal service to investigate crime, it was the duty of the procurator fiscal to make known to the defence any information in their possession which would tend to exculpate the appellants and which the defence were not likely to discover in their own investigations. . . . We regard this ground of appeal as wholly without foundation, not to say impertinent. There is no obligation on the Crown to provide any list of witnesses other than those which are attached to an indictment, and there is no obligation on the Crown to disclose any information in their possession which would tend to exculpate the accused.'

This is a statement of the strict law. As a matter of practice (and as the court went on to recognise in *Higgins*) procurators fiscal and Advocate-depute will disclose to the court anything which is relevant, including material which supports the defence and is damaging to the Crown case. That is not, however, by any means the same as giving the defence a right of access to material in the hands of the Crown.

Documentary productions
Particular rules apply to documents which are to be productions with a view to proof of their contents. Issues arise in relation to copy documents and to business records.

---

[38] 1982 SLT 399.
[39] 1990 SCCR 268.

Copy documents

The general rule, and the starting-point for our consideration, is that a copy is secondary evidence. The best evidence is the original. Therefore in a criminal case unless the absence of the original can be explained satisfactorily—for example, by its loss or destruction—the copy is inadmissible. This rule, for which there was more justification when copies were handwritten rather than nowadays when they are produced photographically, has been heavily modified by statute. Nevertheless, it must be borne in mind because if the statutory requirements are not met it will express the law which applies.

The modification is to be found in Schedule 8 to the 1995 Act, which is derived from Schedule 3 to the Prisoners and Criminal Proceedings (Scotland) Act 1993 and is based on work done by the Scottish Law Commission.

The provisions were enacted following comments made by Lord Justice-General Hope in *Lord Advocate's Reference (No 1 of 1992)*.[40] In that case, he noted that English law had been amended to take account of modern conditions and said that it was regrettable that Parliament had not been invited so to legislate for Scotland. He said that there was an urgent need for consideration to be given to doing so. When the possibility for the legislative vehicle arose, the Scottish Law Commission addressed the issue with some urgency and produced a report, Evidence: Report on Documentary Evidence and Proof of Undisputed Fact in Criminal Proceedings.[41]

The root of the objection to the copy document seems to be Dickson's remark that

'copies are often inaccurate from inadvertence . . . admitting them would afford opportunities for misleading the jury, and . . . a party is most likely to tender such secondary evidence in order to gain an improper advantage from a discrepancy between it and the original document'.[42]

The Commission pointed out inapplicability of the risk of inadvertent error in the light of the existence of the photocopier and thought that the risk of deliberate deception could be sufficiently met by a power in the court to direct production of the original where it is desirable for the court to see the original or where there is any genuine dispute as to its appearance. This was substantially the approach taken for civil evidence in section 6 of the Civil Evidence (Scotland) Act 1988.

Accordingly, paragraph 1(1) of Schedule 8 to the 1995 Act provides:

'For the purposes of any criminal proceedings a copy of, or of a material part of, a document, purporting to be authenticated in such manner and by such person as may be prescribed, shall unless the court otherwise directs, be—
(a) deemed a true copy; and
(b) treated for evidential purposes as if it were the document, or the material part, itself,
whether or not the document is still in existence.'

By sub-paragraph (2) it is immaterial how many removes there are between a copy and the original.

---

[40] 1992 SCCR 724.
[41] Scot Law Com No 137.
[42] W G Dickson, *A Treatise on the Law of Evidence in Scotland* (3rd edn, 1887) para 279.

Essentially, the effect of this is that a copy, provided that it bears what purports to be a proper authentication and the court does not 'otherwise direct', is not only to be deemed a true copy but is also to be treated as if it were the original.

It is also worth noting that in this provision, as throughout the Schedule, 'document' is not confined to written documents. It includes maps, plans, graphs, drawings, photographs, sound recordings and visual recordings (such as videotapes).

Authentication, by rule 26(1) of the Act of Adjournal (Criminal Procedure Rules) 1996, is to be carried out by (i) the author of the original document, (ii) a person who is or who has been in possession and control of the original or a copy of it, or (iii) the authorised representative of such a person. It is to be in the form set out in Form 26.1–A. It is also important to note that all that is necessary is that the copy *purports* to be properly authenticated.

It is *not* necessary for admissibility that the person who authenticates the document actually compares it with the original, though if he gives evidence and it transpires that he has not done so the reliability of the document might become a matter of comment.

In some cases, failure to check the copy with the original might found an application to the court to direct that the document should not get the benefit of paragraph 1. It is emphasised that this will vary from document to document. A banker might well be entitled to assume the accuracy of a copy statement produced from the bank's computer without making any comparison. Indeed there might be little with which it could be compared as the 'original ' is electronic and there is a good case for saying that such a printout is itself an original, rather than a copy.

Other kinds of documents might be less inherently reliable. Two cases in particular require care. The first of these is the production of a monochrome copy of a coloured original, where loss of the coloured material may alter the meaning—for example, where a plan distinguishes different areas by colour. The second applies where what is produced is a copy of a material part of a document. It might well be possible to demonstrate that another part materially alters the meaning of what is produced.

This brings us to the obvious issue of the circumstances in which the court will 'otherwise direct'. So far, we have no case-law on either paragraph 1 or its civil equivalent to assist our interpretation. On the basis that any other approach would defeat the purpose of the statute, it is thought that the court will only 'otherwise direct' where there is some particular reason to doubt the reliability of the copy produced. Some assistance may be derived from the consideration of the Scottish Law Commission, who observed that the mere fact that it is a copy which is produced should not be enough to induce the court to make a direction. It said:

> '[T]he mere fact that the copy, if admitted, will be adverse to the party seeking to demonstrate unfairness is irrelevant since Parliament by enacting the legislation will have impliedly decided that there is nothing intrinsically unfair about the admission of a copy. It will not normally be unfair that there is no opportunity to cross-examine the operator of the copying machine or to examine the original of a tape or other device containing computer instructions or data which would be likely to be meaningless to the court.'[43]

[43] Scot Law Com No 137, p 34.

It is thought that since the thrust of the paragraph is to make the use of copies a normal occurrence, it will be up to the party seeking to challenge the use of a copy to persuade the court to make such a direction. This will be reasonably straightforward where there is a patent defect on the face of the document. There might, for example, be obvious and material alterations and it might be unclear whether they exist on the original. If the authenticator is a witness he or she might be able to resolve that matter but, otherwise, the court might require to direct that the copy is not to get the benefit of the paragraph.

A more difficult question will arise where the party against whom the copy document is sought to be led in evidence maintains that it contains a latent defect. It may be said, for example, that the authentication is not what it purports to be or it may be that serious doubts about the reliability of the copy emerge in the course of evidence, perhaps because it has not been checked with the original. Here, it is thought, the court could be persuaded to make a direction but perhaps the best time to raise the issue in a case under solemn procedure would be at a preliminary diet or a first diet.

Business documents

Paragraph 1 of Schedule 8 to the 1995 Act relates to copies of all kinds of documents. Paragraph 2, by contrast is specific to documents relating to businesses and undertakings and the holders of paid and unpaid offices—though, as we shall see, this is scarcely a major limitation. Paragraph 2(1) provides:

> 'Except where it is a statement such as is mentioned in paragraph 3(b) and (c) below, a statement in a document shall be admissible in criminal proceedings as evidence of any fact or opinion of which direct oral evidence would be admissible, if the following conditions are satisfied—
>> (a) the document was created or received in the course of, or for the purposes of, a business or undertaking or in pursuance of the functions of the holder of a paid or unpaid office;
>> (b) the document is, or at any time was, kept by a business or undertaking or by or on behalf of the holder of such an office; and
>> (c) the statement was made on the basis of information supplied by a person (whether or not the maker of the statement) who had, or may reasonably be supposed to have had, personal knowledge of the matters dealt with in it.'

This too is derived from the Scottish Law Commission report. The Commission treated the law as to business documents as a branch of the law relating to hearsay, essentially because they contain a record of what someone has said or done. After reviewing the existing law, the Commission came to the conclusion that it was 'not well suited to the needs of a society which increasingly depends on information kept or generated by a growing variety of technical methods'.[44] The Commission then looked at the English legislation on the subject and at the effect of the Criminal Evidence Act 1965, which remained in force for Scotland, though not for England and Wales. It was able to identify numerous shortcomings.

In its discussion paper, the Commission noted that

---

[44] Scot Law Com No 137, p 3.

'the system of recording transactions, communications and other events in business and administrative documents will usually be one on which organisations themselves will depend in everyday practice and, therefore, the evidence so generated is likely to be trustworthy. Moreover, in many instances business documents will also be the best evidence, particularly those recording very detailed or unexceptional facts or events of which witnesses are unlikely to have any recollection'.[45]

What the Commission was saying, in other words, is that business records, far from being an inherently unreliable type of evidence, are in fact likely to be highly reliable. They form the basis for just those sorts of important decisions in their own affairs to which juries are invited to have regard when being charged as to the meaning of the concept of reasonable doubt. On such an analysis, reform was overdue.

This approach was carried through to the report itself. In particular the Commission identified three tests of reliability for statements in business documents. First, the statement would have to be based on someone's personal knowledge, so that it would be derived from someone who knew what he was talking about; secondly, the statement should have been made for the purposes of a business; and thirdly, the document containing the statement should have been kept by a business.[46] The point of these requirement was that if a person was making a statement for the purposes of a business and the document was important enough to be kept, there would be a strong incentive to accuracy. These three tests underlie the three conditions which must be satisfied before paragraph 2 can apply.

Where these conditions are satisfied, a statement in the document is admissible in criminal proceedings as evidence of any fact or opinion of which direct oral evidence would have been admissible. The statement in the document stands as evidence in its own right and it does not require to be 'spoken to' by a witness; the sole functions of the witness are to establish that the conditions are met and (perhaps) to interpret a statement which is couched in the jargon of a particular business.

This contrasts with the general rule which is that statements in documents are not evidence unless they are 'spoken to' by a witness. In *Forsyth* v *HM Advocate*[47] it was held that a trial judge should not have allowed an advocate-depute to cross-examine on the basis of a document which had been lodged as a production but which was not spoken to by any witness.

The first test—that the document should have been created or received in the course of, or for the purposes of, a business or undertaking or in pursuance of the functions of the holder of a paid or unpaid office—requires to be satisfied by the evidence of a witness. It defines the breadth of the provision. By paragraph 8, 'business' includes trade, profession or other occupation. By the same paragraph, 'undertaking' includes any public or statutory undertaking, any local authority and any government department. 'Holder of a paid or unpaid office' is not defined but appears to be derived from English legislation.[48] The Scottish Law Commission intended it 'to

---

[45] Criminal Evidence: Affidavit Evidence, Hearsay and Related Matters in Criminal Proceedings (DP No 77) p 52.
[46] Scot Law Com No 137, p 6.
[47] 1991 SCCR 861.
[48] See Scot Law Com No 137, p 11, note 9.

cover such persons as an office bearer in an entity which is neither a business nor an undertaking, such as a charity, kirk session or club, who may keep documents for the efficient discharge of his functions'.[49] It is, in short, difficult to think of any kind of record other than purely personal or private records to which the paragraph does not apply.

The second test is that the document was kept by the business, undertaking or office holder and in terms of paragraph 4 this test can, subject to a discretion in the court to direct otherwise, be satisfied by certification in prescribed form and purporting to be authenticated in such manner as might be prescribed either by a person authorised to do so on behalf of the relevant business or undertaking or by an office holder or a person authorised on his or her behalf, as the case made be. The certificate, by rule 26.1(2) of the Act of Adjournal (Criminal Procedure Rules) 1996, must be in the form set out in Form 26.1–C.

The Law Commission suggested that a court would not be likely to 'otherwise direct' unless the party objecting to the statutory mode of authentication put forward at least *prima facie* grounds for not accepting that the document had been kept by the business concerned.[50]

The provisions of paragraph 4 are derived from section 5 of the Civil Evidence (Scotland) Act 1988. It was the Law Commission's intention to use the expression 'purporting to be signed', rather than 'purporting to be authenticated' and its purpose was to bring into play *Cardle* v *Wilkinson*[51] so that a facsimile signature would suffice.[52] It is suggested that this has been achieved, notwithstanding the draftsman's preference for 'authenticated'.

Service of the indictment

In terms of rule 2.2 of the Act of Adjournal (Criminal Procedure Rules) 1996 service of the indictment may be personal or by leaving it at the domicile of citation specified in the bail order (either in the hands of someone there or by fastening it to the door). It is also competent, where no proper domicile of citation has been specified, to leave the document at a place where the accused is believed, on reasonable grounds, to reside. This approach, however, is rare if not entirely unknown, since the prosecutor cannot be certain that the court will regard the grounds for the belief as reasonable and therefore cannot be certain that the indictment has been served until the accused appears for the first diet or trial and does not challenge the efficacy of the citation.

In the case of an accused which is a body corporate, the indictment may be served (in terms of section 70(2) of the 1995 Act) at its registered office or principal place of business in the UK. The prosecution of bodies corporate on indictment is in fact rather rare.

First diet, preliminary diets and preliminary pleas

After the indictment has been served and before the trial takes place there are two substantial issues which require to be resolved.

One is the state of preparedness of the parties, experience having demonstrated that a significant proportion of cases have to be adjourned at

[49] Scot Law Com No 137, p 11.
[50] *Ibid*, p 30.
[51] 1982 JC 36.
[52] Scot Law Com No 137, p 30.

the trial diet because preparation is incomplete. This causes massive inconvenience and wasted time, especially if jurors and witnesses have attended court.

The other is to deal with preliminary legal challenges. There is no point in convening a trial if, for example, there is some fundamental flaw in the indictment which would mean that the trial should not proceed at all.

These matters are dealt with by sections 71 to 73 of the 1995 Act, under the heading of 'Pre-trial proceedings'. The emphasis in the sheriff court is on ensuring that parties are prepared, with the possibility of dealing also with preliminary pleas. The emphasis in the High Court is on dealing with preliminary pleas and taking the opportunity to check the state of preparation. The differing emphasis is reflected in the procedure by which the issues are brought before the court, but once there the rules are the same.

In the sheriff court, section 66(6) of the 1995 Act requires that the accused be required to attend a first diet not less than fifteen clear days after service of the indictment and not less than ten clear days before the trial diet. The holding of a first diet is, therefore, mandatory.

In the High Court, section 72(1) of the 1995 Act provides for the fixing of a 'preliminary diet' where a party 'within the appropriate period' gives written notice to the court and the other parties that one or more of four situations applies. These are:

(*a*) that he intends to raise a matter relating to the competency or relevancy of the indictment or object (on certain grounds) to the validity of the citation against him;

(*b*) that he intends to submit a plea in bar of trial, to apply for separation or conjunction of charges or trials, to raise a preliminary objection to a special capacity in terms of section 255 of the 1995 Act or to apply in terms of section 278(2) for part of the transcript of the judicial examination not to be read to the jury;

(*c*) that there are documents the truth of the contents of which ought to be admitted or that there is anything else which in his view ought to be agreed; and

(*d*) that there is some other point which could be resolved with advantage before the trial.

By section 72(1) of the 1995 Act written notice of an intention to raise any of these matters must be given to the court and the other parties within 'the appropriate period'. The notice must, by subsection (2), specify the matter or grounds of submission or point to which the notice relates. The appropriate periods are as follows:

Competency, relevancy, objections to validity of citation	Within the period of 15 clear days after service of the indictment
Pleas in bar of trial, separation or conjunction of charges or trials, challenges to special capacities, applications that part of judicial examination be not read to jury	Within the period from service of the indictment to 10 clear days before the trial

Admissions as to documents, agreement of other matters and resolution of other matters	Within the period from service of the indictment to the trial diet

Where such notice is given, the court may (and, in the case of a challenge to relevancy, competency or validity of citation, must) fix a preliminary diet. At the same time, it may postpone the trial for up to twenty-one days (in terms of subsection (4)). At the preliminary diet the court may consider not only the matter originally raised but also any matter raised in a notice intimated to the court and parties not less than twenty-four hours before the diet.

In the sheriff court, section 71(2) of the 1995 Act provides that the court shall, at the first diet, consider any of these matters of which a party has, not less than two clear days before the first diet, given notice to the court and to the other parties.

These do not come to quite the same thing.

In the High Court, the Crown will in practice have several days' notice of the matter to be debated, whereas in the sheriff court that notice can be reduced to as little as two clear days. However, whereas in the High Court the co-accused will have the opportunity to associate themselves with the plea taken by one accused up until twenty-four hours before the diet, in the sheriff court they will have to serve their own notices at least two days before it—and if the accused who first takes the point leaves service of his notice until the last minute, the co-accused will not be able to pursue the matter at all.

It is important to note that, in terms of section 79 of the 1995 Act, except by leave of the court on cause shown, the matters identified in section 72 for consideration at a preliminary diet or first diet cannot be raised except under the procedure provided in those two sections.

We have now to consider the preliminary pleas which can be raised at a preliminary diet or first diet, and we take them in turn.

Challenges to competency or relevancy

Renton and Brown[53] distinguishes the concepts of competency and relevancy thus:

> '[A]n objection to competency implies that the trial of the accused person before a certain court, or at the instance of a certain prosecutor or upon a certain charge is not competent; an objection to relevancy implies that the terms of the indictment to which the accused person is asked to plead are not in accordance with the requirements of the law.'

Competency

Challenges to competency are, therefore, directed essentially to the right to prosecute and the most obvious ground upon which the competency of an indictment may be challenged is lack of jurisdiction. Another ground would be that the time-limits which apply once the accused has appeared on petition have expired.

[53] R W Renton and H H Brown, *Criminal Procedure According to the Law of Scotland* (5th edn, 1983) para 9–18.

Much less frequently the person in whose name the indictment runs will be found not to have a title to prosecute. Section 64(1) of the 1995 Act provides that all prosecutions for the public interest before the High Court or before a sheriff and jury shall proceed on indictment in the name of Her Majesty's Advocate, so that anything which purports to be an indictment and which runs in another name will be incompetent except where the office of Lord Advocate is vacant when section 287 of the 1995 Act permits indictments to run in the name of the Solicitor-General.

Relevancy

Leaving aside silly mistakes (such as failure by the prosecutor to sign the indictment), there are probably two challenges to relevancy which arise more often than any others. The first of these is that what is charged does not amount to a crime and the second is that the charge lacks specification.

The purpose of a criminal trial is not to discover the truth in general but rather to discover the truth or otherwise of the proposition that the accused person committed the particular offence charged against him. It is essential, therefore, that the issue should be properly focused in the charge. The Crown must, in framing the charge, direct the attention of the accused and the court to what it offers to prove and it must do so in a way which is both relevant and, as a sub-branch of this, specific. A challenge to the relevancy of a charge alleges that even if the prosecutor proves everything contained in the charge, it does not amount to an offence. A challenge to specification alleges that the accused has not received fair notice of the allegation against him. Thus a charge will be irrelevant if an essential element of the crime is omitted or if what is charged is a statutory prohibition which does not actually create an offence. So, for example, a charge which alleged that the accused was a law student in a public place without lawful authority or reasonable excuse would not be relevant because that is not a crime.

The cases, of course, are concerned with more subtle criticisms of charges, either where there has been a mistake in the drafting and something has been left out by accident or where the Crown is pursuing a charge which has not previously been applied in quite the way it is used in the instant indictment or complaint.

Khaliq v *HM Advocate*[54] is an example of a challenge to relevancy where the Crown applied a well-recognised type of common law crime to a new type of conduct. That case established that the crime of reckless conduct may be committed by the supply to children of so-called 'glue sniffing kits'— solvents with containers for inhalation—in the knowledge of the intended use and that such use was injurious to health and dangerous to lives. In so deciding, the High Court took the opportunity to reiterate that it is in the nature of Scots criminal law that it does not countenance any precise and exact categorisation of the forms of conduct which amount to crime. Old crimes can be committed in new ways and the law is flexible enough to deal with them. It follows that the fact that a precise precedent for a particular charge does not exist does not necessarily mean that the charge will be irrelevant.

As to specification, the charge must give fair notice of the allegations which the accused will have to meet and, to that end, it is required to be specific as to time (which means date), place and mode. The test to be

---

[54] 1983 SCCR 483.

applied was set out with clarity by Lord Justice-Clerk Ross in *Clydesdale Group plc* v *Normand*,[55] a case on specification in a charge relating to a statutory offence, when, following *Lockhart* v *National Coal Board*,[56] he said:

> 'The appellants must be well able to anticipate what the Crown are seeking to establish, and that is the test of whether the charges are relevant and sufficiently specific.'

Relevancy and specification must be considered in the light of the detailed rules contained in the 1995 Act and especially in Schedules 2 and 3, as given effect for petitions and indictments by sections 34 and 64 respectively.

Schedule 3 sets out the basic rules. We do not require to consider all of them but concentrate instead on the basic essentials, especially time, place and mode.

Specification of quantity

Paragraph 4 of Schedule 3 deals with specification of time, place and quantity. Quantity can be dealt with quite simply by noting that where a quantity of anything is specified in a charge the words 'or thereby' are implied in terms of paragraph 4(6). Accordingly, for example, a prosecution does not fail merely because the Crown alleges the theft of £200 and proves the theft of £195. Indeed, in terms of the same provision, the words 'or some other quantity to the prosecutor unknown' are implied in all statements of quantities. As a result, in the example just given, the Crown can secure a conviction even if the actual amount of money stolen is left shrouded in confusion. That having been said, however, where proof of a particular quantity or the like is essential to the definition of the charge the latitude will not apply. Such will not usually be the case in theft charges and the like but an attempt to rely on the statutory predecessor of this provision in relation to the age of a victim of crime failed in *Lockwood* v *Walker*[57] precisely because the particular offence (lewd and libidinous practices and behaviour) was regarded as only being capable of being committed against a child under the age of puberty (a proposition upon which *Batty* v *HM Advocate*[58] now casts considerable doubt).

Specification of place

Specification of the place of the commission of the crime (often called the locus) matters not only because it is required to give the accused fair notice of the case against him but also because the jurisdiction of the court will depend upon it (as the court pointed out in *McMillan* v *Grant*).[59] Paragraph 4(2) of Schedule 3 implies words such as 'near' in every charge so that some latitude exists as to place in every charge, again where the actual place is not of the essence of the crime.

Specification of time

Latitude as to time is more complex. It is usually possible for the Crown to state the date of the offence with accuracy but in some cases the most that is

[55] 1994 SLT 1302.
[56] 1981 SLT 161.
[57] (1909) 6 Adam 124.
[58] 1995 SCCR 525.
[59] 1924 JC 13.

known is that the crime occurred during a particular period. Paragraph 4(1) of Schedule 3 therefore provides that the 'The latitude formerly used in stating time shall be implied in all statements of time where an exact time is not of the essence of the charge'.

The latitude formerly used was three months[60] and that is the latitude which is implied. Accordingly, a charge which alleges that an offence took place on 1st February in a given year implies the period from 1st January to 31st March, and the Crown can lead evidence of the commission of the offence at any time during that period.

This is subject to the exact time not being of the essence of the charge. There are a few offences where exact time is of the essence and the examples usually given are concerned with poaching where the taking of a creature during the closed season will be an offence but doing so during the open season will not. Of more practical significance (since the offence is more common) is the fact that sexual intercourse with a girl under the age of sixteen will inevitably be an offence even if she 'consents'[61] but consensual sexual intercourse with a girl who has reached her sixteenth birthday is lawful. Accordingly, if the girl is at the time of the offence within three months of that birthday a latitude which extends beyond that birthday cannot be implied.

It was decided in *Howman* v *Ross*[62] that if a defence of alibi is being pled, the prosecutor will have to be more accurate as to date; otherwise the accused is unfairly hindered in his presentation of that defence.

There are some cases in which the period of time during which the offence occurred is longer than three months and sometimes substantially so. This may be because the offence itself is covert and not discovered by the victim for some time or it may be because the victim is a child who, for whatever reason, does not disclose the offence for some time. So, for example, in *HM Advocate* v *Mackenzie*[63] the accused had been stealing from his employer over a period of time but had managed to conceal the fact. The latitude taken and allowed was six years. Again, where the owner of an asset does not check it for a considerable period, the Crown will label the whole of that period. The nineteenth-century cases (*Andrew Hempseed*[64] and *Geo Douglas*)[65] on this refer to sheep on the hill. A more recent example is to be found in *Cuthill* v *Guild*,[66] in which it was held that on a complaint libelling theft of a cheque book and uttering forged cheques, it was reasonable to fix the dates by reference to the last date when the book was seen and the date of the utterings, even though that was seventeen months ago, because theft is in its nature a clandestine act.

An example of a victim not disclosing the offence until a late date is to be found in *HM Advocate* v *AE*[67] in which the Crown took latitudes of nine and a half years on one charge and five years on the other. In that case the charge was incest and the daughters of the accused had been eight and ten years

[60] Hume, ii, 221; Alison, ii, 251.
[61] Criminal Law (Consolidation) (Scotland) Act 1995, s 5(1), (3).
[62] (1891) 3 White 57.
[63] (1913) 7 Adam 189.
[64] (1832) Bell's Notes 215.
[65] (1865) 5 Irv 53.
[66] High Court, Edinburgh, 22nd November 1989; unreported.
[67] 1937 JC 96.

old when the conduct started. The Crown was also proposing to prove a course of conduct and not just isolated acts. Nevertheless, in repelling an objection to the relevancy of the indictment Lord Justice-Clerk Aitchison said that there would be a heavy onus on the Crown to justify such a latitude.

The existence of a course of conduct was also a matter which weighed with Lord Justice-Clerk Grant in *Littlejohn* v *HM Advocate*[68] when he held that twenty-two and a half months was too great a latitude in relation to each of three charges, but the brevity of the judgment makes this case less helpful than it might otherwise be.

Ultimately, it will be for the Crown to justify the taking of an exceptional latitude and inevitably that will depend on the circumstances of the particular case. The test to be met was set out succinctly by Lord Cameron in *HM Advocate* v *Hastings*[69] as follows:

'The basic principle which governs decision in questions of permissible latitude of time in criminal charges is that of fairness: fairness to the legitimate interest of the person accused in being fairly tried on a relevant charge, and fairness to the interest of the public in the detection and suppression of crime.'

Specification of mode
Specification of mode is about setting out in the indictment the conduct by the accused which forms the basis of the alleged charge. By paragraph 2 of Schedule 3, it is not necessary to specify by any *nomen juris* the offence which is charged. Instead, it is sufficient that facts relevant and sufficient to constitute an offence are set forth. So, in *Dyce* v *Aitchison*[70] the accused's conduct in a court formed the basis of a charge of contempt of court; but contempt of court is not a crime. It is a matter *sui generis* with which the court, whether civil or criminal, has inherent power to deal. It was not, therefore, necessary for the Crown to prosecute the matter—the court could have dealt with it on its own initiative. However, the High Court considered that the facts narrated did amount to identifiable offences, even though none of them was named in the charge and the charge was therefore held to be relevant.

Other examples are to be found in *Bewglass* v *Blair*,[71] *Strathern* v *Seaforth*,[72] *Coventry* v *Douglas*,[73] *HM Advocate* v *Grainger and Rae*[74] and *Cameron* v *HM Advocate*.[75]

Forms of charge
Section 64(2) of the 1995 Act provides that an indictment may be in the form set out in Schedule 2 to the Act. That Schedule, which is drawn directly from nineteenth-century legislation, gives examples of charges. It is to be regretted that the examples have not been more substantially updated; they retain a quality which is now somewhat quaint and use language which does not feature in modern practice. So, for example, we still see a charge

[68] 1970 SLT 21.
[69] 1985 SLT 446.
[70] 1985 SCCR 184.
[71] (1888) 1 White 574.
[72] 1926 JC 100.
[73] 1944 JC 13.
[74] 1932 JC 40.
[75] 1971 SLT 333.

relating to the uttering of a forged certificate of character for a domestic servant, and the unfortunate Harriet Cowan, mill-worker, of 27 Tweed Row, Peebles, is still being 'ravished', notwithstanding the well-nigh universal use of the word 'rape' in contemporary indictments for that offence. Section 138(2) gives similar effect to Schedule 5 for summary cases, which (being drawn from 1954 legislation) is less dated but still somewhat so. It is suggested that, although Schedule 5 does not in terms refer to cases on indictment, the existence of a form of charge in that Schedule will nevertheless be at least a powerful argument in favour of its relevancy where it appears on an indictment.

The essential point about these forms of charge is that if they are followed the charge will be relevant even if specification of mode is thoroughly inadequate. In Schedule 2,

'You did, while in the employment of James Pentland, accountant in Frederick Street, Edinburgh, embezzle £4,075 of money'

does not tell the reader how the embezzlement was accomplished at all, and, in Schedule 5,

'You did conduct yourself in a disorderly manner and commit a breach of the peace'

is hopelessly unspecific but is sanctioned by the Act and was given effect to by the High Court in *Anderson* v *Allan*.[76] Lord Justice-Clerk Ross pointed out that the appellant could find out what the case against him was about by interviewing the Crown witnesses.

Paragraph 11 of Schedule 3 provides:

'In an indictment or complaint charging a contravention of an enactment the description of the offence in the words of the enactment contravened, or in similar words, shall be sufficient.'

This can result in greatly reduced specification, but it is not a licence for the Crown to include no specification at all. We have already noted the words of Lord Ross in *Clydesdale Group plc* v *Normand* and can contrast two examples of the application of the principles that what matters is whether the defence can anticipate what the Crown is seeking to establish. In *Yeudall* v *William Baird & Company*[77] the complaint libelled a failure to produce adequate ventilation in a pit but did not specify what should have been done. It was held that the complaint was relevant on the basis that it gave fair notice that the system of ventilation was said to be inadequate to perform its statutory function. In *Blair* v *Keane*,[78] on the other hand, the complaint libelled a contravention of the Trade Descriptions Act and specified the extravagant claims made for the vehicle in question but none of its actual defects. It was held that as the complaint did not tell the accused the defects upon which the prosecution would lead evidence it did not give fair notice and was therefore lacking in specification.

A question which the courts do not appear to have considered so far is how paragraph 11 of Schedule 3 interacts with Schedules 2 and 5, which contain a number of examples of statutory charges. For example, Schedule 5 sanctions a charge in these terms:

[76] 1985 SCCR 399.
[77] 1925 JC 62.
[78] 1981 SLT (Notes) 4.

'You did drive a motor car recklessly contrary to section 2 of the Road Traffic Act 1988.'

This describes the offence in the words of the statute contravened and so is within paragraph 11 of Schedule 3 and, on the basis of *Anderson*, is relevant as sanctioned by Schedule 5; but it gives no inkling as to the manner of driving and, had it not appeared in Schedule 5, it is likely that it could have been attacked on the basis of *Blair*. (It also, incidentally, misrepresents section 2 of the Road Traffic Act 1988 which makes it an offence to drive *dangerously*, not recklessly.)

Paragraph 3 of Schedule 3 makes it unnecessary for the Crown to use words such as 'wilfully', 'maliciously' or 'knowingly' in charges; such words, which apply to *mens rea*, are implied in charges. So in *Gallacher* v *Paton*[79] it was held that a fraud complaint was relevant without the words 'falsely' or 'fraudulently' and in *HM Advocate* v *Colquhoun*,[80] an embezzlement case, it was held to be unnecessary to narrate that the accused knew of the trust purpose for which money was received since the word 'knowingly' was implied by statute.

Paragraph 3 has, however, to be read with two qualifications. The first of these is that it probably does not apply to statutory charges, where failure to libel a word contained in the offence creating provision specifying the *mens rea* might well render the charge defective. The second is that in *HM Advocate* v *Flanders*[81] the trial judge (Lord Cameron) held that this provision did not relieve the Crown from the need to give notice in the indictment of its intention to lead evidence that the accused had at some time earlier than the date of the offence evinced malice and ill will towards the victim. In so holding, he said:

'It is no doubt true that in terms of the Act of 1887 for purposes of relevancy malice is implied in the indictment, but my experience of matters criminal is that the practice has always been that there should be an express allegation of previous malice as matter of fair notice when it is the intention of the Crown to lead evidence of such matters. . . . It seems to me that the argument against admission of this evidence without proper notice rests upon a broader and sounder foundation, namely, that the principle of fair play and of fair notice, which underlies the practice of our criminal law, forbids the introduction of evidence of this kind unless fair and proper notice is given to the accused person of the intention of the Crown to submit it to the decision of a jury.'

There is, therefore, a potential distinction between the rules which apply to the indictment so far as relevancy is concerned and those which apply so far as admissibility of evidence is concerned, though in *Anderson* v *Allan*[82] Lord Justice-Clerk Ross was to point out that the appellant could find out what the case against him was about by interviewing the Crown witnesses and such an approach would not support the making of such a distinction except, perhaps, as to matters which would not necessarily arise in the course of such interviewing (such as malice evinced six months before the crime, as in *Flanders*).

[79] (1909) 6 Adam 62.
[80] (1899) 3 Adam 96.
[81] 1962 JC 25.
[82] 1985 SCCR 399.

Amendment

An issue which is related to that of the content of charges is that of amendment of charges, as provided for by section 96 of the 1995 Act. Section 96(2) and (3) provides as follows:

> '(2) It shall be competent at any time prior to the determination of the case, unless the court see just cause to the contrary, to amend the indictment by deletion, alteration or addition, so as to—
> (a) cure any error or defect in it;
> (b) meet any objection to it; or
> (c) cure any discrepancy or variance between the indictment and the evidence.
> (3) Nothing in this section shall authorise an amendment which changes the character of the offence charged. . . .'

The effect of this section is that it will be open to the Crown, if it considers it necessary to do so in course of a debate about relevancy, to seek to amend the indictment so as to cure some sorts of defect.

This is a wide power but not an unlimited one. As Lord Justice-Clerk Moncrieff put it in *Stevenson* v *McLevy*,[83] 'However wide the power of amendment . . . may be, it cannot extend to the essential requisites of a criminal charge.' Lord McLaren expressed a similar idea in *MacIntosh* v *Metcalfe*[84] when he said, 'Now, to remedy a defect does not mean to transform into a libel what never was a libel.'

In both these cases the complaints omitted to specify the locus of the alleged offence and the sheriff had allowed them to be amended by inserting a locus; but the court held that these amendments were incompetent. This, however, must be seen in the context of *Herron* v *Gemmill*,[85] where the locus libelled in the complaint read 'on the road on the Glasgow Inner Ring Road, at a part thereof near Charing Cross underpass' but did not say that this was in Glasgow. The procurator fiscal sought to amend by inserting the word 'Glasgow' after the word 'Road' and the sheriff refused to allow that amendment. The High Court, however, held that the amendment should have been allowed. Lord Justice-Clerk Wheatley said that a sensible reading of the description given of the locus made it abundantly clear that it was within the jurisdiction of Glasgow Sheriff Court. He went on to distinguish the situation in which no locus is given at all from that in which (as in the instant case) the locus is very fully specified 'but might be lacking in some technical point of description'.

Obviously there are shades of grey between these two extremes and it will be a question for the court in each case where that particular case falls. In *Yarrow Shipbuilders Ltd* v *Normand*[86] it was held that 'on Unit 5, Ship 1047' was inadequate to demonstrate that Glasgow Sheriff Court had jurisdiction and the procurator fiscal was not permitted to amend by adding the words 'South Street, Glasgow'. Lord Justice-General Hope said that 'an amendment . . . cannot be made if the complaint is in the first instance incompetent'.

---

[83] (1879) 4 Couper 196.
[84] (1886) 1 White 218.
[85] 1975 SLT (Notes) 93.
[86] 1995 SCCR 224.

It seems, then, that if a sensible reading of what is in the charge gives the necessary information, an amendment to put the charge into proper form will be allowed but that amendment to provide the basic information is not competent. That sort of approach was applied to the benefit of the Crown in *Duffy* v *Ingram*.[87] In that case the complaint had three charges. No date was given for the commission of the alleged offence in the first charge; the second charge began 'date and place above libelled' and the third charge began 'on said 30th November 1985'. It was held that the date could be inserted in charges (1) and (2) by amendment. The High Court did not say so but, reading the charges together, it is clear that the Crown was alleging that the offences were all committed on 30th November 1985 and it is suggested that the case is to be understood on that basis.

Whether or not to allow an amendment is primarily a matter for the discretion of the court but it is clear that prejudice to the accused will be an important factor. In *Lockhart* v *British School of Motoring*[88] a sheriff refused to allow an amendment, partly because it proposed to narrate (but not charge) a further offence by one of the accused (which the sheriff characterised as 'a radical change to the character of the offence charged') but also because the amendment would have deprived the accused of a statutory defence which would have been available in respect of the unamended version and which he considered to be prejudicial.

By contrast, in *Matheson* v *Ross*[89] an alteration to the date of the offence after the prosecutor's case had been closed was permitted, there being no prejudice to the accused. An adjournment was offered but was declined.

Absence of prejudice to the accused also weighed heavily with the court in *Tudhope* v *Chung*.[90] In that case the Crown had charged the accused with having done certain things in the capacity of one who had management and control of premises; but the particular regulation contravened related to occupiers of premises. The Crown sought to amend so as to substitute the latter status for the former. The sheriff refused to allow that to be done but the High Court allowed the Crown's appeal. Lord Justice-Clerk Wheatley said:

> 'The character of the offence is the breach of the regulation and that has not been changed. . . . This was a classical example of curing an obvious error or defect . . . just the sort of things which [the section] has in contemplation. If the amendments are allowed it is the same person who is being charged with the same offence . . . it was not suggested that the respondent would be prejudiced in any way in his defence on the merits if they were allowed.'

Challenges to validity of citation

The whole purpose of serving the indictment on the accused is to give him notice of the charge which he is to face. Accordingly, failure to serve the indictment is fatal to the proceedings and trial on that indictment cannot go ahead. In *Hester* v *Macdonald*[91] an accused person had been granted money bail (the usual procedure at that time), and a domicile of citation was fixed. However, he failed to lodge the money and so remained in custody. The

[87] 1987 SCCR 286.
[88] 1982 SCCR 188.
[89] (1885) 5 Couper 582.
[90] 1985 SCCR 139.
[91] 1961 SC 370.

indictment was served at the domicile of citation and the accused, who was in prison, never received it, either actually or constructively. The domicile of citation had not taken effect. The case went to trial and the accused was convicted unanimously, but when the Crown learned of the failure in service of the indictment they did not support the conviction when it was appealed. As reported, the case is concerned with the accused's (unsuccessful) attempt to get damages against the procurator fiscal and others in respect of his conviction.

Plea in bar of trial

Nonage
Since it is conclusively presumed that a child aged less than eight years old cannot be guilty of any crime it is a valid objection to trial that the accused is below that age.

Insanity in bar of trial
The primary duty to identify the existence of doubt about the accused's mental condition rests on the prosecutor, in terms of section 52(1) of the 1995 Act. Where it appears to the prosecutor in any court that the person charged may be suffering from mental disorder, it is his duty to bring before the court such evidence as may be available of the mental condition of the accused. Section 52 of the 1995 Act does not prescribe any form for the evidence which the prosecutor is to lay before the court but section 54, which provides a means for the court to deal with a case in which the accused is found to be insane in bar of trial, speaks of the court being satisfied 'on the written or oral evidence of two medical practitioners' that a person charged is insane.

The test for insanity in bar of trial remains that adumbrated by Lord Justice-General Dunedin in *HM Advocate* v *Brown*.[92] It is a mental disorder which 'prevents a man from doing what a truly sane man would do and is entitled to do—maintain in sober sanity his plea of innocence, and instruct those who defend him as a truly sane man would do'.

By section 54 of the 1995 Act unless the prosecutor deserts the diet *pro loco et tempore*, the court which finds an accused to be insane in bar of trial must do three things. First, it must make a finding to that effect and state the reasons for that finding. Secondly, it must discharge the trial diet and order that an examination of facts be held. And, thirdly, it must remand the accused in custody or on bail or, where the written or oral evidence of two medical practitioners satisfies the court that the accused's mental disorder is such as would warrant his admission to hospital under Part V of the Mental Health (Scotland) Act 1984, it must make a temporary hospital order (assuming that a suitable hospital is available) until after the examination of facts.

The purpose of the examination of facts is to determine, so far as possible, whether the accused actually did the act which forms the basis of the prosecution. The point of this is that it is perceived as unsatisfactory that a person who might in fact not have done what is alleged should nevertheless be subjected to compulsory hospitalisation simply because he is not fit to

---

[92] (1907) 5 Adam 312 at 343.

stand trial. A person who is not mentally disordered and who is found not to have done the act charged would, of course, be entitled to be acquitted and Parliament's desire has been to place the mentally disordered person as nearly as possible in the same position as the sane.

So far as possible, the rules of evidence and procedure at an examination of facts are to be as nearly as possible those applicable in respect of a trial (section 55(6) of the 1995 Act). However, those rules inevitably require some modifications, the first and most obvious of which is that, where the accused is not already legally represented the court must appoint counsel or a solicitor to represent his interests (section 56(3) of the 1995 Act). It is axiomatic, of course, that a person who has been found to be insane in bar of trial cannot do so for himself.

The other significant alteration to the usual rules is made by section 55(6) of the 1995 Act which allows the court to order that an examination of facts shall proceed in the absence of the accused if it is not 'practical or appropriate' for him to attend. Ordinarily, of course, proceedings cannot competently take place in the absence of the accused (see *Walker* v *Emslie*[93]) unless he so misconducts himself as to prevent a proper trial from taking place, in which case section 92(2) of the 1995 Act permits the court to exclude him.

By section 55 of the 1995 Act at the examination of facts the court must, on the basis of evidence, determine whether it is satisfied to the criminal standard that the accused did the act or made the omission constituting the offence. It must also determine whether it is satisfied on the balance of probabilities that there are no grounds for acquitting the accused. If it is not so satisfied—in other words, if it is not provided that the accused did the relevant act or if there is a ground for acquitting him—the court must acquit the accused of the charge. However, by section 55(4), if the court holds that the accused did the act charged but acquits him on the ground of insanity at the time it must state that ground. In such cases, the court may (by section 57 of the 1995 Act) proceed to make a hospital order in the same way as if the accused had been found to be insane in bar of trial.

In a case where the accused is found to be insane in bar of trial and is not acquitted at the examination of facts, the court is to proceed in one of the ways set out in section 57(2) of the 1995 Act. There are four options and the court has a large measure of discretion, except where the offence is murder.

First, the court may make an order that the accused shall be detained in such hospital as the court may specify, and may, in addition, make an order that the person shall, without limit of time, be subject to the special restrictions on discharge and leave of absence from hospital set out in section 62(1) of the Mental Health (Scotland) Act 1984. In a murder case the court must make an order for detention in hospital and make the additional order for such restrictions.

Secondly, the court may make an order placing the person under the guardianship of a local authority or a person approved by a local authority.

Thirdly, the court may make a supervision and treatment order. Such orders are provided for by Schedule 4 to the 1995 Act. They are only available where the court is satisfied of four things. The first of these is that the making of such an order is the most suitable means of dealing with the

[93] (1899) 3 Adam 102.

person, though since it is unlikely that a court would deal with any offender in a way other than that which it considered the most suitable it is not obvious why legislative space is taken up with this provision. The second is that the mental condition of the person is such as requires and may be susceptible to treatment but is not such as to require a hospital order; and the court is only entitled to be so satisfied on the written or oral evidence of two or more medical practitioners. The third is that the supervising officer to be named in the order is willing to undertake the supervision. And the fourth is that arrangements have been made for the treatment, details of which must be specified in the order.

The fourth option the court has is to make no order.

There are cases in which a person who has been found to be insane in bar of trial subsequently recovers. In such cases, it is open to the Crown to reactivate the prosecution, upon the basis that it is in the public interest to have guilt or innocence determined by a proper trial. Accordingly, section 56(7) of the 1995 Act provides that, where a finding has been made that the accused did the act or made the omission constituting the offence and that person is subsequently charged with an offence arising out of the same act or omission, any order made under section 57(2) shall cease to have effect.

Res judicata

Res judicata refers to the principle that no one can be required to face a court for a second time on a matter which has been disposed of already by either conviction or acquittal. Accordingly, if a court has held a charge to be irrelevant, or incompetent, the prosecutor cannot place the accused before the court again on a charge or (in relation to competency) in circumstances not materially different. So in *HM Advocate v McNab*[94] an attempt to reindict in circumstances which had already been held to be incompetent was the foundation of a successful plea in bar of trial (applying a much older case, *Longmuir v Baxter*).[95]

HM Advocate v M[96] is an example of a case in which, the first indictment having been dismissed as irrelevant, the Crown served a fresh indictment in which sufficient changes had been made to defeat the plea of *res judicata*.

Where the accused has stood trial on, or pled guilty to, the matter already, he is said to have 'tholed his assize'. The parameters for this are, however, quite strict. In *Hilson v Easson*[97] Lord Ormidale said that 'the essence of the plea is that the person tendering it has already been brought to trial by the prosecutor and has then stood his trial for, or pleaded guilty of a specific offence duly set out in an indictment or other competent form of complaint'. In *HM Advocate v Dunlop*[98] Lord Cameron summarised the position by saying:

> '[I]n order that the plea of *res judicata* will lie the former proceedings must have been orderly and regularly conducted to a conclusion and in the case of solemn procedure this involves the return of a verdict by a properly constituted jury . . . where no verdict has been received or returned . . . the whole proceedings are vitiated and in the absence of a verdict the plea of "tholed assize" cannot lie.'

[94] 1994 SCCR 633.
[95] (1858) 3 Irv 287.
[96] 1986 SCCR 624.
[97] 1914 SC (J) 99.
[98] 1974 SLT 242.

It was a matter of concession in that case that the first prosecution does not have to have proceeded to sentence.

It is of the essence of the plea that the first proceedings were competent. In *Hilson* the Lord Justice-General described as 'downright nonsense' the proposition that the accused had tholed his assize because an English court had, in apparent ignorance of the fundamental principles of criminal jurisdiction and the provisions of the Treaty of Union which address the separate identity of Scots law, purported to take untried Scottish offences into account in sentencing him for English offences. This is a mistake which English courts still make from time to time.

Mora

Mora is concerned with delay. The court has an inherent jurisdiction to refuse to deal with a prosecution, whether under solemn procedure or summary procedure, which has become oppressive as a result of delay. The law was reviewed by a Full Bench in *McFadyen* v *Annan*.[99]

The facts in *McFadyen* were that a man was arrested in August 1990 by two police officers, one of whom was McFadyen. In September 1990 he complained that McFadyen had assaulted him. The man was tried and acquitted a few days later and investigation began into the complaint against the officer. At the beginning of November he was interviewed under caution. The case against him was reported to the (district) procurator fiscal in January 1991 and sent by him to the regional procurator fiscal (who has responsibility for complaints against the police) in March. He reported it to Crown counsel (who decide whether there is to be a prosecution in police complaint cases) in April. They instructed summary proceedings and the officer was charged on 17th April, the complaint being served on 14th May. Although not stated in the judgments, the practice is for the regional fiscal to have the case precognosced before reporting to Crown counsel and this is most likely to have been done between January and March by the district fiscal. In holding that the prosecution had not become oppressive, Lord Justice-Clerk Ross formulated the law thus:

> 'What the court has to ask itself is if the delay, whether caused by the Crown or not, has been such as to prejudice the prospects of fair trial. The court is not really in a position to determine whether delay which took place before the Crown raised proceedings was justified or not. The Crown has to determine its priorities and it is, for example, for the Crown and not the court to determine whether, in cases like the present, proceedings should be taken first against the accused civilian or the accused policeman. On the other hand, if the Crown concede that delay before raising proceedings was due to some failure on the part of the Crown, that would appear to me to be relevant; it would also be a relevant consideration that delay at that stage was due to fault on the part of the accused. Further, irrespective of fault, the court is certainly entitled to consider any delay before the Crown raised proceedings as part of the overall delay which is allegedly prejudicial. Moreover, where there has been delay after the Crown has raised proceedings, the court can determine whether such delay has been due or undue, and that is a circumstance to which the court is entitled to have regard. However, the real question which the court has to consider in all cases where delay is alleged is whether the delay has prejudiced the prospects of a fair trial. This

[99] 1992 SCCR 186.

involves the court asking itself whether the risk of prejudice from the delay is so grave that no direction by the trial judge could be expected to remove it. In the case of summary procedure the question must be whether the risk of prejudice from the delay is so grave that the sheriff or justice could not be expected to put that prejudice out of his mind and reach a fair verdict. I would again stress that cases where such a plea in bar of trial will be upheld will be rare and exceptional cases. The test to be applied where oppression is alleged to have been the result of delay is the same as that which falls to be applied in cases where oppression is alleged to be the result of pre-trial publicity or any other cause.'

The test would seem, then, to be whether the delay itself has resulted in prejudice, though it will be relevant whether the blame for the delay lies at the door of one of the parties.

Hitherto, what has been significant is whether the passage of time has been such that evidence has been lost, as by the death of witnesses or the destruction of documents, but this is not really the same sort of thing as unfair publicity or the accidental disclosure of a previous conviction which can be dealt with by being consciously ignored. The point about lost evidence is that the accused is hampered in his defence and if that has happened to such an extent that any conviction would be unsafe the trial should not go ahead. Lord Cowie, Lord Cullen and Lord Milligan concurred and adopted a similar formula. Lord Morison concurred in the result but dissented on the reasoning.

Lord Justice-General Hope, with Lord Brand and Lord Cowie considered this question, under reference to *McFadyen* in *Normand* v *Rooney*,[100] another police complaint case, and observed that the question of 'putting the prejudice out of one's mind' required some explanation. The Lord Justice-General formulated the test, in a summary prosecution, as being 'whether the prejudice is so grave that no sheriff or justice could be expected to reach a fair verdict in all the circumstances'. This, it is suggested, recognises the particular nature of the prejudice rather better, especially when the Lord Justice-General went on to say:

'I see no reason to doubt on this information that the sheriff who hears the evidence at the trial will be able to arrive at a fair verdict, after making such allowance as may be appropriate for any disadvantage which the respondent may suffer due to the lapse of time which has occurred.'

Separation or conjunction of charges or trials

It is fundamental that the trial must be fair and it is arguable that if some combinations of unrelated charges appear on the indictment the mere presentation of the combination to the court will be so prejudicial that the Crown should not be permitted to proceed to trial upon all of them at once.

This is the theory but it is rare that such an argument succeeds. An example of a case in which it did is *HM Advocate* v *McGuinness*,[101] in which the Crown combined charges of assault on one date with an unrelated charge of murder on another date. However, the Lord Justice-Clerk in that case explained that the test is 'whether it is fair to the person or persons accused to put a particular accumulation of charges in one indictment' and stressed that the decision is one for the discretion of the court.

[100] 1992 SCCR 336.
[101] 1937 JC 37.

In *Brown* v *HM Advocate*[102] Lord Justice-General Hope had to deal with a case in which the accused was charged with 'a catalogue of different crimes alleged to have been committed in different places and under different circumstances'. He said:

'It is well settled that the combination in a single indictment of charges relating to different kinds of crime committed at different times in different places and circumstances does not of itself give rise to a material risk or prejudice to the accused, and it would not be appropriate on this ground alone for the charges to be separated. . . . It is common ground that it is only where a material risk of real prejudice can be demonstrated that the granting of a motion to separate charges can be justified.'

In *Brown* the fact that the accused would need to attack the character of Crown witnesses on some of the charges (thus exposing himself to the risk that his own criminal record would be in issue) was held not to be a sufficient ground for separating charges, since the trial judge would have a discretion whether or not to allow his record to be put in issue. That judge could take the risk of prejudice into account in so deciding.

Separation of trials is a related matter and arises where there are multiple accused. The starting-point is that it has been recognised since at least *HM Advocate* v *Parker and Barrie*[103] that related offences committed by two or more persons should in general be tried together. Separation is possible, but Lord Moncrieff said in *Robt Turner and Others*[104] that 'It generally requires some specification of peculiar circumstances to render it necessary or desirable.' Slightly more recently, in *Gemmell* v *MacNiven*,[105] the Lord Justice-General said:

'Persons accused of the joint commission of a crime have no right to insist on a separation of trials; and there is nothing oppressive in refusing a separation, unless it is asked for on some ground which goes to the conditions of a fair trial.'

A common situation in practice is that of multiple accused who face one or more charges in common but against each of whom there is on the same indictment a series of other, unrelated charges, which he alone faces. It is clear that such an indictment is competent but it remains to be seen whether the court might regard a disparity in the seriousness of the combination of charges against one accused as compared with another as an appropriate ground upon which to grant separation of charges and/or trials.

The conjoining of charges or trials is rare in the extreme but it is possible that by proceeding separately against accused persons for an offence which they are alleged to have committed in concert the Crown may produce unfairness and in such circumstances such a motion may be made.

Special capacity

Certain crimes can only be committed by a person who possesses a particular qualification, such as being the holder of a licence, the master of a vessel or the occupier of a house. In terms of section 255 of the 1995 Act such 'special capacities' are held to be admitted unless challenged. In *White*

[102] 1992 SCCR 59.
[103] (1888) 2 White 79.
[104] (1881) 18 SLR 491.
[105] 1928 JC 5.

v *Allan*[106] the special capacity (that of being a prostitute in relation to a charge of importuning under section 46(1) of the Civic Government (Scotland) Act 1982) was challenged and, since the Crown failed to lead any evidence to prove that capacity, the accused was acquitted. By contrast, in *Allan* v *McGraw*[107] the court affirmed that being a female prostitute is a special capacity in relation to section 46(1) and that, since it had not been challenged at the appropriate time, it was to be held as admitted.

As a general rule, a special capacity exists in any statutory offence where the prosecutor would otherwise have to prove the capacity as part of the proof of the case. As the appeal court put it in *Smith* v *Allan*.[108]

> 'We are of opinion that "any special capacity" . . . applies to all persons who are specifically charged in a particular capacity with committing an offence which can only be committed by persons in that special capacity.'

Special capacities do not apply to common law crimes, for the simple reason that such crimes can be committed by anyone at all and not only by those possessing particular qualifications.

Perhaps the commonest special capacity is that of being disqualified for holding or obtaining a driving licence, and this is relevant to a charge of driving while disqualified. In *Paton* v *Lees*[109] the High Court held on appeal that to be disqualified by order of the court is to possess a special capacity and in *Smith* v *Allan* it was held that to be disqualified by reason of age is also to possess such a capacity. In *Aitchison* v *Tudhope*[110] it was held that to be subject to a bail order is a special capacity; and in *Newlands* v *MacPhail*[111] the provision was held to apply to contraventions of section 58(1) of the Civic Government (Scotland) Act 1982, which can only be committed by persons who have two or more unspent convictions for theft.

Applications for part of the transcript of judicial examination not to be read
The grounds upon which such applications should be granted are not specified in the Act but the obvious one is that a passage in the transcript is inadmissible (perhaps because the procurator fiscal overstepped the limits on questioning) or prejudicial (for example, because the accused disclosed something which is irrelevant to the charge but which goes to his character).

Admissions as to documents and other matters
It is understood that the Crown has occasionally used this provision, with varying success, to try to force the hand of the defence in relation to apparently non-contentious evidence in fraud trials. It may be that it will become of increased importance in light of the duty under section 257 of the 1995 Act to take all reasonable steps to secure agreements as to evidence.

---

[106] 1985 SCCR 85.
[107] 1986 SCCR 257.
[108] 1985 SCCR 190.
[109] 1992 SCCR 212.
[110] 1981 SCCR 1.
[111] 1991 SCCR 88.

Other points which could be resolved with advantage

This is a catch-all, but would seem to cover the circumstances of *Styr* v *HM Advocate*[112] in which the admissibility or otherwise of statements made by the accused and recorded in a transcript which was lodged as a production was canvassed at a preliminary diet rather than by objection in the course of the trial. Since the debate took several days, to hold it before the trial avoided massive disruption of the trial itself and also, incidentally, allowed the matter to be considered on appeal before the trial.

Conduct of first diets and preliminary diets

The accused is required to attend the first diet or preliminary diet (in terms of sections 71(4) and 73(1) of the 1995 Act) and a warrant may be granted for his arrest if he fails to do so. The grant of such a warrant does not seem to result automatically in the discharge of the trial diet but, where the accused has failed to attend at the first diet or preliminary diet, there must be substantial grounds for doubting whether he will attend at the trial and for the taking of steps (such as the desertion of the indictment *pro loco et tempore* coupled with any necessary motion for an extension of the twelve-month time-limit) to ensure that jurors and witnesses are not inconvenienced.

At the first diet, section 71(6) of the 1995 Act requires that the accused be asked how he pleads to the indictment. Section 73(1) makes the same requirement at the conclusion of a preliminary diet. Where he pleads guilty, he may be dealt with for the offence. Where, however, the accused pleads not guilty, and after disposal of any preliminary pleas, the diet will take the course provided for by sections 71(1) and 73(3). The court is required, so far as is reasonably practicable,

> '[to] ascertain whether the case is likely to proceed to trial on the date assigned as the trial diet and, in particular—
> (a) the state of preparation of the prosecutor and of the accused with respect to their cases; and
> (b) the extent to which the prosecutor and the accused have complied with the duty under section 257(1) of [the] Act'.

To that end, the court is permitted to ask the prosecutor and the accused any question in connection with any matters to be ascertained.

The duty to seek to agree facts

Section 257(1) of the 1995 Act imposes a duty on the prosecutor and the accused to identify facts which each would be seeking to prove, which are considered to be unlikely to be disputed by the other party and as to which it is not desired to lead oral evidence. When such facts have been identified, the party identifying them must 'take all reasonable steps' to secure agreement of such facts and the other party is required to 'take all reasonable steps to reach such agreement'.

No sanction is provided for failure in this duty (which only applies where the accused is legally represented) but it may be that a court will take into account the extent to which it has been fulfilled in deciding any motion for adjournment.

[112] 1993 SCCR 278.

Where it appears to the court that the case is unlikely to proceed to trial on the date assigned, the Act requires that the trial diet be postponed, and permits the fixing of a further first diet.

Section 71(8) of the 1995 Act permits the sheriff to adjourn a first diet, a course which will presumably be taken where the results of the original first diet are inconclusive or where more time is required for debate.

Notice of special defences, defence witnesses and defence productions

The fact that the burden of proof is at all times on the Crown is reflected in the obligations placed on the Crown as to the content of the indictment, the list of Crown witnesses and the list of Crown productions. However, it must not be forgotten that the law aims to *balance* the interest of the accused in securing a fair trial with that of the public in securing the effective prosecution of crime, and that Scottish criminal procedure is adversarial in its nature. It is as much in the public interest that the prosecutor has fair notice of the defence case as it is that the accused has notice of the case against him; only in that way can the prosecutor in the public interest make proper investigation of any substantive case which the accused proposes to advance, or either confirm or rebut it. Accordingly, section 78 of the 1995 Act provides for the giving of notice by the accused of any special defence, of any witnesses whom he proposes to call and of any productions to which he intends to refer.

Special defences

There are four 'special' defences. These are alibi, incrimination, insanity at the time and self-defence. Alibi simply means that the accused was elsewhere at the time when the alleged offence was said to be committed and so cannot have committed it. Incrimination means that the accused blames some other person for the crime. Insanity at the time negates *mens rea* and so the accused falls to be acquitted; this is properly dealt with in a text on the general principles of criminal law rather than here. And self-defence means that any violence used by the accused was in legitimate defence to an attack, actual or apprehended, upon him or another; this is properly dealt with in the context of offences of violence, rather than here. *Procedurally*, however, these defences have it in common that section 78 of the 1995 Act requires that in the High Court notice shall be given to the Crown and any co-accused of the plea not less than ten clear days before the trial, while in the sheriff court it must be given at the first diet. If such notice is not given, the special defence cannot be pled unless the court otherwise directs. The same is true of the leading of evidence calculated to exculpate the accused by incriminating a co-accused and, by section 78(2) of the 1995 Act, of the pleading of automatism (which also negates *mens rea* and is properly dealt with in a text on general principles of criminal law) and of coercion.

So far as evidence is concerned, the position is best summarised in the words of the High Court in *Lambie* v *HM Advocate*:[113]

---

[113] 1973 SLT 219.

'The only purpose of the special defence is to give fair notice to the Crown and once such notice has been given the only issue for a jury is to decide, upon the whole evidence before them, whether the Crown has established the accused's guilt beyond reasonable doubt. When a special defence is pleaded, whether it be of alibi, self-defence or incrimination, the jury should be so charged in the appropriate language, and all that requires to be said of the special defence, where any evidence in support of it has been given, either in course of the Crown case or by the accused himself or by any witness led for the defence is that if that evidence, whether from one or more witnesses, is believed, or creates in the minds of the jury reasonable doubt as to the guilt of the accused in the matters libelled, the Crown case must fail and they must acquit.'

Notice of defence witnesses and productions

Section 78(4) of the 1995 Act deals with defence witnesses and productions. By that section, it is not competent for the accused to examine any witnesses or to put in evidence any productions not intimated to the prosecutor at or before the first diet (in the sheriff court) or at least ten clear days before trial (in the High Court) unless the court otherwise directs.

Postponement of trial

Section 80 of the 1995 Act makes provision for the adjournment of trials. Procedurally, by subsection (2), a party may apply at any time before the trial for a postponement. Ideally, this is done by lodging a minute for postponement well before the trial, but it is often done on the morning of the trial itself.

Upon such application being made the court may, by subsection (3), discharge the trial diet and either fix a new trial diet or give leave to the prosecutor to serve a notice fixing a new trial diet. By subsection (1), the court may adjourn the case into any subsequent sitting of the court commencing within two months of the date of the trial diet.

Whether or not to grant an adjournment is a matter for the discretion of the judge who deals with such an application. However, the High Court gave some guidance as to the proper approach to such a motion in *Skeen* v *McLaren*,[114] where the Crown sought to have a summary trial adjourned because witnesses were not available. Lord Justice-General Emslie said:

'When a motion is made by one party or the other to adjourn a diet of this kind on this ground and no question arises as to whether it is well founded in fact, there are two questions to which the sheriff must address his mind if he is to arrive at a proper decision upon the motion. The first question is whether the grant or refusal of the motion will be prejudicial to the accused and if so what is the probable extent of that prejudice. The second question is whether prejudice to the prosecutor would result from the granting or refusal of the motion and once again the degree of probable prejudice must be estimated. . . . To these two questions we would add a possible third, namely prejudice to the public interest which may arise independently of prejudice to the accused or to the prosecution in the particular case in which the motion is made.'

This was reiterated in *Tudhope* v *Lawrie*.[115]

[114] 1976 SLT (Notes) 14.
[115] 1979 SLT (Notes) 13.

There are clear examples of the kinds of situation in which an adjournment should be granted in *Normand* v *West*[116] and *Stewart* v *Normand*.[117] In *West* it was held that, where the defence sought an adjournment because two essential witnesses were absent and the defence had only recently been instructed in respect of the need to cite these witnesses and could not proceed in their absence and the Crown sought an adjournment on the ground that an essential Crown witness, duly cited, had failed to appear, the relief stipendiary magistrate should have granted the adjournment rather than refuse on the broad basis that it would productive of unacceptable delay. In *Stewart* it was held to be oppressive for a sheriff to refuse an adjournment to an accused who produced a doctor's letter stating that a defence witness was unfit to appear. Lord Justice-Clerk Ross said, 'Unless circumstances are special, it will normally be oppressive to refuse an adjournment which is necessary to allow the defence to obtain an essential witness who has been cited.' Again, in *McSorley* v *Normand*,[118] the defence agent mistook the date for the trial and so failed to cite defence witnesses and could not attend himself. A substitute agent moved for an adjournment which was refused. It was held that this was oppressive and not cured by offering an adjournment after the trial had been part-heard to cite witnesses.

[116] 1991 SCCR 76.
[117] 1991 SCCR 940.
[118] 1991 SCCR 949.

8 : SUMMARY PROCEEDINGS

Although the 1995 Act defers material relating to summary procedure until after it deals with trials under solemn procedure, a different approach is taken here. Trial procedure under solemn and summary procedure is so similar that it can be dealt with in a single chapter, with a large component dealing with those aspects of the law of evidence not already addressed. We deal now with the commencement of summary proceedings and the rules which apply to summary procedure up until the time of the commencement of the trial. There are in fact many analogies with solemn procedure.

Incidental applications

There is in summary procedure no direct equivalent to the petition. If, in connection with a case under summary procedure, the procurator fiscal requires the various warrants which the petition would give him in a case dealt with in that way, he will present to the court an incidental application under section 134 of the 1995 Act. That procedure is open also to the accused.

Section 134 does little more than refer the reader to 'the form prescribed by Act of Adjournal' and that form itself (Form 16.4–A) is skeletal in the extreme. It simply requires the applicant to set out in numbered paragraphs 'the reasons for the order sought and the statutory process' and then to set out the orders sought.

Whether an incidental application is competent falls to be decided according to the competency of the order sought.

The Act of Adjournal (Criminal Procedure Rules) 1996 does not lay down any particular procedure for an incidental application. The most common type of application is for a search warrant.

The remedy of the accused who objects to the granting of an incidental application is to take a bill of suspension. This is dealt with at p 169.

The complaint

The document which embodies summary proceedings is the 'complaint'. Whereas a petition can be regarded for some purposes as a step in investigation, the complaint contains the settled charge against the accused. It equates more easily to the indictment than to the petition. However, unlike the indictment, the complaint is the document upon which the first appearance of the accused is focused, and which commences proceedings. Each time the complaint is called in court the court will fix the date for the next time the complaint is to call. If on any such date it does not call the whole proceedings fall, as a sheriff held in _McDonald v Knight_.[1] Whether the procurator fiscal can start the proceedings again with a fresh complaint will

[1] 1990 SCCR 641.

be subject to the same rules as to competency as applied to the first complaint.

Petition appearance by definition involves an arrest warrant, even if the accused has come to court voluntarily and is committed for further examination on bail without ever seeing the inside of the cells. By contrast, however, there are two ways in which an accused person can appear on complaint. He may appear from custody, whether that results from arrest without warrant, from arrest on a warrant obtained as a result of the presentation of the complaint to the court with a request for such a warrant (usually called a summary warrant), or from his release by the police on undertaking to attend on a particular day (which is custody in theory only). Or alternatively he may be 'cited' to attend court.

Appearance from custody

Where the accused is the subject of a summary warrant or is arrested on any other basis he must, by section 135(3) of the 1995 Act, be brought before a court competent to deal with the case not later than the first day after he is taken into custody (not counting weekends and holidays). It was held in *Robertson* v *MacDonald*[2] that failure to bring the accused before the court in this way does not vitiate the subsequent proceedings on the complaint, though it might give rise to civil damages.

A copy of the complaint is given to the accused before he appears in court.

Citation to appear

In the great majority of cases, however, summary proceedings are commenced by service of the complaint with a citation to come to court on a given date, which must, by section 140 of the 1995 Act, usually be at least forty-eight hours after service.

Section 141 of the 1995 Act provides for a variety of ways in which service can be effected.

Service may be to the accused personally; the citation may be left with someone at the accused's residence or place of business; it may be left with someone on a vessel on which the accused is a master or member of the crew; if the accused is a company it may be left at their place of business; if the accused is a body of trustees, the citation may be left with any one of them who is resident in Scotland or with their solicitor in Scotland; or it may be sent by recorded delivery post. If the accused is on bail in connection with the charges (which can happen where he has originally appeared on petition but the case has been reduced to summary procedure) section 25(3) of the 1995 Act provides for the service of documents at the 'domicile of citation', which is an address in the UK included in the bail order as the address at which documents may be served and intimations given.

Time bar

By contrast with petition proceedings, the commencement of summary proceedings is in some cases subject to a statutory time-limit in terms of section 136 of the 1995 Act. That section provides that proceedings in

---

[2] 1992 SCCR 916.

respect of offences to which the section applies can only be commenced within six months after the contravention occurred or, in the case of a continuous contravention, within six months after the last date of such a contravention.

The offences to which this rule applies are, in terms of section 136(2), statutory offences which can only be prosecuted summarily and in respect of which the enactment which creates them does not fix a different time-limit.

Common law offences are not subject to time bar. Neither are statutory offences which can be prosecuted either on indictment or summarily, even if they are prosecuted summarily in fact.

This represents a change in the law. Until the 1995 legislation all statutory offences which were in fact prosecuted summarily were subject to that time-limit. The provision as it now stands applies to a much smaller range of offences, and in particular it does not apply to many of the offences dealt with in the case-law on the subject.

That case-law arises in the context of section 136(3) which, for time-bar purposes, deems proceedings to be commenced on the date the warrant to apprehend or cite the accused is granted, provided that warrant is executed without undue delay.

Undue delay

What will amount to undue delay will depend on the particular circumstances and it may be necessary to lead evidence of the circumstances in order to determine the position. It is clear from *McCartney* v *Tudhope*[3] that the onus of establishing that there has not been undue delay lies with the Crown. It has also been said in a number of cases, such as *McNeillie* v *Walkingshaw*,[4] that the question is one of fact and degree for the sheriff and the appeal court will be slow to interfere.

Examples of situations in which it has been held that there was undue delay are *Tudhope* v *Mathieson*,[5] in which there was five months' delay in the execution of a warrant because clerks of court were on strike and courts were being convened only for the most serious cases, and *Carmichael* v *Sardar & Sons*,[6] in which there was an unexplained delay of six days in postal service of a complaint where warrant to cite had been granted just within the six-month period. However, in *Stagecoach Ltd* v *Macphail*[7] execution of the warrant to cite through normal channels took seven days and a plea to the competency was rejected, as it was in *Buchan* v *McNaughtan*,[8] in which the accused was at sea when the police attempted to serve the complaint. They waited for him to report to the police station to accept service of the complaint on his return (the actual delay being six days after the expiry of the six-month period). In another case *Young* v *MacLeod*,[9] a middle-aged first offender charged with a drink driving offence failed to appear when cited. The case was continued for three weeks and when she

[3] 1985 SCCR 373.
[4] 1990 SCCR 428.
[5] 1981 SCCR 231.
[6] 1983 SCCR 433.
[7] 1986 SCCR 184.
[8] 1990 SCCR 688.
[9] 1993 SCCR 479.

failed to appear a warrant was granted. That was passed to the police about six weeks before the time bar, with instructions to execute it with discretion (namely to try to get the accused to appear without actually being arrested). They made repeated attempts to get her to answer the warrant but she deliberately failed to co-operate. Eventually the procurator fiscal instructed that she should be arrested without further ado and that was done on the day he gave that instruction but seventy-six days after the grant of the warrant. This took the case about one month beyond the time bar. She took a plea to the competency, which was repelled, and she appealed. In refusing the appeal, the court observed that for the police to have arrested her when they first made contact with her about the warrant would have been unnecessarily severe and oppressive; that the accused was given ample opportunity to comply with the warrant voluntarily and that it was entirely her own fault that she did not do so; that the Crown could not be criticised for giving her the opportunity; and that the case was quite different from those in which the Crown or the police took no steps or left the accused in ignorance of the warrant for a long time.

The content of the complaint

Section 140(2) of the 1995 Act contemplates that the complaint will be accompanied by a 'citation', though this is not appropriate where the accused appears from custody. Rule 16.1 of the Act of Adjournal (Criminal Procedure Rules) 1996 provides that the citation and the complaint are to be in the form of Forms 16.1–B and 16.1–A respectively. As Form 16.1–B makes clear, the citation tells the accused on what date and in which court his case will be first called.

Rule 16.1.–(3) requires the procurator fiscal to send with the citation and complaint a reply form which the accused can use to state whether he pleads guilty or not guilty and a means form which the accused can complete and return to inform a sentencing court about his circumstances.

Section 166(2) of the 1995 Act requires that a notice of any previous convictions should be served with the complaint.

By section 138 of the 1995 Act the complaint must be signed by the procurator fiscal (or, in the rare cases in which someone other than the procurator fiscal is the prosecutor, by a solicitor). In *Lowe* v *Bee*[10] it was held that failure to sign the complaint renders it fundamentally null and that a signature cannot be added by amendment. 16.2.–(1) requires the prosecutor to sign the citation also.

Section 138 goes on to require that the complaint be in the form set out in Schedule 5 or prescribed by Act of Adjournal, and to give effect to Schedule 3 as regards complaints in the same way as for indictments.

The effect of the application of Schedules 3 and 5 is to confirm that the principles of relevancy and specification which apply to complaints are identical to those which apply to indictments.

By rule 16.3 failure by the prosecutor to comply with the requirements as to the reply form and the means form does not invalidate the complaint.

[10] 1989 SCCR 476.

...he first diet in summary procedure

The complaint having been served, either upon the accused in custody or with a citation to appear on a particular day, the case will call in court.

The accused who has been cited to appear is able to answer the charges by post, pleading guilty or not guilty in writing. He is also able to answer the charges through his solicitor without appearing himself. Often, however, he will appear and, of course, accused persons in custody will always appear in court.

If the accused simply fails to appear in answer to a citation, by section 144(2) of the 1995 Act the court may adjourn the case to another diet or may grant warrant to apprehend him. Such warrants are not usually granted unless there is proof, in the form of a completed execution of citation, that the complaint was either served on the accused personally or served on him at his domicile of citation.

Where the accused does appear (as the overwhelming majority do), procedure at the first diet is governed in the first instance by section 144(1) of the 1995 Act. By that subsection, where the accused is present at the first calling of the case in a summary prosecution and the complaint has been served on him or read to him or he has legal assistance he is to be asked to plead to the charge unless the court adjourns the case in terms of section 145. That section permits adjournment to allow time for inquiry into the case or for other reasonable cause. Such adjournments are referred to as 'continuation without plea'.

The accused who is called upon to plead must do one of two things. Either he must plead guilty or not guilty or he must state any challenge which he makes to the competency or relevancy of the complaint. If he fails to state such a challenge at the first diet, section 144(5) prohibits him from stating any such challenge at any future diet in the case except with the leave of the court which may be granted only on cause shown.

In addition, the accused must, by section 144(4) state any denial that he is the person charged by the police. Section 144(5) operates to bar the stating of any such denial thereafter except with leave on cause shown.

Finally, in terms of section 255 of the 1955 Act the accused must state any challenge he makes to an alleged special capacity, otherwise that capacity is held as admitted.

Pleas to relevancy and competency have been dealt with in relation to indictments, as have special capacities. The principles are exactly the same under summary procedure. However, we require to deal here with denials that the accused is the person charged.

Denial that accused is the person charged

So far as the identity of the accused as the person charged is concerned, it must be understood that the identification of the accused is always an issue at trial; indeed forgetting to have the accused identified in the dock is the classic prosecutor's mistake. If the accused is not identified as the perpetrator of the crime, usually by being pointed out in the dock, he must be acquitted. In limited circumstances, however, the prosecutor in a summary trial can derive assistance from section 280(9) of the 1995 Act under which there is a presumption that the person who appears for trial in answer to the complaint is the person charged by the police. *Smith* v

Paterson[11] was decided shortly after the statutory precursor of that provision came into force and concerned a case in which the procurator fiscal depute did not ask the police to point out the accused but did take evidence that they had cautioned and charged the person they had seen committing an offence. It was held that the effect of statutory presumption was precisely what it said and that the person answering the complaint is presumed to be the person charged; and that accordingly the sheriff erred in holding that identification of the accused was essential.

Hamilton v *Ross*[12] takes this further. At a summary trial the sheriff upheld a submission of no case to answer on the footing that only one officer had formally identified the respondent in court as the driver of the vehicle in question. Neither the respondent's solicitor nor the procurator fiscal depute referred the sheriff to the section and he reached his decision without considering the effect of the statutory presumption. On appeal it was suggested that it was now too late to rely on this method of establishing the respondent as the driver. The appeal court disagreed, allowed the appeal and remitted the case to the sheriff to proceed as accords.

Debate on preliminary pleas

Where the accused challenges the relevancy of the complaint and/or the competency of the proceedings, the case will usually be adjourned for debate. There is in law no reason why the debate should not take place immediately on the plea being stated and occasionally, where the plea is obviously either well founded or without any basis it may be so dealt with. Usually, however, the prosecutor will have had no notice of the plea and will require an adjournment to consider his position and prepare.

At the debate, which equates to the preliminary diet in the High Court or the preliminary pleas aspect of a first diet on a sheriff court indictment, the defence will present their argument and the Crown will answer it. If a preliminary plea to the relevancy succeeds, the affected charge or charges will be dismissed unless the prosecutor is allowed to amend and can do so in such a way as to make the charge relevant. If a preliminary plea to the competency succeeds, the whole complaint will be dismissed.

If the preliminary plea does not result in the dismissal of the complaint as a whole, the accused will be called upon, at the end of the debate, to state his plea to however much of the complaint survives. The procedure is then exactly the same as if he had stated his plea at the first calling of the case but (obviously) without the option of stating a preliminary plea.

Where the accused pleads guilty at the first diet (or after a debate, though a plea of guilty after debate is very rare) the court will proceed to sentence. Sentencing is dealt with in Chapter 10 below. For the remainder of this chapter we are concerned with the accused who pleads not guilty.

Procedure on not guilty plea

The starting-point when a plea of not guilty is tendered is section 146 of the 1995 Act. In terms, the section applies where there is a straightforward plea of not guilty or where there is a plea of guilty to only part of the charge and the prosecutor does not accept the partial plea.

[11] 1982 JC 125.
[12] 1991 JC 36.

Where there are several charges on the complaint and the accused pleads guilty to some but not to others the practice is to defer sentence on the charges to which he has pled guilty until the end of the trial on the other charges. In such a case, section 146 applies to these charges to which the accused has pled not guilty.

Adjournment for trial

By section 146(2) it is open to the court to proceed to trial at once unless either party moves for an adjournment and the court considers it expedient to grant it. In practice it almost never happens that the trial takes place immediately. Such a course is only taken in cases involving foreign nationals who are scheduled to leave the jurisdiction and whom it is not appropriate to keep in custody. The typical cases are those of the foreign lorry driver who is charged with offences in connection with his hours of work or record-keeping or the skipper of a foreign fishing vessel alleged to have contravened the fisheries legislation and arrested by fisheries protection officers. In other cases, the Crown is unlikely to have witnesses immediately available and the defence will want time to obtain legal aid and to prepare. Accordingly, it is section 146(3) which is usually operated and that section requires the court to adjourn the case for trial to as early a diet as is consistent with the just interest of both parties. Indeed, where the accused is in custody, section 146(4) gives him an absolute right to an adjournment for not less that forty-eight hours unless a shorter adjournment is necessary in order to obtain the evidence of witnesses who would otherwise not be available.

Intermediate diet

At the same time as it adjourns the case for trial, the court is entitled, by section 148, to fix what is known as an 'intermediate diet' between the first diet and the trial. By section 148(5) the accused is required to attend any intermediate diet of which he is given notice unless he is legally represented and the court considers that there are 'exceptional' circumstances justifying him not attending.

Bail

Where the accused has been cited to the first diet he will be ordained to appear at the intermediate diet and the trial diet. This means that he is ordered to attend. In terms of section 150(8) an accused who without reasonable excuse fails to attend any diet of which he is given due notice is guilty of an offence.

Where the accused is in custody, ordaining him to appear is an option but it is more likely that if he is released it will be on bail. The principles which apply to the granting (or withholding) of bail in a summary case are identical to those which apply in a petition case at full committal; in other words, the prosecutor can oppose bail on some substantive ground but not on the ground that there are further investigations to be made.

As at full committal on petition, both the prosecutor and the accused can appeal in connection with bail.

Prevention of delay in trials

Where the accused is remanded in custody in connection with a summary prosecution he gets the benefit of section 147 of the 1995 Act, which provides that a person charged with an offence in summary proceedings shall not be detained in that respect for a total of more than forty days after the bringing of the complaint in court unless his trial is commenced within that period, failing which he shall be liberated forthwith and thereafter shall be for ever free from all question or process for that offence. This, of course, is the direct equivalent of section 65(4)(b) which applies the so-called '110-day rule' to solemn proceedings where the accused is in custody and the case-law on that subject applies by analogy. Section 147(2) contains a provision similar to section 65(7) permitting an extension—in this case by the sheriff.

It is worth noting two cases. The first of these is *Lockhart* v *Robb*[13] in which a sheriff held that, although the serving of another substantive sentence could interrupt the running of the forty days as it can the 110 days where that applies, a remand in custody on deferred sentence on another case could not do so.

The second case is *Grugen* v *Jessop*[14] in which the fiscal began the trial on the fortieth day, knowing that it could not be completed that day because witnesses were unavailable. One was still suffering from serious injuries inflicted by the accused and two others were police officers who were required to give evidence on that day in the High Court. The trial was adjourned part-heard for eight days with the accused being further remanded in custody. The accused took a bill of advocation, arguing that what had been done was an abuse of process. The High Court was not impressed with that argument and held that it was not. The Lord Justice-General pointed out that if the procurator fiscal had sought an extension it would almost certainly have been granted. He also pointed out that the accused was only in custody at all because he failed to turn up at an earlier calling of the case for trial.

Intermediate diet

The intermediate diet under summary procedure is the direct equivalent of the first diet in solemn procedure in the sheriff court but only so far as regards the ascertainment by the sheriff of the state of preparedness of the parties (preliminary pleas having been dealt with by debate after the first diet under summary procedure). Accordingly, as under section 71, the court is to ascertain whether the case it likely to proceed to trial on the date assigned as the trial diet and, in particular, the state of preparation of the parties and the extent to which they have complied with the duty under section 257(1) to seek to agree evidence; and as under solemn procedure the court is permitted to ask the prosecutor and the accused any question in connection with any matters to be ascertained.

Special defences, lists of witnesses and productions
By contrast with solemn procedure, there is no requirement to lodge lists of witnesses or productions. Nor is there a requirement to give notice of any special defence except alibi, which is dealt with by section 149 of the 1995 Act. That section makes it incompetent in a summary prosecution for the accused to found on a plea of alibi unless before the first witness is sworn he

[13] 1988 SCCR 381.
[14] 1988 SCCR 182.

gives notice to the prosecutor of the plea with particulars as to time and place and of the witnesses by whom it is proposed to prove it. Where such notice is given the prosecutor is entitled to an adjournment, though often in practice he will not avail himself of that entitlement.

9 : THE TRIAL

Trial procedure under solemn and summary procedure is very similar indeed, and it may be said in general that such differences as do exist are entirely attributable to the presence of the jury.

Failure of accused to appear

Since the general rule is that it is not competent to proceed in the absence of the accused (and section 92 of the 1995 Act makes this explicit in relation to proceedings on indictment), his presence becomes the first essential for a trial except in the limited case of summary proceedings for a statutory offence which does not carry a potential prison sentence. In those limited circumstances, section 150(5) allows the trial to proceed in his absence. Otherwise, the usual response to the failure of the accused to appear will be a warrant for his arrest, provided it can be shown that he had received intimation of the diet either in fact or by intimation at his domicile of citation (if he has one). Under solemn procedure that warrant takes the accused straight to prison on his arrest and the 110 days start to run—though he can submit a bail application. In due course a new indictment will be served and that indictment is very likely to contain a charge under section 27(1)(a) of the 1995 Act of failing to appear at the time and place appointed for a diet of which he has been given due notice.

Under summary procedure the accused will be brought before the court when he is arrested and may find himself remanded in custody for his trial (the situation in *Grugen* v *Jessop*).[1] If he has been on bail he might well find himself served with an additional complaint containing a section 27(1)(a) charge, or with a new complaint combining the original charges and such an additional charge. If he has been ordained to appear he is likely to find himself facing a charge under section 150(8), which makes it an offence for an accused person to fail without reasonable excuse to attend any diet of which he has been given due notice. Even if the procurator fiscal does not institute proceedings for such an additional charge, the sheriff or justice might decide to treat the failure to appear as contempt of court and deal with the accused in respect of that.

Section 65(2) of the 1995 Act provides that the twelve-month rule does not bar the trial of an accused for whose arrest a warrant has been granted in respect of failure to appear and this, it is thought, must apply equally to summary procedure in the *Gardner* v *Lees*[2] situation.

Selection of jury

Assuming the accused turns up and pleads not guilty, the trial under solemn procedure begins with the selection by ballot of the jury of fifteen persons,

[1] 1988 SCCR 182.
[2] 1996 SCCR 168.

as provided for in section 88 of the 1995 Act and rule 14.2 of the Act of Adjournal (Criminal Procedure Rules) 1996. The name and address of each potential juror is written on a separate piece of paper. Each piece is folded and placed into a container. There they are mixed and from there the clerk of court draws out the names one at a time. Each juror thus elected takes his or her place in the jury box, unless challenged, until all fifteen places are filled.

It is no longer open to the parties to make objections to jurors other than on cause shown. Objections on cause shown remain competent in terms of section 86(2) of the 1995 Act. Such objections have hitherto been rare in practice, though this may have been a result of the former entitlement of parties to object to up to three jurors each without giving reasons.

Once fifteen jurors have been selected, section 88(5) of the 1995 Act requires that the indictment be read to them. Where the indictment is long and complex, the section contemplates that a summary approved by the judge may be read instead. Copies of the indictment, without lists of witnesses or productions, are provided for the jury. Where the accused has lodged a special defence, that is read to the jury after the indictment, as required by section 89 of the 1995 Act and a copy of that is given to the jury as well.

After the indictment and any special defence are read, the jury take their oath. At this point, it is said that the indictment has been 'remitted to the assize' and it is proper to refer to the accused as 'the pannel'.

By section 90 of the 1995 Act, where juror dies or, for some other reason (illness is the obvious example) cannot appropriately continue to serve, the court may direct that the trial shall proceed before the remaining jurors, though their number may not fall below twelve.

The framework of the trial

Evidence
The trial under both solemn and summary procedure begins with the prosecutor calling the first witness in support of the charges. There is no opening statement of any kind. Each witness is examined in chief by the prosecutor and may then be cross-examined by the defence and re-examined by the prosecutor. After all the prosecution witnesses have been called the defence are entitled to argue that there is no case to answer. If that submission is successful, the accused is acquitted.

The defence are entitled to call evidence. If the accused is to be a witness he should give evidence before any other defence witnesses. If he is not a witness his personal account of the facts cannot be heard, except in the special circumstances contemplated in *Morrison* v *HM Advocate*.[3] That case concerned a statement, which was partly incriminatory and partly exculpatory, made to the police by the accused in a rape case. The particular statement was incriminatory to the extent that it admitted intercourse but exculpatory in that it claimed that there had been consent. A Full Bench (of seven judges) held that where the Crown leads in evidence or where the defence lead without objection from the Crown a statement made by an accused person prior to trial which is capable of being both incriminatory and exculpatory the whole statement is admissible as *evidence of the facts*

[3] 1990 SCCR 235.

contained in it. This must be contrasted with the prior statement which purely exculpatory, as to which the court in *Morrison* observed that although these may not be led as evidence of the truth of their contents they are admissible for the limited purpose of proving the demeanour of the accused at the time the statement was made and the consistency of his position on the charges throughout. This assumes, of course, that the accused gives evidence to be supported thus.

Further evidence

Sections 268 and 269 of the 1995 Act make provision for the leading of further evidence under both solemn and summary procedure, even though witnesses might have to be recalled for that purpose and even though (under solemn procedure) the witnesses and productions which it is sought to use have not been listed in terms of sections 66 to 68 of the Act. Section 268 deals with additional evidence and is available to both prosecution and defence. Section 269 deals with 'evidence in replication', which is evidence led by the prosecutor either to contradict defence evidence or to establish that a witness has previously made a statement which is inconsistent with the evidence which he has given.

Additional evidence to which section 268 applies is, by subsection (2), evidence which the judge considers is *prima facie* material and in respect of which he accepts that at the commencement of the trial either the additional evidence was not available and could not reasonably have been made available or the materiality of the additional evidence could not reasonably have been foreseen by the party.

It may be said that if evidence is not *prima facie* material it is likely to be inadmissible in any event upon the principle that evidence which is not relevant is not admissible. That principle is discussed in more detail below at p 127. So far as the criterion that evidence was not available and could not reasonably have been made available at the commencement of the trial is concerned, we have to note that the test applied to the hearing of fresh evidence on appeal is, in terms of sections 106(3) and 175(5) of the 1995 Act, almost identical to this and that a Full Bench of the High Court adopted a somewhat restrictive interpretation of that test in *Elliott* v *HM Advocate.*[4] Further consideration is given to this at p 165 in the context of appeals.

The final criterion is that the party seeking to lead such additional evidence could not reasonably have foreseen its materiality and this will inevitably depend on the particular circumstances of each case.

By section 268(1) an application to lead such additional evidence may be made at any time before the commencement of the speeches to the jury (in a trial on indictment) or the prosecutor's address to the judge on the evidence (in a summary case).

The leading of evidence in replication in terms of section 269 is open only to the prosecutor, who may apply to do so after the close of the defence evidence and before the commencement of the speeches to the jury or his own address to the judge on the evidence. The test in relation to evidence to contradict defence evidence is whether the evidence of the defence witness could reasonably have been anticipated by the prosecutor and, as was made

[4] 1995 SCCR 280.

clear in the related cases *MacGillivray* v *Johnston (No 2)*[5] and *Neizer* v *Johnston*,[6] evidence in replication cannot be used to palliate inadequacies in the Crown preparation or presentation of the prosecution. In the latter case, Lord Sutherland drew a clear distinction between the situation in which the Crown had received clear intimation of a line of defence (as in the instant case) and that in which a line of defence had been sprung on the Crown during the course of the trial.

Part-heard trials

Section 91 of the 1995 Act provides that a trial on indictment is to proceed from day to day, unless the court sees just cause to adjourn over a day or days—in other words, for some longer period. Such a longer adjournment occurred in *Kyle* v *HM Advocate*,[7] where the trial judge began his charge to the jury (at the end of the trial) on a Friday afternoon, it being a holiday weekend. He had not completed it by 5 pm and gave the jury the choice of sitting on the Saturday or adjourning until the Tuesday; they chose the Tuesday and the case adjourned over the Monday to the Tuesday. There was an appeal on the ground that there had been a failure to comply with the requirement to proceed from day to day, but the appeal court gave that short shrift, Lord Justice-Clerk Ross commenting that the decision was one for the trial judge, who had no obligation to consult either prosecution or defence on the matter, and that it is impossible to define exhaustively what would amount to 'just cause'.

If trials under summary procedure are not concluded within the first day (and most are) they are adjourned part-heard to another convenient day as soon as possible after the first day.

Jury speeches/address on the evidence

After all the evidence has been led the prosecutor addresses the jury or (in a summary case) the judge. The accused or his legal representative then do so in their turn, in the order in which their names appear on the indictment or complaint of there are multiple accused. Sections 98 and 161 of the 1995 Act specifically preserve the right of the accused to speak last.

Charge and verdict

Finally, under solemn procedure, the judge will charge the jury, giving them directions as to the law but making it plain to them that it is for them to decide what facts they hold to be proved but that they must rely on his directions as to the law. One of those directions, in terms of *Affleck* v *HM Advocate*,[8] must be

> 'to explain the verdicts which are open to them, to inform them that they may return a verdict by a majority, and then to emphasise the only matter of importance: that no verdict of guilty can be returned unless eight members of the jury are in favour of that verdict'.

The requirement for at least eight members of the jury in favour of a guilty verdict before that verdict can be returned remains even if the size of the jury is reduced below fifteen.

[5] 1994 SLT 1012.
[6] 1993 SCCR 772.
[7] 1987 SCCR 116.
[8] 1987 SCCR 150.

The jury then retire to consider their verdict, returning once the verdict has been reached. Under summary procedure the judge simply announces his verdict after both parties have addressed him (and perhaps after a short adjournment to consider the matter).

Verdicts

There are three verdicts open to a jury or to a judge under summary procedures. These are guilty, not proven and not guilty. The guilty and not proven verdicts are self-explanatory. Although in *Neil* v *HM Advocate*[9] the High Court held that it is not necessary to explain the not proven verdict to a jury on the ground that it is well understood in Scotland, it does need to be said that it is a verdict of acquittal and that it founds a plea of tholed assize.

Schedule 3 to the 1995 Act provides for a range of alternative verdicts. In terms of paragraph 8 offences of dishonesty are very nearly interchangeable, and in particular on an indictment or complaint charging theft it is open to the jury or judge to convict of reset. In terms of paragraph 10 a person charged with a completed crime may be convicted of attempt at that crime and, indeed, where the charge is one of attempt the accused may be convicted of attempt even if the evidence is enough to establish the completed crime. In *Muldoon* v *HM Advocate*[10] the crime charged was assault with intent to rape but the evidence established a completed rape. He was convicted of the offence libelled and the conviction was upheld on appeal.

Within this basic framework, there is much (especially in relation to evidence) which requires elaboration.

The witnesses

Presence in court

It is unusual for a witness to be in court before he himself gives evidence, although section 267 of the 1995 Act does make provision for the court to permit this to happen if it appears that the presence of the witness would not be contrary to the interests of justice. Where it happens that a witness is in the court before giving evidence but without such permission, section 267(2) leaves it to the discretion of the court whether to admit the evidence of the witness. The issue, of course, is whether the evidence of the witness has been coloured by what he has heard and so the subsection limits the exercise of the discretion to cases in which it appears to the court that the presence of the witness was not the result of culpable negligence or criminal intent and that the witness has not been unduly instructed or influenced by what took place in his presence or that injustice will not be done by his examination. *MacDonald* v *Mackenzie*[11] makes it clear that the onus is on the party tendering the witness's evidence to satisfy the court that the discretion should be exercised in his favour.

Use of aides-mémoire

The Scottish criminal courts rely heavily on oral evidence. Memory, however, can be an unreliable thing, especially in relation to details which

[9] 1948 JC 12.
[10] 1967 SLT 237.
[11] 1947 JC 169.

do not, at the time of the incident, strike the observer as being of critical significance. On the basis that notes made while an incident is fresh in the memory are more likely to be reliable than unaided memory months—or years—later, the courts allow witnesses to refer to such notes in the course of giving their evidence.

It is not, however, every note which can be used in this way. The notes must be original notes (not transcriptions) made by the witness himself (otherwise they fall foul of the rule against hearsay) and made at the time of the incident or so soon after that the incident is still fresh in the memory (otherwise their value as an objective and accurate note of events disappears).

Police officers in particular are in the habit of giving evidence under reference to their notebooks in this way. There is, however, no reason at all why other witnesses who possess such notes should not have their assistance.

Such notes do not require to be lodged as productions in the case.

So far as the notes of police officers are concerned, it should be noted that in the first instance it is only the Crown which can require that these are referred to. The defence in a criminal case are not entitled to require production of the notes of police officers unless the officers have referred to them in examination in chief. This is on the basis that the notes have been made for the police report and are therefore confidential on public policy grounds. In *Hinshelwood & Another* v *Auld*[12] two men were charged with contravening the Police Act 1919 by attempting, in speeches which they made at a public meeting, to persuade police officers to go on strike and to assault senior officers. Certain police officers who gave evidence at the trial had made notes during the meeting but did not refer to the notes when being examined in chief. In cross-examination they were asked to produce the notes but the procurator fiscal objected successfully, on public policy grounds.

In holding that the sheriff had been right to refuse the defence access to these notes, Lord Justice-General Clyde explained that, where the witness has looked at the notes when giving his evidence in chief, considerations of fairness compel their production to the defence. However, he went on to say that there is a broad general rule that any communication which is made by an inferior official to a superior officer in the same department is on the grounds of public policy, a confidential document, and is not producible in evidence. To decide otherwise, would, he said, render police work impossible. If the actual report made by police witnesses was thus protected, so should notes and drafts be.

Competence—children

Some categories of witness are subject to special rules as to their competency as witnesses and the most obvious of these relate to children. The High Court pointed out in *Rees* v *Lowe*[13] that the essential question in relation to a child who is proffered as a witness is whether the child, however young, understands the need to tell the truth. The trial judge must satisfy himself on that point by examination of the child and, if need be, of others (though it was held in *P* v *HM Advocate*[14] that it is a matter for the trial judge whether

[12] 1926 JC 4.
[13] 1989 SCCR 664.
[14] 1991 SCCR 933.

he requires the evidence of others to be so satisfied). In *Kelly* v *Docherty*[15] Lord Justice-General Hope said that the process has two stages, the first being to discover whether the child knows the difference between truth and lies and the second being to admonish the child to tell the truth. In that case the conviction was quashed because the sheriff did not attempt to carry out the first of these stages.

Whether the child should be sworn is a matter for the discretion of the judge but in general those over the age of fourteen are sworn and those under the age of twelve are not. If a child is not sworn he must be admonished to tell the truth. Whether or not the child is sworn, the law regards his evidence as no better and no worse than the evidence of any other witness.

Competence—those with learning disabilities

The witness with learning disability is in a similar position to children so far as competency as a witness is concerned. Where the disability is alleged to be such as to go to the root of the person's ability to give truthful testimony, objection may be taken to him being called as a witness and the question settled by evidence; otherwise such disability might sometimes affect reliability.

The spouse of the accused

At common law one spouse is not a competent witness against the other except where he or she is the victim of the offence in which case the spouse is both competent and compellable for the prosecution. This is modified by section 264 of the 1995 Act which makes the spouse of the accused a competent, but not compellable, witness for any party except the accused. In *Hunter* v *HM Advocate*[16] the accused sought to incriminate his wife in connection with assaults on their child. He sought to call her as a witness but the trial judge informed her that she was not compellable and she declined to give evidence. The High Court held that this was incorrect and that one spouse is a compellable witness at the instance of the other in the trial of the other. The court did say, however, that the spouse called as a witness is not obliged to answer any question which might incriminate her in a criminal offence and is not obliged to disclose any communication made between the spouses within the marriage.

Care must be taken in the case where there are two or more accused and the spouse of one of them gives evidence. That was the position in *Bates* v *HM Advocate*[17] and the wife of one accused was called by the Crown. That accused had been incriminated by another accused, whose counsel in cross-examination asked her questions designed to incriminate her husband. These she declined to answer but on appeal the High Court said that once she had agreed to give evidence she was obliged to answer all questions put to her (subject, presumably, to the right not to disclose communications within marriage).

Finally, it should be noted that these rules only apply to a spouse. *Casey* v *HM Advocate*[18] makes it clear that a mere cohabitee, as in that case, is not in

[15] 1991 SCCR 312.
[16] 1984 SLT 434.
[17] 1989 SLT 701.
[18] 1993 SLT 33.

any special position, and Renton and Brown[19] suggests that a former spouse is always compellable.

Expert or skilled witnesses

In most matters, judges or juries, presented with the facts, can draw their own conclusions. However, there are occasions on which some assistance is required. In such cases, evidence may be led from a 'skilled witness' whom the Walkers[20] describe as 'a person who, through practice or study or both, is specially qualified in a recognised branch of knowledge, whether it be art, science or craft'.

Who is an expert?

The expression, 'skilled witness' is more appropriate in Scots law than the expression 'expert witness' and reflects the fact that such evidence is competent in relation to any area beyond everyday understanding and to the importance of practice as well as of formal qualifications. In *Hewatt* v *Edinburgh Corporation*[21] the court, in a civil case, accepted that a police constable who had special duties in respect of road safety could give such evidence as to the degree of danger represented by a particular hole in the road. An example of this in a criminal case is *White* v *HM Advocate*.[22] Police officers had expressed an opinion that the quantity of LSD found in the possession of the accused was greater than could be expected if the drug was for the use of the accused alone; in short, that it was a dealer quantity. Appealing against conviction, the accused contended that it was incorrect to allow police officers to give opinion evidence on the dosage of drugs a user would consume and that such opinions ought only to be expressed by medically qualified persons.

Lord Justice-Clerk Ross said that this submission was not well founded. He went on to say:

> 'Police officers who served for some time with the Drugs Squad do acquire knowledge of such matters as the quantity of drugs which a drugs user would consume in a day or in a week and so forth. Provided such a witness's qualifications as a police officer and his experience in the Drugs Squad are first established, such evidence, in our opinion, is clearly competent. Evidence of this nature is not competent only to medically qualified witnesses.'

As Pattenden[23] has pointed out in relation to expert evidence in England:

> '[A]n expert witness in a criminal trial can give 2 types of evidence. He can testify to the facts and he can give opinion evidence. The distinction is one of degree for in a broad sense everything which an expert says within his own field of expertise contains an element of opinion.'

The distinction may be one of degree but it is, nevertheless, a useful one and it is helpful in assessing the evidence of a skilled witness to determine whether at a particular point that witness is giving evidence of fact or is giving evidence of opinion.

---

[19] R W Renton and H H Brown, *Criminal Procedure According to the Law of Scotland* (5th edn, 1983) para 18-19.
[20] A G Walker and N M L Walker, *The Law of Evidence in Scotland* (1964) para 413.
[21] 1944 SC 30.
[22] 1986 SCCR 224.
[23] R Pattenden, 'Expert Opinion Evidence Based on Hearsay' [1982] Crim LR 83.

The factual basis for the expert's opinion

The importance of laying the basis of fact for the opinion evidence of an expert is emphasised by the Walkers.[24] They call attention to *Forrester* v *HM Advocate*[25] in which opinion evidence which was intended to link the accused with the crime following a comparison between material used for the crime and material said to have been found in the accused's pocket turned out to be useless when the Crown failed to establish by sufficient evidence that the material had indeed been found there.

The importance of laying the appropriate factual foundation was particularly stressed in *Blagojevic* v *HM Advocate*,[26] a murder case in which the police subjected the accused to two interviews, each quite short, and separated by a period of about three quarters of an hour. During the first interview the accused denied his presence at the locus. During the interval a police officer told him that he was not doing himself any favours by that denial. During the resumed interview he admitted his presence at the locus and stabbing a man. The defence did not call the accused, but sought to call a psychologist to show that the accused was 'suggestible' to a degree which could explain the shift of his position. The Crown objected, successfully, to this evidence.

The defence appealed, arguing that the general issue of fairness, relating to the break in the interview and what then transpired, provided a sufficient foundation for the leading of the psychologist's evidence. The defence founded on passages in *R* v *Ward*[27] to suggest that the evidence of a psychologist is admissible as to the raw liability of a confession. However, the High Court declined to refer to that case on the basis that 'questions relating to the admissibility of evidence in an English criminal trial may depend on rules of English law or practice with which we are not familiar'.

The court identified the issue as whether a proper basis had been laid for the leading of the evidence. It referred to *HM Advocate* v *Gilgannon*[28] for an example of a case in which it was clear from the evidence led for the Crown that the accused was mentally incapable of giving an accurate account. It pointed out that in Blagojevic's case, however, the accused was not suffering from either mental illness or a personality disorder. His only area of vulnerability was that it was said that stress modified his response pattern. It then said:

> 'In the absence of evidence from the appellant himself that his statement was influenced . . . or from the police that he was seen to be suffering from emotional stress or was under any pressure . . . the jury could only speculate as to whether his vulnerability affected him. On this occasion [the psychologist's] evidence lacked therefore any proper basis.'

The factual basis for the skilled witness's evidence is likely to come from one of two sources. Often, the skilled witness will be presented with facts spoken to by other witnesses. Indeed, in order to facilitate this, the skilled witness is generally allowed to be present in court and to hear the evidence of the witnesses to fact unless objection is taken, though he is

[24] Walker and Walker, *op cit*, para 413.
[25] 1952 JC 28.
[26] 1995 SCCR 570.
[27] [1993] 1 WLR 619.
[28] 1983 SCCR 10.

excluded from court while other witnesses giving opinion evidence are in the witness box.[29]

The other source for the factual basis on which a skilled witness's opinion is based is the examination which may have been made by the skilled witness himself. Where the factual basis is being laid in the first part of the skilled witness's own evidence, he will not be permitted to be in court during the evidence of other witnesses as to fact.

Typically, in such a case, a forensic scientist will speak to an analysis of, say, two or more blood samples and that analysis is a question of fact. Thereafter, he will go on to express an opinion about the possibilities in relation to the source of one or more of these samples. There, his evidence is a matter of opinion. A pathologist will speak first to the findings at post-mortem and these will be matters of fact. He will then speak to the conclusions which he draws as to the cause of death and this part of his evidence is opinion. In the case of a fingerprint expert, the particular ridge characteristics identified in a fingerprint are a matter of fact. The proposition that the fingerprint comes from the accused is a matter of opinion.

The function of the expert

The classic statement of the function of a skilled witness who gives opinion evidence is to be found in a civil case, *Davie* v *Magistrates of Edinburgh*[30] where Lord President Cooper said:

> 'Expert witnesses, however skilled or eminent, can give no more than evidence. They cannot usurp the functions of the jury or judge sitting as a jury . . . their duty is to furnish the judge or jury with the necessary scientific criteria for testing the accuracy of their conclusions, so to enable the judge to form their own independent judgment by the application of these criteria to the facts proved in evidence. The scientific opinion evidence, if intelligible, convincing and tested, becomes a factor (and often an important factor) for consideration along with the whole other evidence in the case, but the decision is for the judge or jury. In particular the bare *ipse dixit* of a scientist, however eminent, upon the issue in controversy, will normally carry little weight for it cannot be tested by cross-examination nor independently appraised, and the parties have invoked the decision of a judicial tribunal and not an oracular pronouncement by an expert.'

It will be apparent from this that there are real limits on the function of the skilled witness. To begin with, the evidence which such a witness gives must relate to matters beyond everyday experience. Matters within everyday experience will be regarded as matters within judicial knowledge and these include such matters as the normal period of human gestation[31] and the elementary principles of dynamics.[32]

The courts are anxious to ensure that the skilled witness does not usurp the function of the tribunal of fact, as the passage from Lord President Cooper's judgment in *Davie* makes clear. If a judge or a jury are in a position to draw their own conclusions from the facts then, as Lord Avonside observed in *Assessor for Lothian Region* v *Wilson*,[33] an expert witness is not essential. Moreover, questions which invite an expert to put himself in the

---

[29] Walker and Walker, *op cit*, para 413.
[30] 1953 SC 34.
[31] *Williamson* v *McClelland* 1913 SC 678; *Preston-Jones* v *Preston-Jones* [1951] AC 391.
[32] *Ballard* v *North British Railway Co* 1923 SC (HL) 43; *Carruthers* v *Macgregor* 1927 SC 816.
[33] 1979 SC 341 at 349.

position of expressing a view on the very matter for the determination of the jury will be objectionable. In *Ingram* v *Macari*[34] it was held that a sheriff had been wrong to hear expert evidence on the question whether particular magazines were liable to deprave and corrupt the morals of the lieges. That was the very issue which he had to determine. In *Hendry* v *HM Advocate*[35] in a question whether an assault had caused a fatal heart attack (the charge being culpable homicide) it was held that a doctor could be asked his opinion on the matter and how confident he was of that opinion, but could not be asked in terms whether he was satisfied on the matter beyond reasonable doubt. This case modified the rule in *HM Advocate* v *McGinlay*.[36] That was a case in which one doctor said that it was possible that a stressful situation could have precipitated a heart attack and the second doctor was prepared to say that it was more likely than not that there was a connection. As modified by *Hendry*, the opinion of the court in *McGinlay* was that

'where the medical experts were not prepared to express a more confident opinion it cannot be maintained that there was material before the jury which would have justified them in reaching a conclusion beyond reasonable doubt. The experts would only admit of, on the one hand, the possibility or, on the other hand, at best the probability on a balance of the evidence as a whole'.

It follows from this that the opinion of the skilled witness, if it is to be the foundation for the determination of the jury, must be an opinion expressed with some certainty, but that an opinion expressed with certainty will not bind the jury.

Use of literature
One obvious question which arises is the relationship between the evidence of a skilled witness and the literature in the relevant field. Strictly, that literature is hearsay, but this will not result in reference to the literature being excluded. The principle was stated by Pattenden[37] as follows.

'To some extent all opinion evidence by an expert contains hearsay. Very few experts acquire a specialist's skills entirely through first hand experience. Provided the hearsay on which the expert relies is of a sufficiently general nature to be regarded as part of the corpus of knowledge with which an expert in his field can be expected to be acquainted, no objection will be taken to his evidence on this ground.'

This was the point at issue in *R* v *Abadom*[38] in which the appellant argued that an expert on the analysis of fragments of glass could not rely on statistics collated in a research establishment except for those few examples with which he might have been personally concerned. The court, however, was not impressed with this argument and Kerr LJ said:

'In the context of evidence given by experts it is no more than a statement of the obvious that, in reaching their conclusions, they must be entitled to draw upon material produced by others in the field in which their expertise lies. Indeed, it is part of their duty to consider any material which may be available in their field and not to draw conclusions merely on the basis of their own experience, which

[34] 1982 SCCR 372.
[35] 1987 SCCR 394.
[36] 1983 SLT 562.
[37] R Pattenden, 'Expert Opinion Evidence Based on Hearsay' [1982] Crim LR 85.
[38] [1983] 1 WLR 126.

is inevitably likely to be more limited than the general body of information which may be available to them ... it is also inherent in the nature of any statistical information that it will result from the work of others in the same field, whether or not the expert in question will himself have contributed to the bank of information available on the particular topic on which he is called upon to express his opinion. Indeed, to exclude reliance upon such information on the ground that it is inadmissible under the hearsay rule might inevitably lead to the distortion of unreliability of the opinion which the expert presents for evaluation by a judge or jury.'

It is suggested that this passage accurately reflects Scots law as well as English. Moreover, in *Davie* the court made it clear that passages from published work may be adopted by a witness and made part of his evidence or may be put to the witness in cross-examination for his comment; though the court warned against the practice of the judge at first instance scrutinising published work for himself and using passages not referred to in evidence with a view to determining the issue or assessing the testimony of the expert witness.

The availability of the literature for expert evidence is not confined to published work. Some of the literature in *Abadom* was not published and Kerr LJ said:

'It does not seem to us, in relation to the reliability of opinion evidence given by experts, that they must necessarily limit themselves to drawing from material which has been published in some form. Part of their experience and expertise may well lie in their knowledge of unpublished material and in their evaluation of it.'

However, the court in *Abadom* desiderated explicit reference to the sources upon which the expert has based his opinion.

Vulnerable witnesses

Most witnesses give their evidence in open court but there are special rules which apply to witnesses in trials for sexual offences and to the evidence of children generally.

Sexual offences

So far as sexual offence cases are concerned, section 92(3) of the 1995 Act permits the judge in trial under solemn procedure for 'rape or the like' to cause all persons other than the accused and counsel and solicitors to be removed from the courtroom. There is no general equivalent under summary procedure. However, in terms of section 50(3) (which applies to both solemn and summary procedure) where a child is called as a witness in a case relating to an offence against decency or morality the court may direct the exclusion of all persons except court members and officers, parties and their lawyers, the press and anyone specially authorised by the court to remain.

Children

Much has been done in recent years to make it possible for child witnesses to give evidence with as little stress as possible, consistent with the overriding need to ensure a fair trial. The starting-point is the relatively informal one of a practice note issued by the Lord Justice-General in 1990 in which he desiderated the removal of wigs and gowns while a child is giving evidence. Judges should sit in the well of the court and a relative or other person should be allowed to sit near the child to provide support while the child gives evidence (but must not prompt the child in any way).

The other principal protections for children giving evidence are contained in section 271 of the 1995 Act.

The first of these is the possibility of the evidence of the child being taken on commission, as provided for by subsections (1) to (4).

By subsection (1), the court may appoint a commissioner to take such evidence in solemn proceedings before the oath is administered to the jury and in summary proceedings before the first witness is called. In exceptional circumstances a commissioner may be so appointed during the course of the trial. Proceedings before such a commissioner must be video recorded (subsection (2)) and the accused may not, except with leave of the commissioner, be present in the room where the child's evidence is being taken (subsection (3)). He is, however, entitled to watch and hear the proceedings 'by such means as seem suitable to the commissioner'.

By subsection (7) the court may grant an application only on cause shown having regard in particular to three things. These are (*a*) the possible effect on the child if required to give evidence without application being granted, (*b*) whether it is likely that the child would be better able to give evidence if the application were granted, and (*c*) the views of the child. By subsection (8) the court is permitted (but not required) to take into account the age and maturity of the child, the nature of the charge and the evidence to be given and the relationship between the child and the accused.

Beyond this, applications for the taking of a child's evidence on commission are governed by section 272(2) to (6), (8) and (9) of the 1995 Act, as applied by section 271(4). The effect of this is that an application may be granted only if the judge is satisfied that the evidence which it is averred the witness is able to give is necessary for the proper adjudication of the trial and that there would be no unfairness to the other party if the evidence were to be taken in that form.

Where an application is granted and a record is made of the taking of the evidence on commission (as it must be), section 272(4) of the 1995 Act provides that the record shall, without being sworn to by witnesses, be received in evidence insofar as that can be done without unfairness to either party. It, therefore, open to either party to object to the admissibility of the evidence, notwithstanding the fact that an application has been granted for the taking of evidence on commission. Presumably, in that event, the child can be led as a witness, though the Act does not make that clear.

Section 271(5) to (11) provides for the taking of the evidence of children (*a*) by closed circuit television (subsection (5)), and (*b*) with the child behind a screen (subsection (6)). Where a screen is used, the Act requires that arrangements are made to ensure that the accused is able to watch and hear as the evidence is given by the child.

In terms of rule 22.1(2) of the Act of Adjournal (Criminal Procedure Rules) 1996 applications require to be made at least fourteen clear days before the trial.

The evidence which the witnesses give

Objections

We have seen that the approach which Scots law takes to the admissibility of evidence is exclusory; that is, there are certain rules the breach of which will render the evidence in question inadmissible. The means by which a party secures compliance with those rules by his opponent, and the exclusion by the court of evidence which breaches them, is by objecting when an attempt is made to lead that evidence. Before we consider the rules as to admissibility we need to look at the procedure upon an objection being made.

The party making the objection must do so immediately the evidence is sought to be led. If he does not do so, the evidence becomes part of the case to be considered by the court in due course no matter how strong the objection might be. The court will, not except in the most flagrant cases, itself take notice of inadmissibility. For all the judge knows, the parties may have agreed that the evidence can be led, and in an adversarial system—that is, one in which the parties fight the case out and the judge is a kind of referee—it is not for the judge to descend into the arena of controversy.

In *Skeen* v *Murphy*,[39] a drink driving case, the defence sought at the end of the case to contend that service of the analyst's certificate as to the accused's alcohol level had not been proved. Such certificates, if served on the accused, are (in terns of the road traffic legislation) evidence in their own right—witnesses are not needed to establish the facts set out in the certificate. However, if the certificate had not been served it was not evidence and the prosecution would have failed to establish an essential of the case (that is, that the accused's alcohol level was over the limit). If the certificate was not evidence it was not admissible and it should not have been put in evidence; but the defence had not objected to it being so put. The High Court held that the end of the trial was too late to raise the question and that the certificate had become evidence in the case. Again, in *Cordiner* v *HM Advocate*[40] the prosecutor asked a question of the accused which suggested that he had committed a crime not charged, namely subornation of perjury, by attempting to persuade a witness to give false evidence at his trial. On appeal, it was held that there was a technical breach of law on admissibility of evidence but that since no objection had been taken at the time the appellant was to be regarded as having waived compliance with the rule.

A similar (but not identical) point arose in *Higgins* v *HM Advocate*.[41] In that case, which was one of a murder, the Crown led evidence that the dying victim said to a police officer, 'They three bastards tore into me. They stabbed me.' As we shall see, a statement made by a person who has since died may in some circumstances be admissible evidence but it is not like the evidence of a witness who goes into the witness box. In particular, it cannot be tested by cross-examination. The trial judge should have pointed out to the jury but did not do so. The accused appealed, arguing that this was a miscarriage of justice. The High Court noted, however, that not only had the judge not pointed out the particular character of the evidence but neither

[39] 1987 SLT (Notes) 2.
[40] 1991 SCCR 652.
[41] 1993 SCCR 542.

had defence counsel done so in addressing the jury. The court concluded, 'The value or quality of this evidence was not put in issue by the defence and there is accordingly no reason to think that the failure or the judge to give the correct direction in law led to any miscarriage of justice.' The conviction was upheld.

Accordingly, the time to take issue with an attempt to lead evidence which a party to criminal proceedings considers to be inadmissible is the time when that attempt is made and before the witness has had a chance to answer the offending question.

Once an objection is made, the judge will want to know its content. It will often be undesirable to allow the witness to hear what the objection is, much less to hear the arguments presented, because to do so might colour his evidence and perhaps defeat the whole point of objecting. If, for example, the objection is to a leading question (by which is meant a question which merely asks the witness to confirm information provided by the questioner), the party objecting will not want the witness to hear the whole of that information, still less any explanation which might be put forward as to why the evidence is of particular significance. In such circumstances, the judge will direct the witness to leave the courtroom while the matter is being argued.

The need to exclude those who should not hear the detail of the objection becomes most acute in a jury trial. Very often the judge will have to be told the nature of the evidence likely to be elicited by the question objected to, and that information will often be capable of being agreed between the parties (though without its truth being agreed). Manifestly, it would be unsatisfactory that the jury, which will eventually decide the facts of the case, should hear such information. Accordingly, except where the point is very short, obvious and cannot conceivably colour the jury's deliberations, the jury will be asked to retire while the point is debated.

The party making the objection will state what it is, preferably formulating the objection as a proposition of law, though this will often be implicit rather than explicit. The party who asked the question objected to will then reply and, after hearing the objector further if need be, the judge will rule on the point.

Trial within a trial
There is a procedure, now in some disfavour, known as the 'trial within a trial' under which the judge in a jury trial will hear evidence on the disputed point outwith the presence of the jury in order to form a view on the admissibility of the evidence objected to. If the objection is then upheld that is an end of the matter. If it is repelled, however, the evidence will then be led again in the presence of the jury.

The procedure was criticised by Lord Justice-General Clyde in *Thompson v HM Advocate*[42] on account of its tendency to allow witnesses to reconstruct their evidence for the second runthrough, before the jury. He pointed out that the usual question in such a procedure is whether confession evidence was freely and voluntarily given and that there is much to be said for leading that evidence once and for all before the jury and allowing them to decide whether it is admissible. Griffiths has suggested

[42] 1968 JC 61.

that remarks made by Lord Cameron in *HM Advocate* v *Whitelaw*[43] indicate that 'a trial within a trial should only be held if the court is "teetering on the brink" of holding a statement inadmissible and . . . the Crown declines to concede the point'.[44]

For obvious reasons the judge in a summary trial where there is no jury, cannot hold a trial within a trial. In a summary trial, the best practice is to allow the evidence to be led 'under reservation'—that is, reserving the possibility that it will be excluded from the court's consideration at the end of the day. This was the course laid down by the High Court in *Copeland* v *Gillies*[45] and it means that the evidence exists and is available for the appeal court if need be. The difficulty occasioned by excluding evidence altogether in a summary trial was demonstrated in *Aitchison* v *Rizza*[46] in which the High Court hearing the appeal was obliged to remit the case back to the sheriff to hear the evidence which he had wrongly excluded.

The admissibility of evidence

We have already noted Dickson's classic statement of the purpose of the law of admissibility of evidence:

> 'to exclude valueless and deceptive proofs, to secure regularity in the investigations and to confine within reasonable limits the duration and expense of judicial proceedings'.[47]

This falls naturally into three parts and we can consider the admissibility of evidence in those parts.

The exclusion of valueless and deceptive proofs—hearsay

Hearsay is the most obvious, and perhaps the classic, example of a type of evidence which is regarded as inherently unreliable and misleading, and hence objectionable.

Hearsay is simply reported speech or that which is analogous to it. When a witness attempts to give evidence about what someone else has said to him, that is hearsay.

Primary hearsay

The Walkers distinguish two categories of hearsay, which they call primary and secondary.[48] Primary hearsay refers to statements so clearly connected with the action or event in time, place and circumstances as substantially to form part of it. These statements are said to form part of the '*res gestae*'—the 'whole thing that happened'—and this is true whether the maker of the statement is the accused or another person, whether or not a participant.

Primary hearsay is admissible and it is possible to find many examples of cases in which it has been essential to conviction, though hardly any in which its admissibility has been challenged. The challenges tend to relate to the borderline between primary hearsay and *de recenti* statements, to which

[43] 1980 SLT (Notes) 25.
[44] D B Griffiths, *Confessions* (1994) p 112.
[45] 1973 SLT 74.
[46] 1985 SCCR 297.
[47] W G Dickson, *A Treatise on the Law of Evidence in Scotland* (3rd edn, 1887) Preface.
[48] Walker and Walker, *op cit*, para 370.

we shall come very shortly. However, by way of examples of primary hearsay, we may note two cases.

The first case is *Crosbie and Others*[49] in which a gang chased and killed a man, shouting as they did so, 'Kill him' or 'Get him'. A few minutes later one of them was seen near the body, brandishing a bayonet and shouting, 'Here's your victim'. The shouts of 'Kill him' and 'Get him' were plainly primary hearsay; they formed part of the incident just as much as the chasing did. A further example is to be found in *Glover* v *Tudhope*[50] in which a man solicited a motorist for a homosexual act. The motorist was not called as a witness but the arresting officer's account of the conversation between the parties and of the circumstances was admitted as evidence. That conversation, of course, was the whole essence of the soliciting.

Other examples could be multiplied. In a fraud, the words by which the false pretence is made will, if spoke to by a person who heard them said, be primary hearsay and admissible as such. In a breach of the peace, the obscenities shouted by the accused will likewise be admissible as primary hearsay provided that the witness who gives evidence about them actually heard them shouted. And so on.

Secondary hearsay

Secondary hearsay is another matter altogether. If someone gives evidence about an event without himself having observed it directly, his evidence must be based on what someone else has told him. That evidence will be inadmissible as secondary hearsay. It is in this sense that the word 'hearsay' is usually used in court and in which it will be used in the remainder of this section.

Hearsay is in its nature not susceptible to meaningful cross-examination and is therefore open to attack as being dangerous to rely upon because it cannot be tested properly. Suppose A is charged with killing B, C is being an eyewitness and D having been nowhere near the scene of the crime. If, instead of calling C as a witness, the Crown was simply to call D to say what C told him about the crime, the court could not test that account at all. D would be unable to elaborate on the account given to him, unable to clear up ambiguities, unable to help to clear up discrepancies with the evidence of other witnesses and unable to respond (with any certainty) to the accusation that C had a motive to lie. Moreover, through repetition there is a danger of the original sense of what was said being distorted, especially if it had passed through a number of intermediaries before it reaches the court. For these reasons, the law excludes from evidence all forms of assertion other than those made by the witness on the basis of his own direct observation. The traditional explanation for this was articulated by Lord Normand in *Teper* v *R*,[51] when he said:

> '[Hearsay] is not the best evidence and it is not delivered on oath. The truthfulness and accuracy of the person whose words are spoken to by another witness cannot be tested by cross-examination and the light which his demeanour would throw on his testimony is lost.'

---

[49] High Court, Glasgow, December 1945; unreported. This case is discussed in G H Gordon, *The Criminal Law of Scotland* (2nd edn, 1978) p 156.

[50] 1986 SCCR 49.

[51] [1952] AC 480.

Typically, the objection will be made to reported speech but the form of the evidence or of the matter reported does not matter and the reported cases tend to concern hearsay in written reports which are submitted as evidence. In *Grant* v *HM Advocate*,[52] for example, the accused was charged with putting ear lotion containing carbolic into a bottle of milk intended for his wife's illegitimate daughter; the child consumed the milk and became ill as a result. The wife gave evidence that the accused put carbolic in the child's milk and the doctor who had examined the child was also called as a witness. His report was a production and contained the following passage.

'The child was crying in extreme pain, and on asking the mother what was wrong with the child she told me that it had been poisoned. She said that her husband had done it.'

The conviction was quashed on appeal on the ground that this passage had been hearsay and therefore incompetent; and that its being given in evidence was so prejudicial to a fair trial that it was fatal to the conviction. In giving his opinion, Lord Justice-Clerk Aitchison said:

'[I]t is really too plain for argument that it was incompetent to put to the jury that passage in the medical report. The evidence was hearsay and it did not cease to be hearsay because the wife had been called as a witness and had deponed to the same effect.'

Scientific and other reports

Hitherto, difficulties have arisen for the Crown in relation to scientific and other reports where it turned out that the scientist who gives the report delegated some of the analysis upon which it is based to a lab technician or some other person. The reporting by the scientist of the results which had been reported to him by the technician fell to be excluded as hearsay, as the High Court decided in *Normand* v *Wotherspoon*.[53]

In *O'Brien* v *McCreadie*,[54] however, the High Court held that *Normand* does not apply where statute provides that the report is sufficient evidence of any fact stated in it. That case concerned a certificate as to the analysis of a drug under a provision which now finds its statutory expression in section 280(1) of the 1995 Act. By that subsection, for the purposes of certain specified offences, a certificate as to specified matters purporting to be signed by specified persons is, provided it has been served on the accused not less than fourteen days before the trial and not challenged within seven days of service of the copy, sufficient evidence of the matter so certified. In *O'Brien* the Lord Justice-Clerk recognised explicitly that such documents might contain hearsay but held that the wording of the statute was decisive and that *Normand* was to be distinguished.

The effect of section 280(4) of the 1995 Act seems to be to extend this exception to the rule against hearsay to a great many scientific reports. That subsection provides that for the purposes of any criminal proceedings a report purporting to be signed by two authorised forensic scientists (and served and not timeously challenged) is to be sufficient evidence of any fact or conclusion as to fact contained in the report and of the authority of the

[52] 1938 SLT 113.
[53] 1993 SCCR 912.
[54] 1994 SCCR 516.

signatories. By contrast with subsection (1), no limit is placed on the nature of the matters which may be certified.

By subsection (5), a forensic scientist is authorised if he comes into one of two categories. He may be authorised by the Secretary of State or he may be a constable possessing the qualifications and experience prescribed by the Secretary of State and authorised by the chief constable of the area concerned.

Even where there is a challenge, section 280(8) provides that the evidence of both forensic scientists is to be sufficient evidence of any fact or conclusion as to fact contained in the report. It seems to follow that the reasoning in *O'Brien* must extend to that oral evidence and that the possibility of objecting to hearsay in such a report no longer exists. Not only that, but whereas the Lord Justice-Clerk in *O'Brien* noted that the certificates with which the court had to deal in that case could only be granted in cases under summary procedure, certificates under section 280(1) and reports under section 280(4) are both explicitly capable of being granted in *any* criminal proceedings.

De recenti statements

Difficulty arises at the borderline between primary and secondary hearsay because in some circumstances *de recenti* statements—that is, statements which are made shortly after the events in question made by one who is called as witness—may be admitted in evidence for the limited purpose of supporting the credibility of that witness. *De recenti* statements are not, however, substantive evidence of the facts.

The Walkers suggest that *de recenti* evidence may be theoretically admissible in any case but in practice it tends to be tendered mainly in cases of physical injury.[55] Field, on the other hand, maintains that *de recenti* statements are now almost certainly restricted to circumstances in which the victim of a sexual assault is allowed to consistency in her claim to have refused consent,[56] though he cites no authority for this proposition and it might well be an unduly restrictive view.

Distinguishing res gestae and de recenti

The distinction between that which is part of the *res gestae* and statements which are *de recenti* can be a difficult one. It is certainly the case, following a line of cases starting with *Yates* v *HM Advocate*,[57] that distress observed in a rape victim shortly after the alleged attack can amount to substantive evidence to prove that she was subjected to force. In many cases, that distress will be evidenced by what the victim says as well as by how she acts. The theory is that her reaction to the assault is spontaneous and part of the *res gestae*.

The distinction between that which is part of the *res gestae* and that which is *de recenti* is somewhat blurred by *HM Advocate* v *Stewart*[58] when evidence was allowed, as *de recenti*, of what a seven-year-old boy had said about forty-eight hours after seeing a murder and evidence was also allowed as '*de recenti* and in fact . . . part of the *res gestae*' of what the accused had said about the

---

[55] Walker and Walker, *op cit*, para 376.
[56] D Field, *The Law of Evidence in Scotland* (1991) p 324.
[57] 1977 SLT (Notes) 42.
[58] (1855) 2 Irv 160 at 179.

victim within twenty-four hours of the crime and of what a deceased witness had said about the accused within forty-eight hours of the crime. It might have been better for the court to proceed on the basis that evidence which has the accused as its source is always admissible (subject to fairness in the manner in which it is obtained) and that the statement of a dead witness is a recognised common law exception to the rule against hearsay.

HM Advocate v *Murray*[59] also confuses the issue. In that case, the first statement made by a mentally defective girl when she got home after she was alleged to have been raped was admitted in evidence as part of the *res gestae* even though she was not herself a witness (being incapable of understanding the oath and therefore, at that time, disqualified).

Some remarks of the court in *Andersons* v *McFarlane*[60] suggest that evidence that a servant girl, who had been assaulted by her employers, had reported the matter to her mother at the first opportunity some days later was admissible as *de recenti* but the issue in the case was its effect in relation to sufficiency of evidence. On the admissibility of *de recenti* statements it requires to be treated with some care.

Perhaps the safest thing that can be said is that in any case where a statement might be *de recenti* the whole circumstances will have to be examined with care to determine exactly what the status of that statement actually is.

Prior inconsistent statements

De recenti statements are concerned with supporting the credibility of the maker of the statement. Section 263(4) of the 1995 Act is, perhaps, the direct opposite. That section authorises the leading of evidence as to a previous statement made by *any* witness for the limited purpose of demonstrating that his story has not been consistent throughout and thus affecting his credibility adversely. Typically, this relates to what a witness has told the police at an early stage.

The statements which can be put to witnesses in terms of such a provision as relevant to their credibility were considered in *Coll, Petitioner.*[61] In that case, the court distinguished three categories. Statements made in the course of the initial investigation can be put and this will include most statements made to the police. Precognitions, which are defined as statements taken by those engaged in preparing the case for one of the parties, cannot be put because of the risk that their content is affected by the partisan interest of the precognoscer. Into this category fall virtually all statements taken by procurators fiscal and defence solicitors and also statements taken from defence witnesses by the police on the instructions of the procurator fiscal in response to the intimation of a list of witnesses to be called by the defence at trial. The final category consists of precognitions on oath, where the procurator fiscal (or, rarely, the defence solicitor) interrogates a witness in the presence of the sheriff, the questions and answers being recorded by shorthand writer, transcribed and signed by the witness. In this case the court considered that the presence of the sheriff was a safeguard against the content being affected as might happen in an ordinary precognition.

[59] (1866) 5 Irv 232.
[60] (1899) 2 Adam 644.
[61] 1977 SLT 58.

In *HM Advocate* v *McGachy*[62] Lord Sutherland held in the course of a trial that statements taken by the police on their own initiative the day after they charged the accused did not fall to be regarded as precognitions simply because the police had passed the stage of charging. With this we may compare *Low* v *HM Advocate*,[63] in which it was held that it was open to the jury to take the view that a statement taken by a police officer twenty-four hours after the crime when only three out of eight accused had been arrested was not a precognition. The formulation of this decision suggests that the issue is one of fact for the jury to decide, rather than of law for the court, but this might be influenced by the fact that this case was a substantive prosecution of the maker of the statement for perjury by denying making the statement in the original trial.

We must contrast *Kerr* v *HM Advocate*[64] in which it was held that a statement obtained on a question and answer basis after the accused had appeared on petition was a precognition and hence could not be put to the witness.

Exceptions to the rule against hearsay

There are a number of exceptions to the rule against hearsay recognised at common law, though not all of them are likely to be of much practical significance. One which should be noted is that relating to a statement made by a person who has since died, admissible in terms of *HM Advocate* v *Monson*[65] (but the party wishing to lead such evidence needs first to prove the death, usually by an extract death certificate).

Another more recently recognised exception arose in *Lord Advocate's Reference (No 1 of 1992)*.[66] In the trial which gave rise to that, the Crown sought to lead evidence of a remittance advice produced by a computer. That document was to be spoken to by the computer operations controller of the organisation in question but he had not made the entries himself. Although, as we shall see below, changes in the law have meant that this particular situation should no longer cause problems, at that time it did. The evidence was rejected as hearsay by the presiding sheriff.

In dealing with the reference, the Lord Justice-General said:

> 'This court has shown itself willing to adapt the criminal law of this country in order to meet changes in social conditions and attitudes. . . . In my opinion that is a proper exercise of the judicial function and it is within the inherent power of this court, subject always to recognition . . . that development of the law on these lines must never be arbitrary but ought only to be done by developing the application of well-established principles of our law.'

Upon this basis, and noting that it was in the particular case impossible to identify the authors of the records, the Lord Justice-General articulated an exception to the hearsay rule where it was not merely impracticable but was in fact impossible to identify the author of the records.

Muldoon v *Herron*[67] has also been regarded by some as an exception to the rule against hearsay though it is important to realise that the High Court in

[62] 1991 SLT 921.
[63] 1987 SCCR 541.
[64] 1958 SLT 82.
[65] (1893) 1 Adam 114.
[66] 1992 SCCR 724.
[67] 1970 SLT 229.

deciding the case did not regard it as such. In *Muldoon* police officers said that shortly after a breach of the peace two witnesses had pointed out the accused as the perpetrators. At court, neither witness could identify him. One of them was not sure if the accused were those he had pointed out and the other denied that they were those she had pointed out. The High Court held on appeal that the evidence of the police was available to link the accused with the crime and upheld the conviction. This approach was developed in *Frew* v *Jessop*[68] in which two witnesses gave evidence that they had provided police officers with a description of the driver of a vehicle (who was alleged to be guilty of offences) but that they could neither recall that description nor identify the accused. The police officers gave evidence of what the witnesses had told them, which included the registration mark of the vehicle. On appeal, it was argued that this evidence was hearsay and ought not to have been admitted but Lord Justice-Clerk Ross, under reference to *Muldoon*, said:

> 'We do not see why any different principle should be applied to evidence of this kind than is frequently applied to evidence of positive identification which the witness has been able to make shortly after an offence has been committed but which he is unable to recall by the time he gives his evidence in court. . . . No doubt [such] evidence is hearsay evidence but it is hearsay evidence which forms an exception to the general rule that hearsay evidence is inadmissible.'

Evidence of this sort can only be given if the witness who viewed the identification parade or pointed out the accused attends court and gives evidence. In *McNair* v *HM Advocate*[69] a police officer was asked whether a man listed as a defence witness but not present to give evidence had been asked whether he saw a particular person on the identification parade and whether he had been able to identify anyone. It was held that both questions sought to elicit inadmissible hearsay.

Jamieson v *HM Advocate (No 2)*[70] might, perhaps, be seen as a development of the *Muldoon* principle. In that case, a witness gave evidence that she had given a true statement to the police at the time but that she could not now remember the details of what she had said. Evidence was led from the police officer as to the content of her statement and this was held by the trial judge to have had the effect of incorporating her statement to the police into her own evidence. The argument that the police officer's evidence had been inadmissible hearsay was rejected on appeal.

The *Jamieson* principle now finds statutory expression in section 260 of the 1995 Act. Subsection (1) provides that, subject to the other provisions of the section, where a witness gives evidence in criminal proceedings, any prior statement made by the witness shall be admissible as evidence of any matter stated in it of which direct oral evidence by him would be admissible if given in the course of those proceedings. Section 262(1) excludes statements in precognition (other than precognitions on oath) from the ambit of this section, no doubt for the reasons contemplated in *Coll, Petitioner*[71] (essentially that a precognition is 'filtered through the mind of the precognoscer' and hence is of questionable accuracy). Section 261(1)

---

[68] 1989 SCCR 530.
[69] 1993 SLT 277.
[70] 1994 SCCR 610.
[71] 1977 SLT 58.

excludes statements made by the accused from the ambit of section 260, except where the evidence is taken from him by a co-accused.

The restriction to those matters as to which the witness could competently give direct oral evidence guards against the risk that otherwise inadmissible evidence could come to be given under cover of this provision, and the particular criteria to which the provision is subjected by subsection (2) (except in the case of precognitions on oath and statements made in other judicial proceedings) are intended to provide further safeguards.

First, such a statement is not admissible unless it is contained in a document, though 'document' is defined widely by section 262(3) and section 262(2) provides that a statement is 'contained' in a document where the maker makes the statement in the document personally, makes a statement which is embodied in a document by any means, whether he knows it or not, or approves a document as embodying the statement.

Secondly, such a statement is not admissible unless the witness in the course of evidence indicates that the statement was made by him and that he adopts it as his evidence. Accordingly, a prior statement cannot be substituted for the evidence of the witness.

Thirdly, and last the statement is not admissible unless the maker would have been a competent witness at the time it was made. This may restrict the availability of the provision in the case of statements made by very young children.

These common law rules have been modified by section 259 of the 1995 Act, which gives effect to recommendations of the Scottish Law Commission Report, Evidence: Report on Hearsay Evidence in Criminal Proceedings.[72]

The policy proposed by the Commission was

> 'to confirm the traditional preference for direct oral evidence over hearsay but to provide both for the prosecution and for the defence new categories of exception . . . which would allow hearsay evidence of a statement to be admitted if there were truly insurmountable difficulties in the way of obtaining the evidence of the maker of the statement from the maker personally'.[73]

The section allows hearsay evidence (other than of the content of precognitions) subject to the satisfaction of several conditions. By section 261, section 259 does not apply to statements made by the accused.

The first, and most important, condition is that one of five limited sets of circumstances exists. It is with this condition that we are here primarily concerned. The second and third conditions seek to avoid giving hearsay a higher status than direct evidence. They are that the evidence must be evidence which would be admissible if given as direct oral evidence and that the maker of the statement must be a competent witness. The fourth condition is that there exists evidence which would entitle a jury or judge to find that the statement was made and, more significantly. That the witness has direct personal knowledge of the making of the statement—in other words, that the witness who gives evidence had the account directly from an eyewitness. This excludes 'double' hearsay, where A comes to court to say that B told him that C said that he had seen something.

[72] Scot Law Com No 149.
[73] *Ibid*, para 4.48.

e five situations are set out in subsection (2). In the first three, hearsay
nly be led if notice has been given before the trial or with leave of the

he first situation is that the maker of the statement is dead or is, by
reason of his bodily or mental condition, unfit or unable to give evidence in
any competent manner. So far as it deals with death and insanity this places
common law exceptions on a statutory footing. However, it does represent
an extension when it includes unfitness by reason of bodily condition.

The second situation is that in which the maker of the statement is named
and otherwise sufficiently identified but is outwith the UK and it is not
reasonably practicable to secure his attendance at the trial or to obtain his
evidence in any other competent manner. This deals with a somewhat
difficult situation, because, although witnesses in foreign jurisdictions can
be cited, with the assistance of the foreign authorities, in terms of section 2
of the Criminal Justice (International Co-operation) Act 1990, they are not
compellable.

The third situation contemplated by section 259 is that in which the
maker of the statement cannot be found, and all reasonable steps have been
taken to find him. This reverses Lord Justice-Clerk MacDonald's observation in *Monson* that 'If parties are unable to find a witness, that is a
misfortune to the litigant, and a misfortune to which he must just submit.' It
is also, of course, inimical to the interests of justice if such a witness has
something relevant to say and the content of his statement is known but it
still cannot be considered by the court.

Section 259(3) would exclude the evidence in such a case if the dis-
appearance had been engineered by the party tendering the statement;
though in practice it might be hard to make that connection out.

The fourth situation dealt with is that in which a witness refuses to answer
questions on the ground that the answers might incriminate him. This will
only apply, of course, where the witness has made such a statement to
someone else already. The Scottish Law Commission thought that, in such
a situation, it 'should not be acceptable for a criminal to disclose his criminal
activity to a person outside the court and then to claim the privilege in order
to prevent the disclosure of his crime to a court which requires information
relevant to the guilt or innocence of an accused person'.[74]

The fifth and final situation contemplated is that in which a person called
as a witness refuses to give evidence. Such a person would, of course, be
guilty of contempt but this does not assist the party seeking to lead that
person's evidence. There is an evident utility in relying on the hearsay. Any
evidence may be seen as better than none.

Although these new statutory exceptions to the hearsay rule have been
introduced, it is not open to a party simply to spring hearsay evidence upon
his opponent at trial. Section 259(5) of the 1995 Act provides that (except
where the evidence is that of someone who has refused to give evidence
because it might incriminate him or who has refused to take the oath)
hearsay evidence cannot be led under these provisions unless notice in
writing has been given of that intention and of the witnesses and productions
to be adduced in connection with the hearsay evidence. Rule 21.3 of the Act
of Adjournal (Criminal Procedure Rules) 1996 and Form 21.3 make more

[74] *Ibid*, para 5.61.

detailed provision and, in particular, Form 21.3 requires that the notice be accompanied by an affidavit of the person who will give the evidence stating what that witness will say. In this connection it is important to note that section 59 of the Solicitors (Scotland) Act 1980, which makes it lawful for notaries public to administer oaths and affirmations and take affidavits, explicitly does not apply to 'any matter . . . relating to . . . the prosecution, trial or punishment of any offence'. It seems to follow, therefore, that for such a notice to be effective the affidavit will have to be sworn before a sheriff or JP, and this might well diminish the practical utility of the provisions considerably.

Excluding valueless and deceptive proofs—irrelevant evidence
The first paragraph of Dickson on Evidence begins thus:

> 'The first and most general of the primary rules of evidence is this—that the evidence led be confined to matters which are in dispute or under investigation.'

Facts which are not relevant are referred to as 'collateral' and the reasons for excluding evidence of such facts were noted by Lord Justice-Clerk Ross in *Brady* v *HM Advocate*.[75]

> 'The general rule is that it is not admissible to lead evidence on collateral matters in a criminal trial. Various justifications have been put forward for this rule. The existence of a collateral fact does not render more probable the existence of the fact in issue; at best a collateral matter can only have an indirect bearing on the matter in issue; a jury may become confused by having to consider collateral matters and may have their attention diverted from the true matter in issue. Whatever the justification for it, the general rule is clear.'

In short, evidence which is not relevant has the potential to be 'valueless and deceptive'. It may also be said that the leading of irrelevant evidence does nothing to help to 'confine within reasonable limits the duration and expense of judicial proceedings' as desiderated by Dickson.

In practice, however, it is not always easy to know exactly when a particular fact will be regarded as collateral. This difficulty becomes especially acute in relation to circumstantial evidence. The concept of relevance can, therefore, become extremely complex. Moreover, the facts which the law will regard as irrelevant will not necessarily be so perceived by the layman. For example, evidence that there are more housebreakings in a particular area when a particular person is our of prison than when he is locked up might be regarded as a piece of circumstantial evidence which would tend to support (though fall far short of proving) the proposition that the person in question is a housebreaker. However, even if it would tend to support the general proposition that the person is a housebreaker, that is all it would support. It does not offer any assistance whatever with the determination of whether that person committed the particular house-breaking with which he is charged. For that reason, it is irrelevant. It is also regarded by the law as prejudicial and is an example of the most obvious category of collateral material, namely evidence of a crime not charged against the accused on the indictment or complaint upon which he is standing trial. An attempt to lead such evidence is, subject to what was said in the Full Bench decision in *Nelson* v *HM Advocate*,[76] objectionable.

[75] 1986 SCCR 191.
[76] 1994 SCCR 192.

ence of a crime not charged

elson, the appellant was charged with drug trafficking offences. Evidence led that when he was being detained he had obstructed the police. It objected that the indictment did not contain a charge of obstruction and argued that, this being evidence of a crime not charged it should be excluded as irrelevant. However, the High Court held that the Crown could lead the evidence because what the accused did when approached by police officers was relevant to the proof of the crime which was charged. The fact that the behaviour of the accused fell within the definition of another crime, not charged, was not enough to exclude the evidence unless fair notice requires that the other crime be expressly referred to in the indictment. This would be the situation if, for example, the other crime was significantly different in time, place and character from the crime charged.

It is not clear how far this decision goes; passages of the judgment are less than clear. Gordon has suggested, however,[77] that notice will now only be required where the Crown requires to prove guilt of the crime in question or where the evidence either reflects badly on the accused's character (in a way which minor road traffic violations, for example, do not but other, unspecified housebreakings in the example above do) or relates to some offence so different in time place or character from that libelled that the accused could not expect it to be led as evidence relevant to that charge.

Character of victim

Evidence of the character of the victim is generally inadmissible. It has no relevance to the merits of the case before the court. However, proof may be led in relation to offences of violence that the injured party was quarrelsome. Alison justifies this by suggesting that, where provocation is claimed as a defence, the relevancy of inquiry into the generally quarrelsome nature of the victim lies in the fact that 'it is much more likely that a person of bad temper and quarrelsome habits has been betrayed into some of his usual excesses on the occasion libelled, than one who has always been remarkable for his meekness and serenity of disposition'.[78]

Alison also suggests that, where such evidence is to be led 'without doubt it will be held indispensable that due notice of the intention to bring forward such proof should have been given by the pannel, that the prosecutor may be on his guard to support his own witness's temper by his own witnesses'.[79] This observation is treated by the Walkers as authoritative in itself.[80]

It is not clear how such notice is to be given, but presumably anything would do provided the prosecutor is put on notice that the temperament of the victim will be an issue. No doubt the simplest approach would be to adapt the type of notice which is given of a special defence and, in Alison's example, one can imagine that a notice of a special defence of self-defence could readily be adapted.

It may, of course, be that the prosecutor will wish to take the initiative and lead evidence in chief of the sanguine character of the victim and this

[77] *Ibid* at 203, Commentary.
[78] A J Alison, *Practice of the Criminal Law of Scotland* 1833 ii, 532.
[79] *Ibid*.
[80] Walker and Walker, *op cit*, para 20.

seems to be permissible,[81] though the authorities are silent on the matter of the notice.

In general, evidence may not be led of specific act of violence, though Macphail has cited two cases in which this was allowed,[82] these being *HM Advocate* v *Kay*[83] and *HM Advocate* v *Cunningham*.[84] The prohibition on proof of specific acts of violence must in general make it very difficult to prove the proposition that the victim was quarrelsome. It must make cross-examination even harder because the obvious question to ask a witness who alleges that a particular person was bad tempered is what examples he can give (with a view to suggesting that anger was, on the particular occasions, fully justified or alternatively that the assessment of his temper is exaggerated). This is, however, precisely the question which the rule forbids.

Prior sexual conduct of the victim

The other issue which has confronted the courts is that of the character of a woman who has been sexually abused. The prosecutor may set up her respectability in general terms, while the defence may in such cases prove her bad reputation during the immediately preceding period but not specific acts of unchastity unless they are so closely related as to form part of the *res gestae*. The matter was discussed by Lord Justice-Clerk MacDonald in *Dickie* v *HM Advocate*.[85]

> '[I]t seems a relevant subject of enquiry whether the woman was at the time a person of reputed bad moral character, as bearing upon her credibility when alleging that she has been subjected to criminal violence by one desiring to have intercourse with her. Such evidence may seriously affect the inference to be drawn from her conduct at the time. But such evidence is something very different from evidence of individual acts of unchastity with other men at an interval of time. I am not aware that such evidence has ever been allowed and indeed it could only be allowed upon the footing that a female who yields her person to one man will presumably do so to any man—a proposition which is quite untenable. . . . Every woman is entitled to protection from attack upon her person. Even a prostitute may be held to be ravished if the proof established a rape, although she may admit that she is a prostitute.'

The underlying basis of this reasoning seems to be that the credibility of a person who claims to have acted out of character on a particular occasion must be open to doubt. Whether psychologists would agree with such a broad proposition is, of course, questionable. It seems clear, however, that it will be only in exceptional cases that evidence as to the victim's sexual character will be relevant. We have in *Green* v *HM Advocate*[86] an example of such evidence being allowed in relation to an appeal, it being claimed that the evidence was not available for trial.

The case was one of rape and the appellants tendered, *inter alia*, evidence that the victim (who seems to have been aged about sixteen) had had sexual intercourse previously with one of them, that she had had sexual intercourse with a number of others on prior occasions, that she had twice falsely reported having been raped and that she suffered psychiatric disturbance

[81] *Porteous* (1941) Bell's Notes 293.
[82] I D Macphail, *Evidence* (1987) para ˙16.07.
[83] 1970 JC 68.
[84] High Court, Glasgow, 14th February 1974; unreported.
[85] (1897) 2 Adam 331 at 337.
[86] 1983 SCCR 42.

used her to fantasise and have delusions. The High Court remitted
al judge to hear the evidence of certain witnesses. The first spoke to
reputation of the victim, which seems to have been for promiscuity.
nd and third spoke to the victim's somewhat irrational reaction on
being caught red-handed in theft. The fourth spoke to the victim's obsession
with sex and to an allegation of rape which she made but which was not
pursued. The fifth was a consultant psychiatrist specialising in adolescent
and child psychiatry and his evidence was that the complainer did indeed
have an obsession with sex and had a readiness to make allegations of sexual
assault upon her which the psychiatrist was not prepared to accept as having
a foundation in fact. Faced with this evidence, the Crown did not seek to
support the conviction.

The policy behind allowing such evidence, and its actual significance,
could be debated at great length. We, however, are concerned here with
admissibility. It is suggested that the critical point in this case was the fact
that there was psychiatric evidence available as to the complainer's tendency
to make up stories about being sexually assaulted. Such evidence is plainly
both relevant to her credibility on such an issue and also scientifically based,
which is more than can be said for 'local reputation'.

This area of law must be seen in the light of section 274 of the 1995 Act
which applies to both solemn and summary procedure and to prosecutions
for rape, sodomy, assault with intent to rape, indecent assault, indecent
behaviour (including 'any lewd, indecent or libidinous practice or
behaviour'), contraventions of section 106(1)(a) or section 107 of the
Mental Health (Scotland) Act 1984 and to contraventions of certain
sections of the Criminal Law (Consolidation) (Scotland) Act 1995 which
relate to sexual offences. In such cases, unless the defence can bring the case
within the exceptions provided by section 275, the court must not admit or
allow questioning designed to elicit evidence (from any witness) that the
alleged victim is not of good character in relation to sexual matters, is a
prostitute or associate of prostitutes or has at any time engaged with any
person in sexual behaviour not forming part of the charge.

These prohibitions do not apply to the Crown, in terms of section 274(5).

The exceptions are, first, that the evidence which it is desired to lead is to
explain or rebut evidence led or to be led other than by the party wishing to
ask the questions, secondly, that it relates to sexual behaviour on the same
occasion as that charged or that it relates to a special defence of
incrimination, or, thirdly, that to exclude the questioning would be contrary
to the interests of justice.

The meaning of this, and especially of the 'interests of justice' exception,
was canvassed in *Bremner* v *HM Advocate*.[87] That was a rape case in which
the defence sought leave to ask whether a relationship between the victim
and the accused, which had ended eight months before the date of the
offence, had involved regular sexual intercourse. The trial judge (Lord
Mayfield) refused and, following conviction, the accused appealed on the
ground that the exclusion of that evidence had been an error.

In his report, Lord Mayfield explained that he regarded the statutory
prohibition as absolute and that the defence had not satisfied him that it
would be contrary to the interests of justice to exclude the questioning,

[87] 1992 SCCR 476.

having regard to the facts of the particular case which involved sexual intercourse at a roadside, accompanied by violence, which led passers by to stop and ask 'Are you being raped?'

In a short judgment, Lord Justice-Clerk Ross noted that the matter is one for the discretion of the trial judge. The appeal court is slow to interfere in the exercise of discretion. As counsel for the appellant had recognised, the question for the appeal court was whether it could be said that no reasonable judge could have arrived at the decision to which Lord Mayfield came. The court recognised that another judge might have taken a different view but, having regard to the length of time which had elapsed between the end of the relationship and the offence, it could not be said that Lord Mayfield was wrong. The conviction was not disturbed.

It seems to follow from this that the question of the interests of justice exception will always depend on the particular circumstances of the case (which is obvious enough). It can also be said that, where there had been a relationship between the parties to an incident which forms the subject-matter of a charge to which the prohibition applies, it will be relevant to consider the passage of time since that relationship ended in deciding whether questions about the sexual content of that relationship will be allowed. *Bremner* is clearly not authority for its converse, which would be the proposition that such questions should be allowed if the relationship was current at the time of the alleged offence, though it is not difficult to imagine an argument, based on the reasoning in *Dickie*, that if the female victim has been in the habit of 'surrendering her person' to the particular accused very shortly before the alleged offence, that will be relevant to her credibility when she says that he forced her on the particular occasion. Such an argument would be weaker if there was other significant evidence of force (such as injuries or distress) and might, in any event, be met by pointing out that the development of the law on rape within marriage has been such that the proposition that permitting intercourse on one occasion can offer any guide to whether there was consent on another must be highly questionable. It remains to be seen what further guidance the courts will give.

General character of witnesses

It will be recalled that the reasoning in *Brady* v *HM Advocate* was that it is not admissible to lead evidence on collateral matters in a criminal trial because the existence of a collateral fact does not render more probable the existence of the fact in issue. It will also be recalled that the exception for the moral character of the victim of a sexual assault in *Dickie* v *HM Advocate* proceeded upon the basis that the moral character of the victim was in such cases relevant to credibility. The same principles underlie the general law on admissibility of evidence as to the character of witnesses. The witness himself may be asked questions about his general character but if the blemish on his character which it is sought to demonstrate has nothing to do with his credibility and nothing to do with the issue which the court has to decide—namely whether the particular accused committed the particular crime charged—those questions will be objectionable as irrelevant.

A conviction for dishonesty will always be relevant to credibility. The witness has undertaken to tell the truth. If he has been guilty of dishonesty, especially involving a false pretence and especially recently, most people will have a doubt about relying on him unless there is some other source of evidence to confirm what he says or it is clear that his evidence is contrary to his own interests (it being assumed that liars do not lie in such a way as to deliberately make their own position worse). However, there is a limit. The witness can be asked about his character, but it is not permissible to lead other evidence to prove his bad character. The court is not there to decide whether the witness is in general a liar but only whether the charge being prosecuted against the accused is proved.

This is not, however, to say a witness can with impunity tell lies about his criminal record, for example. It is not possible to prove his dishonesty in the case in which he is a witness, but telling lies on oath may well be perjury, for which he can be prosecuted.

The character of the accused

Evidence as to the criminal record and character of the accused is dealt with by sections 266 and 270 of the 1995 Act.

Section 266 contains, at subsection (4), a prohibition on the asking of questions of the accused which tend to show that he has committed, or been convicted of, or been charged with, any offence other than that with which he is then charged, or is of bad character, unless—

'(a) [T]he proof that he has committed or been convicted of such other offence is admissible evidence to show that he is guilty of the offence with which he is then charged; or

(b) the accused or his counsel or solicitor has asked questions of the witnesses for the prosecution with a view to establishing the accused's good character, . . . or the accused has given evidence of his own good character, or the nature or conduct of the defence is such as to involve imputations on the character of the prosecutor or of the witnesses for the prosecution . . . ; or

(c) the accused has given evidence against any other person charged in the same proceedings.'

It is clear, then, to begin with, that where the witness is the accused the asking of questions about crimes not charged is not only objectionable as irrelevant upon the principle that where the question is whether a person did something on one occasion it is not relevant to show that he did a similar thing on another. It is also specifically prohibited by statute. Presumably the prohibition is now to be understood subject to *Nelson* v *HM Advocate*.[88] To this is added a prohibition on asking the accused questions 'tending to show' that he has been charged or convicted of any offence not on the indictment or complaint and also on asking questions tending to show that he is of bad character.

The simplest situation relates to previous convictions. Section 266 has to be read with sections 101(1) and 166(3) of the 1995 Act. Section 101(1) provides for solemn procedure that previous convictions shall not be laid before the jury and that reference must not be made to them in the jury's presence before the verdict is returned. Section 166(3) prohibits in summary cases the laying of previous convictions before the judge until he is satisfied that the charge is proved. Accordingly, the prosecutor must be assiduous not to make any reference to previous convictions before the accused is convicted, especially in a jury trial. The consequences of the

[88] *Supra*, p 127.

prosecution making such a reference can be fatal to the prosecution, though this will not always be the case where the disclosure of previous convictions is at the hand of someone other than the prosecution. *McCuaig v HM Advocate*[89] was a case in which the presiding sheriff asked a police officer to read out the precise terms of the charge which the police had put to the accused, who was being dealt with for attempting to pervert the course of justice by giving a false name. The charge read out by the officer, in the hearing of the jury, contained the allegation that the accused's motive was to avoid production of a schedule of previous convictions relative to him. The prosecutor did not seek a conviction on this charge but not, presumably, because of a fear that the accused had been prejudiced, but because convictions were sought in respect of other charges on the indictment and obtained in respect of sixteen of them. It was held that there was no miscarriage of justice and the convictions were sustained.

Such laying of convictions does not always happen in the most obvious way. *Cordiner v HM Advocate*,[90] for example, concerned an accused charged with offences said to have been committed at a time when he was in fact in prison. He lodged a special defence of alibi to that effect and his previous convictions were thus disclosed. This was held to be a contravention of the section. The Crown could, of course, have checked this and avoided the problem and so was entitled to little sympathy for its difficulty.

By contrast, we may note *Johnston v Allan*,[91] in which a DVLC printout showing previous convictions and endorsement was accidentally seen by the sheriff in the course of trial. It was held that there had been no contravention of the Act as it could not be said that the document had been laid before the court by the prosecutor. A further variation was *O'Neill v Tudhope*[92] in which the service copy notice of previous convictions was returned to the fiscal by the accused with his letter pleading guilty and was handed to the sheriff at court. However, the guilty plea was not accepted and a trial diet was fixed. Unfortunately the notice of previous convictions remained with the court papers, where it was seen by the trial sheriff. On appeal, it was held that there was nothing to suggest that the previous convictions came to the notice of the sheriff as a result of any decision of the prosecution nor was there any constructive 'laying' of convictions by prosecutor. Accordingly, the section was not breached.

It will be recognised that this sort of approach depends upon the proposition that a sheriff can act properly and put things out of his mind, a principle elaborated in *Kerr v Jessop*,[93] where the prosecutor elicited from a witness that the appellant had been previously convicted of driving while disqualified. The appeal court held that the prosecutor had been careless in framing the question and pressing that line and that there had been a breach of the section; but nevertheless found that a sheriff ought to be able to disregard such evidence and in this case that there had been no miscarriage of justice. It would not be possible to be confident that the result would have been the same had the trial been under solemn procedure, notwithstanding the principle that properly instructed juries can put prejudicial

---

[89] 1982 JC 59.
[90] 1978 JC 64.
[91] 1983 SCCR 500.
[92] 1984 SCCR 424.
[93] 1991 JC 1.

material out of their minds (in *Lambert* v *HM Advocate*,[94] for example, a person accused of ill-treating elderly people argued that media coverage had been such that she could not get a fair trial but it was held that the matter could be cured by adequate directions to the jury).

Again, where a witness ultroneously reveals the existence and nature of a warrant outstanding against an accused that is not *per se* a breach of the section. This was the situation and result in *Carmichael* v *Monaghan*.[95]

Exceptions

The prohibition in section 266 is subject to three exceptions. If one of them applies, the accused who gives evidence can be asked questions on the matters which the section would otherwise prohibit.

The first exception relates to the situation where the proof of the commission of or conviction for another offence is admissible to show that the accused is guilty of the offence with which he is presently charged. The most obvious example of this is the offence of driving while disqualified by order of the court (rather than by reason of age). In such a case, proof of the disqualification inevitably involves proof of the conviction which resulted in the disqualification. However, this does not give the prosecutor complete *carte blanche* as to that conviction. Rather, he will require to restrict what he proves to what is essential to proof of the new charge.

It may well be, for example, that the conviction was imposed in respect of a complaint which contained a number of offences, only some of which resulted in disqualification. In such a situation an extract of the earlier conviction may be produced but only the charge which founded the disqualification may be referred to. In *Boustead* v *McLeod*[96] the extract conviction produced to prove disqualification contained a charge in addition to the charge required to prove the disqualification and the conviction was quashed. In another case, *Mitchell* v *Dean*,[97] the extract conviction produced by the prosecutor to prove disqualification disclosed that 'the accused admitted six previous convictions'. This was enough to vitiate the proceedings.

The practice is to charge the disqualified driving on a separate complaint or indictment from any other charges arising out of the same incident so as to confine the exposure of the previous conviction to that charge in respect of which is it strictly necessary and this is done in any other similar case also. The one exception to this is where the second charge follows inevitably from the first, as where the charge of driving without insurance appears on the same complaint as driving while disqualified. If a man is disqualified from driving he cannot possibly have insurance and is not prejudiced by the two charges appearing together. This was the position in *Moffat* v *Smith*.[98]

Graham v *HM Advocate*[99] was a case in which one of the accused's replies when charged by the police with a series of offences which included assault on his wife was 'that cow's got me the jail again'. The prosecutor led evidence of that reply. The sheriff held this to be a breach of the Act and

[94] 1993 SLT 339.
[95] 1986 SCCR 598.
[96] 1979 JC 70.
[97] 1979 JC 62.
[98] 1983 SCCR 392.
[99] 1984 SLT 67.

directed the jury to ignore it. The High Court, however, took the view that the breach was 'deliberately engineered quite unnecessarily and without any justification by the procurator fiscal' and in the circumstances was so grave a breach that the conviction must be quashed. By contrast, *Deeney* v *HM Advocate*[100] was a case in which Crown witness, unprompted, gave evidence that the accused 'was on licence'. This was held not to be an infringement of the section. It may well be that one factor which influenced the court in *Graham* was the fact that the reply had no evidential value at all. It neither assisted the Crown on the merits (because it did not constitute any kind of admission) nor the defence (because it was neither a denial nor an explanation). It was, in short, pure prejudice.

The second exception had two alternatives. It applies either where the defence has, by evidence from prosecution witnesses or the accused himself, attempted to set up the accused's good character or where the nature or conduct of the defence has involved imputations on the character of the prosecutor or of prosecution witnesses.

The reference to imputations upon the character of the prosecutor is of virtually no practical significance in the Scottish system under which almost all prosecutions are conducted by a public prosecutor. Evidence directed to the prosecutor's character will almost inevitably be inadmissible as irrelevant and so the situation will not arise. The presence of this element in the subsection is thought to be a product of the fact that the provision is ultimately derived from one which applied in both Scotland and England. Clearly, under a system such as the English one where private prosecution has a significant part to play, attacks on the character of the prosecutor can assume greater significance, because the prosecutor will often also be the victim of the crime. The provision might be of some significance in those rare Scottish cases which do involve private prosecution but even here, it is suggested, the hurdle of relevancy will have to be overcome by demonstrating that the imputations on the prosecutor's character actually have some bearing on the merits of the case.

The mounting of an attack upon the character of prosecution witnesses is of more significance. The law on this is now to be found in *Leggate* v *HM Advocate*.[101] In that case the essence of the cross-examination of the police witnesses was that they had conspired to fabricate evidence. It was held that this constituted an attack on the character of the prosecution witnesses sufficient to bring the exception into play and that it did not matter whether the attack was necessary to the defence on the merits. It was also held that the trial judge had a discretion whether or not to allow questions addressed to the character of the accused. In general one may expect that discretion to be exercised in favour of the defence where the attack on the prosecution witness is genuinely necessary to the defence on the merits; and in favour of the prosecution where the defence are merely mud-slinging. There is value in looking also at *Templeton* v *McLeod*[102] in which it was held that an accused is afforded the protection of the section where cross-examination as to the veracity of a prosecution witness is necessary to enable the accused fairly to establish his own defence, albeit it involves an invitation to the judge or jury to disbelieve the witness insofar as he testifies in support of the charge; but

[100] 1986 SCCR 393.
[101] 1988 SLT 665.
[102] 1986 SLT 149.

where such cross-examination goes further and can be seen to involve imputations upon the general character of a witness the accused may forfeit his right to the statutory protection. *Conner* v *Lockhart*[103] also decided that where it is essential for an accused to establish that a Crown witness has fabricated evidence against him, this is not an attack on the character of the witness but is necessary to establish the proposed line of defence. In such circumstances the accused should not have lost his statutory protection under the subsection and been cross-examined on his criminal record.

The exception applies (by section 266(7)) where the reputation attacked is that of a deceased victim.

It is, of course, all very well to permit the Crown to ask questions of the accused as to his criminal record or bad character where he has thrown mud at prosecution witnesses or held himself out as being of good character; but he might not give evidence and, if he does, he might lie. Section 270 therefore permits the Crown to lead evidence of the accused's criminal record or bad character where this second exception applies, even though the witnesses necessary to do so have not been on the list with the indictment.

The third ground upon which questions as to character may be put to the accused is that he has given evidence against a co-accused. The meaning of the expression 'given evidence against' was considered in *McCourtney* v *HM Advocate*[104] and in *Burton* v *HM Advocate*.[105] In *McCourtney*, counsel for the appellant invited the High Court to adopt the test propounded by Lord Donovan in an English case, *Murdoch* v *Taylor*,[106] which was that the evidence given supports the Crown against the co-accused to a material extent or undermines his defence. The court noted that this is a stiff test but found it unnecessary to consider whether any lesser standard was appropriate because even this stiff test was satisfied in the case they were considering. In *Burton*, however, the court came off the fence and said in terms:

> '[A]s a matter of law, evidence against a co-accused within the meaning of the subsection is evidence which supports the Crown case in a material respect or evidence which undermines that of the co-accused.'

McCourtney makes it clear that in a case where this test is satisfied the trial judge has no discretion to refuse the co-accused the right to cross-examine that accused as to his character, while *Burton* establishes that the right arises not only where evidence has been given explicitly against the co-accused but also where an accused has by implication given evidence against a co-accused. In that case, the first accused (Jones) had claimed to have been in possession of items used in a crime only because the second accused Burton had asked him to get them. When the second accused gave evidence he denied this and said that the first accused had obtained certain of the items for his own purposes. Counsel for the first accused cross-examined the second accused as to his criminal record.

On appeal, it was conceded by counsel for the second accused that his evidence had been 'against' the first accused but argued that this was only

---

[103] 1986 SCCR 360.
[104] 1977 JC 68.
[105] 1979 SLT (Notes) 59.
[106] [1965] AC 574 at 592.

so incidentally and by implication. It was maintained that the subsection did not apply in such a case, but the court held that it did, observing that

> 'Nothing could have been more damaging than the evidence of Burton so far as Jones' position was concerned. By giving the evidence which he did Burton stripped or sought to strip from the testimony of Jones his "innocent" explanation of the possession of the instruments which were incriminating in the highest degree. By doing this, Burton supported the Crown case against Jones in a material respect by leaving him with possession of the instruments without an innocent explanation. At the same time he in the very clearest way expressly undermined the defence which Jones had put forward.'

This approach may be contrasted with that in *Templeton* in which questioning by the Crown was not allowed where the imputations on the characters of the Crown witnesses were merely incidental to the substantive defence which it was sought to advance.

Slane v HM Advocate[107] is an interesting variation on the same theme. In that case, evidence of one accused's criminal record was obtained without justification from a Crown witness by counsel for a co-accused in cross-examination. It was held that this did not mean the accused whose criminal record was thus revealed was entitled to have the indictment against him dismissed on the ground that he had been prejudiced. It is possible to regard this outcome with a degree of cynicism. Presumably the High Court was conscious of the need to avoid having a properly conducted prosecution founder because of the outrageous conduct of the representative of a co-accused.

Securing regularity in the investigations

The second purpose of the exclusory approach to the rules of evidence as identified by Dickson is to secure regularity in investigation, the reasoning being that there is a disincentive to improper conduct at the investigative stage if it is known that the product of irregular investigations is likely to be worthless in terms of proof. We have, of course, given detailed consideration to the regularity of investigations in Chapter 4 and it is not necessary to repeat that here. What does bear reiteration, however, is that although irregularity in investigation is a ground of objection to the admissibility of evidence, irregularities may be excused and accordingly mere irregularity will not inevitably result in an objection being upheld.

Confining within reasonable limits the duration and expense of judicial proceedings—routine evidence

Dickson's final reason for the exclusory rules of evidence is to confine within reasonable limits the duration and expense of criminal proceedings. Statute now seeks to achieve this end not merely by excluding evidence which is irrelevant but also by the routine evidence provisions of sections 280 and 281 of the 1995 Act.

Section 280(1) gives effect to Schedule 9 and provides that for the purposes of any proceedings for and under the enactments there specified a certificate purporting to be signed in terms of the Schedule shall be sufficient evidence of the matter and qualifications of the person signing. We have already noticed that in *O'Brien v McCreadie*[108] the High Court took the view

[107] 1984 SLT 293.
[108] 1994 SCCR 516.

that Parliament had meant precisely what it said and the hearsay objection at least is excluded by the words of the section. Whether similar reasoning will apply to other objections remains to be seen.

The enactments specified in Schedule 9 cover a wide variety of offences. Those which are likely to be of particular practical significance are the Misuse of Drugs Act 1971 (as to which the type, classification, purity, weight and description of a substance may be certified) and the Road Traffic Regulation Act 1988 (as to which the accuracy of speed-measuring equipment may be certified).

Before such certificates are evidence they must, in terms of section 280(6), be served on the other party (usually the accused) not less than fourteen days before the trial. The recipient then has seven days within which to challenge the certificate. If such a challenge is made, the evidence of the forensic scientists has to be led to establish the fact or the conclusion as to fact.

Submission of no case to answer

Once all the evidence has been led for the Crown, it is open to the defence to submit in terms of sections 97 and 160 of the 1995 Act that there is no case to answer. The submission must be that there is no case to answer both on the offence charged and on any other offence of which the accused could be convicted, so that if it would be open to the jury to convict of an amended or alternative charge a submission of this sort will be repelled.

Subsection (2) of each section sets out the test which the court must apply to such a submission, which is whether there is insufficient evidence in law to justify the accused being convicted. Considerations of quality of evidence have nothing to do with this, as the High Court made clear in *Williamson* v *Wither*[109] as follows.

> '[The section] provides that the evidence led by the prosecution is insufficient in law to justify the accused being convicted. It is not whether or not the evidence presented is to be accepted and therefore the only question before the court at that stage is whether there is no evidence which if accepted will entitle the court to proceed to conviction.'

What this comes to is that, at the stage of such a submission, evidence in a criminal case is to be taken at its highest for the Crown and looked at to see whether there is enough in law to prove each essential allegation.

If the submission succeeds, then the accused must be acquitted in relation to the charge or charges affected by the submission; and, of course, this may mean all of the charges on the indictment or complaint, in which case the trial is over. The trial proceeds only in respect of charges in respect of which there has been no submission or no successful submission.

Sufficiency of evidence

It is at this stage that we need to consider what will amount to a sufficiency of evidence. As we have noted in Chapter 1, before an essential fact can be held to be proved there must be at least two adminicles of evidence to establish it, though these may be direct evidence or circumstantial evidence.

[109] 1981 SCCR 214.

The adminicles need not be of equal weight. It would be possible to cite a battery of cases to demonstrate this but particular notice should be taken of three.

The first is *Proctor* v *Tudhope*[110] in which a man was convicted of housebreaking with intent to steal; he was identified by the householder and it was held that the fact that a police officer identified him as having run off when pointed out as the perpetrator of the crime was sufficient corroboration. The Lord Justice-General said that 'not very much was required in the way of corroboration of the testimony of the credible and reliable eye-witness who identified the appellant in the act of committing the crime'.

In *Ralston* v *HM Advocate*[111] it was held that where one eyewitness made an unhesitating identification there was corroboration in the evidence of a second that the accused resembled the perpetrator in that his face was the same shape and that of a third that the accused was possibly the perpetrator.

Finally, in *Nolan* v *McLeod*[112] it was held that there was sufficient identification where the first witness was 'eighty per cent' sure and the second 'seventy-five per cent' sure.

Particular difficulties have arisen in connection with sexual assaults, where corroboration of the events themselves, and of the lack of consent, can prove hard to find.

The High Court first addressed this issue in *Moorov* v *HM Advocate*.[113] The accused was a shopkeeper who had, over a period of years, subjected female shop assistants to unwanted sexual attentions, always singly. In upholding his conviction the court applied a principle stated in Hume on Crimes over a century earlier. It is worth noting the way the principle was formulated by the Lord Justice-General.

> 'Before the evidence of single credible witnesses to separate acts can provide material for mutual corroboration the connection between the separate act (indicated by their external relation in time character and circumstance) must be such as to exhibit them as subordinates in some particular and ascertained unity of intent, project, campaign or adventure which lies beyond or behind—but is related to—the separate acts.'

In other words there must be some real connection between the acts other than the identity of the accused as the perpetrator. But it is not the case, as is sometimes thought, that what has become known as the '*Moorov* doctrine' applies only in relation to sexual offences—*Lindsay* v *HM Advocate*[114] is an example of its application to assault and robbery, and further demonstrates that the evidence identifying the accused need not be that of an eyewitness. It is, however, the case, that it only applies where the charges are all on the same complaint of indictment.

In *Reynolds* v *HM Advocate*[115] the accused was charged with a charge of assault, abduction and robbery and a charge of assault and robbery. There were some similarities between them and some dissimilarities. The Lord Justice-General said:

[110] 1985 SCCR 39.
[111] 1988 SCCR 590.
[112] 1987 SCCR 558.
[113] 1930 JC 68.
[114] 1993 SCCR 868.
[115] 1995 SCCR 504.

'As was pointed out in *Carpenter* v *Hamilton*,[116] cases of this kind, while they must be approached with care, raise questions of fact and degree. That is especially so where, to use Lord Sand's expression, the case falls into the open country which lies between the two extremes. . . . We accept that there was a process of evaluation to be conducted, because there were dissimilarities as well as similarities. On the other hand, we do not accept that on no possible view could it be said that there was any connection between the two offences. Where the case lies in the middle ground, the important point is that a jury should be properly directed so that they are aware of the test which requires to be applied. . . . When . . . regard is had to the fact that there are items in the evidence which may on one view be regarded as similarities and then balanced against the dissimilarities, we consider that this case fell within the province of the jury rather than the judge.'

In a case of a single incident, to which *Moorov* by definition cannot apply, it will often be possible to prove from scientific evidence, or even the admission of the accused, that sexual activity has taken place but proof of the absence of consent can be particularly difficult unless there is injury to the victim. However, as a result of *Yates* v *HM Advocate*[117] the emotional state of the victim after the alleged assault can assist the Crown. That was a rape case, intercourse being admitted, in which it was held that the evidence of a witness who spoke to the victim's distressed condition immediately after the incident was enough to corroborate her own evidence as to force and that a knife had been used to threaten her. The court observed that all that was necessary was to find 'evidence in general which supports the broad proposition of force, details of which had been given by the girl'.

In *Moore* v *HM Advocate*,[118] distress twelve or thirteen hours after the incident was too remote in time to afford *Yates*-type corroboration but as *Cree* v *HM Advocate*[119] makes clear, each case will turn on its own circumstances. In that case the allegation was rape; there was an admission of intercourse but a defence of consent. A witness heard screams at the time of the alleged crime and there was evidence from others of distress between five and seven hours later. It was argued, relying on *Moore*, that the interval was too long but it was held that it was a matter for the jury who were entitled to accept that the victim was only prepared to discuss the offence with a close relative, which she had done as soon as reasonably practicable. The matter was put even more clearly by *Cannon* v *HM Advocate*[120] in which, again a 'consent defence' rape, the only substantial corroboration available was evidence of distress twelve hours later. There was also evidence that there was no earlier stage at which the victim was in contact with someone who might have been in a position to observe the distress and it was held that, since the jury had been given a clear direction by the trial judge that they could only convict if they were satisfied that the distress resulted from the accident, the conviction should stand. It follows that there is no outside limit beyond which distress cannot provide corroboration in this kind of case, though in practice the longer the interval and the more people the victim has been in contact with during that time the less likely it

[116] 1994 SCCR 108.
[117] 1977 SLT (Notes) 42.
[118] 1990 SCCR 586.
[119] 1991 GWD 19-1133.
[120] 1992 SCCR 505.

is that distress will assist. In *Stobo* v *HM Advocate*,[121] in which the charge was indecent assault, the sheriff directed the jury, in terms of *Moore*, that they were entitled to look to evidence of the victim's distress if spoken to by another or other witnesses for corroboration. The accused was convicted and appealed, contending that something other than distress was required to corroborate the fact that the crime libelled had been committed. In giving judgment the Lord Justice-General said:

> '[W]here circumstantial evidence is relied upon in order to corroborate the complainer's evidence on this matter the circumstances do not require in themselves to be incriminatory. What is required of the circumstantial evidence is that it is capable of providing support for her evidence and it will be sufficient for this purpose if it is consistent with what she has said ... whether or not distress can afford corroboration of the complainer's evidence must depend upon the nature of the activity she has described. Distress cannot of course corroborate her evidence as to the identity of her assailant, and it cannot provide corroboration in those cases of assault where the evidence that it resulted in physical injury requires to be corroborated ... where corroboration of penetration is required in rape cases distress will be incapable of providing this, because the other acts involved in the rape to overcome the complainer's resistance will be sufficiently distressing in themselves to explain the distress.'

Clearly, it will assist the Crown if there is something to which they can point beyond 'mere' distress. In *Stephen* v *HM Advocate*[122] there was no evidence of injury to the person or clothing of the complainer. There was evidence of scratch marks on the abdomen of the appellant and of the distress of the complainer immediately after the incident. The appeal court held that there was sufficient material for the jury to find corroboration of the complainer's version of the events and refused the appeal.

Corroboration of confessions

Confusion sometimes arises about confessions and from time to time it is thought by some that when a suspect confesses that is all that is required for a conviction. But it needs to be understood clearly that a confession has only one source and that is the accused. That is true no matter how many people hear it made or how often it is repeated. There needs to be some other source of evidence whether the confession is made to one person or to 100, whether it is made once or repeated many times and even if it is repeated in judicial examination. It is only one source of evidence and not by itself sufficient. At the very least what is needed is what is contemplated by Lord Dunpark in *Hartley* v *HM Advocate*:[123]

> 'If ... a jury is satisfied that a confession of guilt was freely made and unequivocal in its terms, corroboration of that confession may be found in evidence from another source or sources which point to the truth of that confession.'

Often a confession will be corroborated by direct evidence (for example, the admission to intercourse in *Yates* v *HM Advocate*, corroborated by the victim's evidence on that point). The law recognises, however, that sometimes there will be material in the confession which can be shown to be

---

[121] 1994 SLT 28.
[122] 1987 SCCR 570.
[123] 1979 SLT 26.

true and which only someone present at the crime could have known; and that will be enough. The rule starts with Alison[124] where he says:

> 'If a person is apprehended on a charge of theft and he tells the officer who seized him that if he will go to such a place and look under such a bush he will find the stolen goods; or he is charged with murder or assault and he says that he threw the bloody weapon into such a pool, in such a river and it is there searched for and found, without doubt these are such strong confirmations of the truth of the confession as renders it of itself sufficient if the *corpus* is established *aliunde* convict the prisoner.'

This was precisely the situation in *Manuel* v *HM Advocate*[125] in which a murderer confessed and told the police accurately where a body and clothing were to be found, and was hanged on the strength of it.

The situation in contemplation in Alison and in *Manuel* was one where the investigator checked afterwards what was disclosed for the first time in the accused's confession; and the possibility of fabrication is for practical purposes excluded. However, the rule is not confined to cases where the information was previously unknown to the police. In *Wilson* v *McAughey*[126] police found a mechanical digger with a broken window submerged in the Clyde. The accused subsequently admitted vandalism and described breaking the window and driving it into the river. The sheriff acquitted him because the digger had not been found as a result of the confession as contemplated in the authorities discussed above; but the High Court overturned that acquittal, holding that it was enough if the confession contained what has become known as 'special knowledge' even if it was known to the police. Where the relevant facts are known to others than the police, *Wilson* v *HM Advocate*,[127] which concerned knowledge of the way in which a murder had been committed and the body position, such knowledge having become public, established that it is a jury question whether the confession can be said to contain knowledge which is special enough to amount to corroborative material.

The detail in such a confession need not be very substantial. In *Hutchinson* v *Valentine*[128] the words 'I canna really mind where aboot in the hotel I got it. I was drunk. I dumped it' were held to be sufficient where there was evidence that a stolen television had been abandoned in the hotel car park.

Demeanour of the accused

Although the emotional state of the victim in a rape may afford corroboration of the proposition of force and the reaction of the suspect upon being accused may sufficiently corroborate a householder's identification of him as the housebreaker, this should not mean that the demeanour of an accused who admits a crime will corroborate his admission. In *McGougan* v *HM Advocate*[129] the trial judge was held to have erred when he directed the jury that the accused's demeanour when making an admission and in particular his attempt to throw himself out of the window were capable of amounting to corroboration.

[124] Alison, ii, 580.
[125] 1958 JC 41.
[126] 1982 SCCR 398.
[127] 1987 SCCR 217.
[128] 1990 SCCR 569.
[129] 1991 SCCR 49.

Fingerprints, etc

Fingerprints, handwriting and the like are a trap for the unwary. Although on one view a fingerprint is only one source of evidence, it was held in *Hamilton* v *HM Advocate*[130] and *HM Advocate* v *Rolley*[131] that it will be sufficient where each step is corroborated—so that there will be two witnesses to the finding of the print at the locus, two to the taking of a print from the accused and two experts to make the comparison (it being clear from *McKillen* v *Barclay Curle & Co Ltd*[132] that expert witnesses require corroboration like anyone else when their evidence relates to the essentials of a case), though section 281(2) of the 1995 Act is authority for only calling one expert in this and similar situations where notice of that intention has been given to the defence. If any of the stages is spoken to by only one witness, the evidence ceases to be sufficient in itself and requires corroboration from some other source.

[130] 1934 JC 1.
[131] 1945 JC 155.
[132] 1967 SLT 41.

10 : SENTENCING

If the accused pleads guilty to or is found guilty of any charge the proceedings enter the sentencing phase. Sentencing can be dealt with on a common basis for solemn procedure and summary procedure, and the 1995 Act does so in Part XI (sections 195 to 254).

There are particular sentencing provisions in particular statutes. Sometimes, for example, an Act will make provision for—or even require that—a disqualification to be imposed as ancillary to a sentence. Obvious examples include disqualification for holding or obtaining a driving licence, imposed under road traffic legislation, and disqualification from acting as a director of a company, imposed in relation to some offences under the Companies Acts. We are not, however, concerned in this book with the minutiae of particular sentences of that sort. Rather, we shall address the sentences which are available to the court for offences in general and the procedures by which they are arrived at.

Motion for sentence

Although the Scottish prosecutor does not ask for any particular sentence, by contrast with some jurisdictions, he does initiate the whole sentencing process, at least under solemn procedure. There, once the guilt of the accused has been established, the prosecutor has a discretion whether or not to move for sentence. If he does not do so, it is not competent for the court to proceed to sentence.[1] The motion for sentence can be made by implication from the prosecutor's actings, as in *Noon* v *HM Advocate*[2] in which, although the prosecutor forgot to say the words 'I move for sentence', he did tender to the court a list of previous convictions—an action consistent only with an intention that the court should proceed to sentence—and the competency of the sentence imposed was upheld on appeal.

Under summary procedure there is no motion for sentence and, although the prosecutor will usually take action such as tendering a notice of previous convictions which under solemn procedure would imply such a motion, Nicholson considers that the court may proceed to sentence even if he does not do so.[3]

Once a motion for sentence is made under solemn procedure, or once the accused has been convicted under summary procedure, the court proceeds to consider sentence. Unless the imposition of sentence is for some reason incompetent, the court does not have the option of making no order. In *Skeen* v *Sullivan*[4] the High Court was sharply critical of a sheriff who had declined to consider sentence.

[1] See C G B Nicholson, *Sentencing: Law and Practice in Scotland* (2nd edn, 1992) p 114.
[2] 1960 JC 52.
[3] Nicholson, *loc cit*.
[4] 1980 SLT (Notes) 11.

Before the coming into force of the 1995 Act it was necessary for the procurator fiscal to serve a notice of penalty in summary cases and failure to do so constituted the most common reason for sentencing to become incompetent. An example, now of historical interest only, occurred in *Geddes* v *Hamilton*,[5] in which a police officer served the notice of penalty on the accused's solicitor in the accused's presence. The conviction was allowed to stand but the sentence was quashed.

Previous convictions

By sections 69(2) and 166(2) of the 1995 Act the notice of previous convictions tendered by the Crown upon the accused being convicted must have been served upon the accused along with the indictment or complaint. The same sections contain prohibitions on references to previous convictions before conviction except where proof of such convictions is necessary to proof of the substantive charge. The most common example of the need to prove convictions in support of a substantive charge is probably that of driving while disqualified by order of the court but even there (as we have noted under reference to cases such as *Boustead* v *McLeod*)[6] the reference made to such convictions is the minimum necessary to proof.

Forms 8.3 and 16.1–E annexed to the Act of Adjournal (Criminal Procedure Rules) 1996 provide the form to be used for notices of previous convictions.

It was held as long ago as 1842, in *HM Advocate* v *John Graham*[7] that previous convictions must predate the offence and not merely the date of service of the complaint or indictment or the date of conviction. In 1911, *McCall* v *Mitchell*[8] established that convictions under appeal could not be referred to. This having been said, social enquiry reports will frequently disclose to the court the existence of such convictions which the prosecutor is prohibited from libelling and Nicholson[9] suggests that it would be absurd if the court was not told, for example, of a long period of imprisonment imposed on the accused in respect of a conviction which could not be libelled, because otherwise any sentence imposed might be wholly inconsistent with the accused's actual situation. A probation order, for example, is pointless in relation to a man who has been sentenced to several years' imprisonment.

Crown narrative

As well as tendering a notice of previous convictions the prosecutor will, in a case of a plea of guilty, give a narrative of the facts to the court.

Forfeiture

It is possible that the prosecutor will also seek an order for forfeiture of some article used in course of the commission of the offence. This is dealt with under Part II of the Proceeds of Crime (Scotland) Act 1995.

[5] 1986 SCCR 165.
[6] 1979 JC 70.
[7] (1842) 1 Brown 445.
[8] (1911) 6 Adam 303.
[9] Nicholson, *op cit*, p 116.

Where the prosecutor certifies that the article in question is perishable, dangerous or worthless or that the possession of it is unlawful, section 24 of the Proceeds of Crime (Scotland) Act 1995 operates to forfeit it at once. In other cases, however, the order made will be a suspended forfeiture order and it will take effect only after the passage of a sufficient period of time to allow third parties claiming an interest in the property to vindicate that interest.

Plea in mitigation

Once the prosecutor has completed his narrative it is up to the defence to make a plea in mitigation. Occasionally the defence version of the facts will be so far removed from that given by the prosecution as to make it impossible for the court to deal with the case. If the defence version is inconsistent with guilt then the case must be adjourned for trial. More commonly, the defence version will still justify a plea of guilty but will vary so far from the prosecution account that the court lacks a proper basis upon which to deal with the case. Where that happens, Nicholson suggests[10] that the court may hear evidence to resolve the issue. Such 'proofs in mitigation' are relatively common.

Adjournment for inquiry

Section 201 of the 1995 Act allows the court to adjourn a case before imposing sentence in order to enable inquiries to be made or to determine the most suitable method of dealing with the case. Such adjournments must not be for any single period exceeding three weeks where the accused is remanded in custody or four weeks (eight on cause shown) where the offender is on bail or ordained to appear.

Deferred sentence

In terms of section 202 of the 1995 Act the court may defer sentence for a period and on such conditions as it may determine. It is quite common for the court to defer sentence for a period of months for the accused to demonstrate that he can be of good behaviour or for a shorter period for the accused to repay the value of stolen or damaged property. The seriousness of the offence is by no means an absolute bar on the taking of this course, and *McPherson* v *HM Advocate*[11] is an example of deferral of sentence in a case of attempted murder.

At the end of the period of deferral the accused is sentenced for the offence, taking into account the facts of the offence but also how well he has complied with the condition imposed.

The power to defer is sometimes used where there are other proceedings current against the offender, with a view to dealing with him at the same time in respect of all matters.

'Discount' for guilty plea

By section 196 of the 1995 Act it is open to a court, in sentencing an offender who has pled guilty to an offence, to take into account the stage in

[10] Nicholson, *op cit*, p 114.
[11] 1986 SCCR 278.

the proceedings at which the offender indicated his intention to plead guilty. This seems to diminish the effect of *Strawhorn* v *McLeod*[12] in which the High Court found the practice of giving a discount for a guilty plea objectionable, though as Nicholson points out[13] that case has never prevented a sentencing court from regarding a plea of guilty as evidence of remorse justifying some reduction in sentence.

Sentencing guidelines

In selecting a sentence, the court is obliged by section 197 of the 1995 Act to have regard to any relevant opinion pronounced by the High Court under section 118(7) or section 189(7). Those provisions allow the High Court, in the context of determining an appeal against sentence, to pronounce an opinion on the sentence or other disposal order which is appropriate in any similar case; in short, to issue sentencing guidelines.

Particular sentences

Death

Although the death sentence remains competent for high treason and piracy with violence, these offences are almost of theoretical interest only and we do not need to spend time on capital punishment.

Custodial disposals

As we have already noted, the High Court of Justiciary can impose a sentence of life imprisonment and (by section 205 of the 1995 Act) must do so in a case of murder. The sheriff sitting with a jury can impose a sentence of up to three years' imprisonment (by section 3(3) of the 1995 Act) or (in terms of section 195 of the 1995 Act), where he holds that any competent sentence which he could impose is inadequate, remit to the High Court for sentence.

In terms of section 5(2) and (3) of the 1995 Act, the sheriff sitting summarily can impose a sentence of up to three months' imprisonment. This limit is increased to six months where the accused is convicted of a second or subsequent offence inferring dishonest appropriation of property or attempt thereat or of a second or subsequent offence inferring personal violence.

By section 7(5) of the 1995 Act a district court constituted by a stipendiary magistrate has the same sentencing powers as a sheriff sitting under summary procedure. In other cases, by section 7(6)(a), the district court may impose up to sixty days' imprisonment.

All the foregoing limits may be varied by statute. Accordingly, many offences carry lesser maximum terms than the court could ordinarily impose but occasionally a statute will provide for an enhanced summary penalty. It is, for example, competent for a sheriff to impose up to twelve months' imprisonment under summary procedure for certain offences under the Misuse of Drugs Act 1971.

The High Court held in *Williamson* v *Farrell*[14] that where (as happens often) an accused person is being sentenced on two or more indictments or

[12] 1987 SCCR 413.
[13] Nicholson, *op cit*, p 191.
[14] 1975 SLT (Notes) 92.

complaints at the same time, the total prison sentence imposed must not exceed the maximum which could have been imposed on any one of them. An exception to this was articulated in *Thomson* v *Smith*[15] for the case in which the charges could not have been dealt with on a single indictment or complaint—for example, because the accused had been convicted on complaint and committed the second offence during the period of deferral. In such a case cumulative sentences may be imposed which exceed the normal maximum.

In all cases in which a custodial sentence is being imposed the court must, by section 210(1) of the 1995 Act have regard, in determining the length of the sentence, to any time spent in custody on remand awaiting trial or extradition.

Although imprisonment is the most obvious custodial disposal, there are others which apply in the case of persons under the age of twenty-one. Section 208 of the 1995 Act provides that where a child is convicted on indictment and the court is of opinion that no other method of dealing with him is appropriate, it may sentence him to be detained in such place and on such conditions as the Secretary of State may direct. 'Child' is defined by section 307 by reference to the Children (Scotland) Act 1995 and means, essentially, one who has attained the age of sixteen or one who has attained the age of sixteen but not eighteen and who is subject to a supervision requirement of a children's hearing under the Children (Scotland) Act 1995.

By section 207 of the 1995 Act it is not competent to impose imprisonment on a person under twenty-one years of age. Instead, the court may impose detention in a young offenders institution on a person aged between sixteen and twenty-one but only where, after obtaining a social enquiry report from 'an officer of a local authority' (that is, a social worker) the court is of opinion that no other method of dealing with the offender is appropriate.

In the case of a person aged twenty-one or over who has not previously been sentenced to imprisonment, section 204(2) of the 1995 Act prohibits the passing of a sentence of imprisonment unless after considering a social enquiry report it considers that no other method of dealing with him is appropriate.

Section 210(1)(b) requires the court to specify the date of commencement of the sentence and subsection (1)(c) requires that where the date specified is 'not earlier than the date on which sentence was passed' (it is hard to see how it could be later) the court must state its reason for not selecting an earlier.

Backdating is essentially a matter for the discretion of the sentencing court but Nicholson has identified a number of general principles.[16] Paraphrasing what Nicholson says, backdating is not an obligation in all cases and the court's obligation is only to 'have regard to' the time spent in custody. The insistence of the accused on his right to go to trial does not justify a refusal to backdate and still less can it be said that time spent on remand pending such a trial is something the accused brought on himself. Backdating probably should occur where the accused is convicted of a lesser charge than that indicted and he would probably have got bail had the lesser

---

[15] 1982 SLT 546.
[16] Nicholson, *op cit*, p 140.

charge been the one he faced throughout. This is especially so where he has been offering to plead guilty to some of the charges and is ultimately convicted of those charges to which he offered to plead guilty.

However, it does not follow from the fact that the court imposes the maximum sentence available to it on a particular charge that the sentence should be backdated.

Community service orders

Sections 238 to 245 of the 1995 Act provide for community service orders, section 238 being the most important for our present purposes.

A community service order is, in terms of section 238, an order requiring the offender to perform not less than forty and not more than 240 hours of unpaid work. It is explicitly an alternative to imprisonment, provided by section 238(1) for the situation in which someone has been convicted of an offence punishable by imprisonment. The subsection says that in the case of such a conviction the court 'may, *instead of imposing . . . a sentence of . . . imprisonment*' (emphasis added) make a community service order.

A number of preconditions exist before a community service order can be made. The most fundamental of these is that arrangements exist in the area for the performance of community service, although since they do exist in most populous areas this is unlikely to be a problem in most cases. The next is that the court must be satisfied, after (obtaining and) considering a social enquiry report, that the offender is a suitable person to perform work under such an order. Next the court must be satisfied that there is a place available on the community service scheme which exists. And, finally, in terms of time (though it comes first in the section) the offender must consent—though since the alternative is prison refusal is rare.

Section 238(4) requires the court to explain certain things to the offender before imposing an order and to do so in 'ordinary language'. The first is the purpose and effect of the order and in particular the obligations laid on the offender. Those obligations are spelled out in section 239(1) to (3). He must report to the social worker and notify him without delay of any change in his address or in the times he usually works, and must perform the hours ordered and do so within twelve months.

Next, the court must explain the consequences of failing to comply with the order. These are set out in section 239(4) to (6). A warrant may be issued for his arrest or he may be cited to attend court. He may be fined for the breach of the order with the order being left to continue. Alternatively the order may be revoked and he may be dealt with for the original offence in any manner which would have been open to the court had the order not been made. This, of course, might well mean a custodial sentence. Finally, the number of hours may be varied.

The third thing to be explained to the offender is that the court has power to review the order in terms of section 240 of the 1995 Act where it appears to the court that it would be in the interests of justice to do so having regard to circumstances which have arisen since the order was made. The options include variation of the order and substitution of another sentence.

Probation

Probation orders have much in common with community service orders and in some areas the two are combined. A probation order, in terms of section 228 of the 1995 Act, is an order requiring the offender to be under supervision for a period of not less than six months and not more than three years.

By section 229 a probation order may require the offender to comply with such requirements as the court considers conducive to securing the good conduct of the offender or preventing the commission of further offences. These may include in particular conditions as to the offender's place of residence and as to the payment of compensation by the offender. Section 230 permits the court to impose conditions requiring the offender to submit to treatment in respect of any mental condition from he suffers.

As in relation to community service order, the court must explain certain things to the offender before imposing a probation order. These are specified in section 228(5) and are the effect of the order, including any additional requirements to be made, and that if he fails to comply with the order or commits another offence during the probation period he will be liable to be sentenced for the original offence. In this connection it should be noted that, strictly, in terms of section 228, a probation order is an alternative to sentencing the offender.

Section 228(5) prohibits the making of a probation order unless the offender 'expresses his willingness to comply with the requirements thereof'.

Section 232 and 233 of the 1995 Act deal with failure to comply with the requirements of a probation order and committing a further offence while on probation.

Under section 232, if it appears to the court on information from certain social work sources that the probationer has failed to comply with a requirement of the order, it may issue a warrant for his arrest or cite him to a hearing. If thereafter it is proved to the satisfaction of the court that there has been such a failure the court may take very similar action to that available on breach of community service. It may impose a fine, sentence the offender for the original offence or vary the order. Proof of breach may be by the evidence of a single witness in terms of section 232(3).

Similar options are available under section 233 in the case of the commission of an offence while on probation.

Financial penalties—fines
The fine is probably the most commonly imposed sentence. Section 211 of the 1995 Act contains a general power to fine, subject to particular provisions in Acts of Parliament. Under solemn procedure, there is no limit to the amount of the fine which can be imposed in either the High Court or the sheriff court. Under summary procedure, fines are structured within levels on what is known as the 'standard scale', which is set out in section 225(2). That scale is as follows.

Level on the scale	Amount of fine
1	£200
2	£500
3	£1,000
4	£2,500
5	£5,000

Level 5 on the scale, £5,000, is also known as the 'prescribed sum' in terms of section 225(8)

By section 5(2) of the 1995 Act a sheriff is empowered, on convicting a person of any common law offence, to impose a fine not exceeding the prescribed sum. Section 7(5) gives a district court stipendiary magistrate the same powers as a sheriff. Otherwise, the district court is empowered, by section 7(6)(b), to impose a fine not exceeding level 4 on the standard scale. Section 7(7) prohibits the district court from imposing any fine greater than level 4 unless the statute explicitly empowers the district court to do so. It is thought that no statute does so.

However, a number of statutes permit fines on summary conviction of up to £20,000 and such fines can be imposed by the sheriff or a stipendiary magistrate.

It should be noted that in *Wann v Macmillan*[17] it was held that the total financial penalty imposed on a complaint in respect of multiple charges can exceed the maximum for a single offence (by contrast with the position as regards imprisonment).

In determining the amount of a fine the court is required, by section 211(7), to take into account the means of the offender so far as known to the court and section 212 specifically permits money found in the possession of the offender to be applied to payment of the fine. The principle of taking into account the means of the offender was applied in *Andrew Redpath & Son v MacNeill*[18] to the case of a corporate offender.

Time for payment of fines is dealt with in section 214 of the 1995 Act and is in general the right of the convicted person. It is also one means of taking account of the means of the accused. The general principle is that the payment of a fine should not take an unreasonably long time but the High Court in *Johnston v Lockhart*[19] disapproved of the proposition that a fine should be capable of being paid within one year.

Where payment is not made timeously, the accused will be at risk of imprisonment in default, the period being calculated according to section 219 of the 1995 Act.

Financial penalties—compensation

The compensation order is closely analogous to a fine and is provided for by section 249 of the 1995 Act. Such orders are available for personal injury, loss or damage arising out of an offence, except most road traffic offences, and provided the court has not dealt with the case by deferred sentence, probation or absolute discharge. The maxima are as for fines and the payments are enforced and collected as if they were fines and remitted to the victim by the clerk of court.

Financial penalties—caution

Caution for good behaviour is another financial 'penalty' and is provided for by section 227 of the 1995 Act. The order is for the offender to lodge a sum of money with the clerk of court as a guarantee of his good behaviour during a period which must not exceed twelve months. If during the specified period of time he stays out of trouble he gets the money back with interest; otherwise, he loses it.

[17] 1956 SLT 369.
[18] 1990 GWD 25-1423.
[19] 1987 SCCR 537.

Admonition and absolute discharge
Admonition and absolute discharge are provided for by section 246 of the 1995 Act and are what they say. No penalty is imposed. Admonition is in effect a formal reprimand and absolute discharge not even that.

11 : APPEALS

Although the 1995 Act deals separately with appeals under solemn and summary procedure and although some of the modes of appeal are somewhat different, they have many common features and identical underlying principles. This chapter will therefore approach appeals according to the nature of the decision appealed against, rather than according to the type of procedure or the type of appeal.

The nobile officium

In extraordinary and unforeseen circumstances, where there is no other avenue of appeal, application may be made to the *nobile officium* of the High Court, which is the power that the court retains to do what is just in circumstances for which the law makes no other provision. In most cases, however, a more orthodox avenue of appeal will be available and it is with such avenues that this chapter is concerned.

Appeals from preliminary diets and from decisions on competency and relevancy

Under solemn procedure section 74(1) of the 1995 Act provides for an appeal to the High Court against a decision at a preliminary diet. Section 174 of the 1995 Act provides a very similar appeal mechanism for summary procedure. Detailed provision is made by Chapters 9, 15 and 19 of the Act of Adjournal (Criminal Procedure Rules) 1996 but sections 74 and 174 of the 1995 Act include two important qualifications to the right of appeal.

The first is that such an appeal is only competent with the leave of the court of first instance, which may be granted upon the motion of the party wishing to appeal or *ex proprio motu*. The sections do not specify when that leave must be sought, but rule 9.11(1) provides that a motion for leave to appeal against a decision at a preliminary diet shall be made 'at that diet immediately following the making of the decision in question, and shall either be granted or refused there and then'.

Under solemn procedure, a judge who grants leave to appeal is required by rule 9.11(2) to consider postponing the trial. The obvious reason for doing so is to allow time for the appeal. Such a postponement might require to be accompanied by an extension of the time-limits applying to the case, so far as that can competently be done by the particular judge. By section 74(3) of the 1995 Act the High Court may postpone the trial diet pending an appeal and, of the High Court does so, the period of the postponement does not count towards any time-limit which applies to the case. Section 174(2) gives the High Court a similar power for summary procedure.

The courts have not had to consider what is meant by 'immediately' in the context of the making of a motion for leave to appeal but Lord McCluskey has used the phrase 'immediately and on the spot'.[1] Certainly,

---

[1] Lord McCluskey, *Criminal Appeals* (1992) p 22.

given the wording of the rule, any time after the preliminary diet will be too late, even if it is only a few minutes. There is no statutory warrant for calling the indictment or complaint again to allow such a motion to be made and it is thought that to do so would be incompetent. Moreover, it will be recalled that in terms of section 73(1) of the 1995 Act the accused must be asked to state his plea to the indictment 'at the conclusion' of the preliminary diet. It seems to follow in theory, as it does in practice, that the stating of that plea marks the end of the preliminary diet. Since the requirement to state that plea is the next thing which happens after the decision on the preliminary plea has been given, it would seem that the only window of opportunity for leave to be sought is after the end of the judge's or sheriff's statement of his decision and before the accused is asked how he pleads. In other words, if leave is not sought instantly upon the adverse decision being given, it will be too late.

For summary procedure, rule 19(1) stipulates that leave can only be sought by the accused after he has stated how he pleads to the charge or charges set out in the complaint and by rule 19(2) the application for leave and the determination of that application are, as under solemn procedure, to be made 'immediately following the decision in question'.

The second qualification in sections 74 and 174 of the 1995 Act is that the appeal must actually be 'taken' within two days after the decision, though by sections 75 and 194 Saturdays, Sundays and court holidays are not counted. Rules 9.12(1) and 19.1(4) provide that such appeals are to be taken by way of note of appeal which is to be in the form of Form 9.12 or 19.1–A and lodged with the appropriate clerk of court not later than two days after the making of the decision in question.

These forms are skeletal but their most important aspect is probably the requirement to specify the grounds of the appeal. In *Templeton* v *HM Advocate*[2] an attempt was made to argue a ground of appeal which had not been specified in the note but the High Court refused to entertain that argument. The particular point had been raised in the original minute of notice which led to the preliminary diet but had not been argued at the preliminary diet. Indeed Lord Clyde noted that the solicitor for the appellant had said at the preliminary diet that 'it was not a line he was insisting upon'. Lord Justice-Clerk Ross pointed out that such an appeal is an appeal against a decision at a preliminary diet and said that it was only the issue which had actually been decided at the preliminary diet which could be considered in the appeal. There is room for an attempt to distinguish this case where the person who argues the appellant's position at the preliminary diet does not explicitly abandon the line in question, though it is thought that the High Court might not be especially sympathetic to such an attempt. Nor does *Templeton* say explicitly that grounds which were argued and decided at the preliminary diet, but *per incuriam*, omitted from the note of appeal will not be considered. There have been cases in other types of appeal, such as *Moffat* v *HM Advocate*[3] in which submissions have been allowed to go beyond the stated grounds, but both the High Court of Justiciary Practice Note of 29th March 1985[4] and judges of that court (in cases such as *Moffat* and *McAvoy* v *HM*

[2] 1987 SCCR 693.
[3] 1983 SCCR 121.
[4] Reproduced in Lord McCluskey, *op cit*, p 35.

Advocate)[5] have stressed the importance of the grounds of appeal not only to the appeal court but also to any judge who has to write a report for the appeal court.

Lord McCluskey has said[6] of grounds of appeal in relation to appeals after conviction that they should 'consist of specific and distinct statements which identify the particular criticism or criticisms . . . which the appellant intends to present at the oral hearing of the appeal'. He has elaborated this[7] to desiderate *inter alia* accuracy, stateability (grounds which cannot seriously be argued help no one), clarity of language and brevity.

Once the note of appeal has been lodged the clerk must request and the judge at first instance must provide a report on the circumstances relating to the decision at the preliminary diet. A copy of the report is then sent to the parties.

Once the appeal has been heard, the High Court may affirm the decision of the court of first instance or remit the case to it with appropriate directions. If the court of first instance has dismissed the indictment, complaint or part of it, that decision may be reversed and the court of first instance may be directed to fix a trial diet.

Finally under this heading, it should be noted that all will not inevitably be lost if this procedure is not followed, however, because the opening words of both sections 74 and 174 expressly preserve other rights of appeal. Accordingly, in *Harvey* v *Lockhart*[8] the High Court was prepared in the context of an appeal against conviction to hear submissions challenging a decision as to competency which had been made at a debate but not appealed at that time. The court did observe, however, that it was 'in no doubt that the better method of proceeding in a case of this kind would have been for leave to appeal to have been sought before the plea was acted upon'.

Appeals against conviction and/or sentence

We are concerned here with appeals by the convicted accused, either against that conviction itself or against the sentence imposed. Of course, a successful appeal against conviction will, by definition, carry with it the quashing of the sentence. What must be remembered at all times, however, is that it is not open to the appeal court to take a different view of the facts than was taken by the tribunal of fact—the jury in a case on indictment or the trial judge under summary procedure. In *McQuarrie* v *Carmichael*[9] the purported ground of appeal was 'Police evidence at the time of trial which was untrue'. Lord Justice-Clerk Ross explained that this is not a matter which can be brought under review in a stated case because the facts are a matter for the sheriff (and, by implication, for the sheriff alone). Similar reasoning may be applied to appeals from conviction by juries, with the added factor that, whereas a sheriff in a stated case sets out the facts he found proved, the jury never explains the process of reasoning by which it arrived at a verdict of guilty. Accordingly, even where the court is prepared to hear additional evidence, the quashing of a conviction will be

[5] 1982 SCCR 263.
[6] Lord McCluskey, *op cit*, p 35.
[7] *Ibid*, p 37.
[8] 1991 SCCR 83.
[9] 1989 SCCR 371.

accompanied by the granting of authority for a new prosecution (though the Crown does not always in fact do so).

It is fundamental that the matter for consideration by the High Court in an appeal is whether or not there has been a miscarriage of justice. That is the expression used in sections 106(3) and 175(5) of the 1995 Act. Accordingly, it is not sufficient for the quashing of a conviction that there has been an error. As Lord Wheatley put it in *Hunter v HM Advocate*,[10] 'an error in law by the trial judge in regard to the evidence of a witness does not *eo facto* necessarily lead to a granting of an appeal . . . the appellant has to show that the error resulted in a miscarriage of justice'. In that case, the court weighed the significance of evidence which had not been given as a result of an incorrect decision by the trial judge against the 'virtually watertight' prosecution case and decided that the result would not have been affected. The evidence was said to be mitigatory only and the conviction upheld. This followed Lord Wheatley's remark in *McCuaig v HM Advocate*[11] that the court possessed 'a discretionary power . . . *inter alia* to quash the conviction or amend the verdict of guilty'.

Lord McCluskey has stated the current approach thus:[12]

'The High Court now tends to look rather at the seriousness, importance and materiality of the error that the appeal brings to light. Whatever the character of the error . . . the High Court in the light of its judgment about the importance of that error in the context of the whole trial, goes on to make the further judgment as to whether or not what went wrong may have affected the understanding and the deliberations of the jury in such a way as to lead them to draw an important inference or inferences adverse to the appellant. If the judgment is that the error was likely to have influenced the jury to reach a material judgment adverse to the appellant it will hold that the ground of the appeal has been made out, that the "alleged" miscarriage of justice was a true miscarriage of justice, and, a miscarriage of justice having occurred, the conviction appealed against must be quashed.'

Under solemn procedure the appeal is by note of appeal. Under summary procedure, the appeal is by stated case. The fact that there are far more summary prosecutions than prosecutions on indictment and that most reported cases relate to appeals after conviction means that most appeals which settle points of law are stated cases. Many investigators tend to be misled by this into assuming, incorrectly, that every appeal is a stated case.

Under solemn procedure, by section 106(1) of the 1995 Act a person who has been convicted on indictment may, with leave granted in accordance with section 107 of the 1995 Act, appeal to the High Court against

(i) conviction
(ii) sentence
(iii) absolute discharge, admonition, probation, community service or deferred sentence—some of these are not strictly sentences and others are imposed without proceeding to conviction; they therefore require separate provision
(iv) both conviction and sentence or other disposal.

By subsection (3) that right of appeal includes *any* alleged miscarriage of justice including a miscarriage of justice based on the existence and

[10] 1984 SCCR 306.
[11] 1982 SCCR 125.
[12] Lord McCluskey, *op cit*, p 174.

significance of additional evidence which was not heard at the trial and which was not available and could not reasonably have been made available at the trial.

The direct equivalent of this for summary procedure is section 175(2); there is no significant difference between the provisions.

Obviously, the first thing which a person who wishes to appeal will have to do is bring that fact to the attention of the court. Under solemn procedure, this is a two-stage process, the first stage being accomplished, in terms of section 109 of the 1995 Act, by the lodging with the Clerk of Justiciary of written intimation of intention to appeal. That intimation must be lodged within two weeks of the final determination of the proceedings and a copy must be sent to the Crown Agent. Application should be made at this point for any necessary interim orders (such as suspension of disqualification from driving).

Determination of the proceedings is defined by subsections (4) and (5) as occurring when sentence is pronounced or when sentence is first deferred. In terms of sections 111(2) and 103(7) of the 1995 Act that period may be extended by a single judge and this was done in, for example, *Boyle* v *HM Advocate*.[13] As was made clear in *Clayton, Petitioner*[14] the provisions allowing extensions of time-limits in both solemn and summary appeals are not themselves subject to time-limits and an application for an extension can therefore be made at any time.

The second stage under solemn procedure, in terms of section 110 of the 1995 Act, is the lodging with the Clerk of Justiciary of a written note of appeal. By section 110(1) that must be done within six weeks of the lodging of the intimation of intention to appeal. Sections 111 and 103 allow the extension of this period also.

The form for the note of appeal is set out in Form 15.2–B and its essence is a 'full statement of all grounds of appeal', as section 110(3) requires. The importance of the grounds of appeal has already been mentioned in connection with appeals from preliminary diets and stands reiteration here. Submissions which go beyond the grounds specified cannot be heard except by leave of the High Court on cause shown. Moreover, inadequate grounds will at the very least irritate the judges who have to deal with the appeal. The Practice Note criticised in particular the bare assertions that there was 'misdirection' or 'insufficient evidence' without further specification. In *Smith* v *HM Advocate*[15] Lord Justice-General Emslie had the following to say:

> 'The note of appeal tells us that the ground of appeal is "Misdirection of jury by judge". Now that, of course, is an irrelevant ground of appeal because it does not specify what the alleged misdirection is ... we are not disposed to entertain appeals containing an attack upon a judge's charge unless the alleged misdirection is clearly specified. There are several good reasons for that: (1) the Crown must have an opportunity to consider its position, (2) the judge must have an opportunity to explain and deal with the alleged misdirection and (3) this court must, in advance of the hearing, be in a position to examine the charge in light of the specific criticisms which are being made.'

Similar comments were made in *Mitchell* v *HM Advocate*.[16]

[13] 1976 SLT 126.
[14] 1991 SCCR 261.
[15] 1983 SCCR 30.
[16] 1991 SCCR 216.

There was some slight comfort for the appellants in both *Smith* and *Mitchell* in that the court observed in each case that so far as it could see there was no merit in the appeal anyway. However, if in any case there was a good point which the court refused to allow to be argued on the basis of the inadequacy of the grounds stated, the result might well be that a conviction or sentence which should have been quashed would be allowed to stand, with all that means. There has also to be borne in mind the fact that the content of the note of appeal will be a major factor in deciding whether or not leave to appeal is to be granted and there is therefore a substantial risk that inadequate grounds will provoke a refusal of leave to appeal.

The two stages in commencing an appeal under solemn procedure are, under summary procedure, combined into one. The provision relevant to appeals against conviction and to appeals against both conviction and sentence is by section 176, subsection (1) of which provides for such appeals to be made by application for a stated case and demands that such an application should be made by lodging it with the clerk (of the court which convicted the appellant) within one week of the final determination of the proceedings. A copy is to be sent to the respondent and the application itself is to 'contain a full statement of all the matters which the appellant desires to bring under review'. Application should be made at this point for any necessary interim orders (such as suspension of disqualification from driving).

There is under summary procedure no equivalent to section 109(5) which defines the final determination of proceedings as occurring when sentence is first deferred. Rather, in *Walker* v *Gibb*[17] it was held that an appeal by stated case by a convicted accused upon whom sentence had been deferred was premature and incompetent because there had been no final determination of the prosecution. The concept of final determination was further refined in *Tudhope* v *Colbert*[18] and *Tudhope* v *Campbell*,[19] in both of which it was held, on the basis of the statutory predecessor of section 167 of the 1995 Act, that the proceedings are not finally determined until particulars of conviction and sentence are entered in the record of proceedings.

Smith v *Gray*[20] made it clear that the application must be in writing and it was held in *Elliot, Applicant*,[21] that the requirement to lodge the application with the clerk within one week means that it must be in his hands within that time and not merely posted. Comments in certain textbooks, based on another part of the decision in *Smith* v *Gray*, to the effect that posting is enough, were disapproved. However, consistent with practice as to other time-limits, the date of the determination of the inferior judge is not counted as one of the days of the week allowed.[22]

Elliot concerned an application which was primarily directed to the obtaining of an extension of the one-week period, which is provided for by section 181(1) of the 1995 Act and that extension was granted. Accordingly, it may be seen that, just as extensions may be obtained under solemn

[17] 1965 SLT 2.
[18] 1978 SLT (Notes) 57.
[19] 1979 JC 24.
[20] 1925 JC 8.
[21] 1984 SCCR 125.
[22] (1884) 5 Couper 274.

procedure, so they may be obtained under summary procedure and that missing a deadline will not inevitably prove fatal. However, it should also be borne in mind that the High Court is not obliged to grant such extensions and that the court might not look kindly on applications for extensions which have become necessary as a result of negligence or a cavalier approach to the requirements of the statute (the time-limits are, after all, there for a purpose). In *Elliot* the textbook references mentioned above provided a substantial excuse for the failure to meet the deadline as it came to be interpreted by the court.

Just as the grounds of appeal are of great importance under solemn procedure, so the statement of matters desired to be brought under review is crucial in a summary appeal by stated case. The High Court pointed out in *Durant* v *Lockhart*[23] that the requirement to give a full statement of the matters to be brought under review was introduced 'so that the sheriff, when he stated the case, could be in no doubt as to what particular issue it was that the applicant was seeking to bring under review, and so that he could state in his findings in fact the matters which were appropriate to that issue'. From time to time, sheriffs have regarded their task as being made impossible by the inadequacy of the grounds in the application and so, in *Galloway* v *Hillary*,[24] for example, a sheriff refused to state a case on the basis that 'insufficient evidence for conviction' was not a statement of matters but merely a 'brute assertion'. That the High Court will support sheriffs who take such a position is clear from *Dickson* v *Valentine*[25] in which the appellant applied for a stated case giving as the ground of appeal 'that the sheriff erred in law', without specification of how and in what respect he was said to have so erred. In the event, the sheriff stated a case, but the High Court commented that he would have been well founded had he declined to do so and said that '[appellants] should understand in the future that if they fail to comply with provisions [requiring a full statement of all matters to be brought under review] the consequences may well be either that the sheriff will decline to state a case or that this court will decline to entertain the appeal'.

Section 182(3) of the 1995 Act makes it incompetent for an appellant to found on any matter not contained in the application, and it is clear that the High Court will not be endlessly indulgent with inadequately formulated applications. In *Anderson* v *McClory*[26] an attempt to argue a detailed point on the basis of a ground which simply invited the High Court to consider whether, on the facts stated, the sheriff had been entitled to convict was rejected. The court held that this came 'nowhere near' the specification required and refused to entertain the argument.

In section 176(3) of the 1995 Act there is provision for the amendment of the application for a stated case, so that an application which is defective when lodged, either because it is unspecific or because it does not refer to a ground which it is hoped to argue, can be corrected. The alternative, following *Singh, Petitioner*,[27] is to lodge a second application within the permitted

---

[23] 1986 SCCR 23.
[24] 1983 SCCR 119.
[25] 1988 SCCR 325.
[26] 1991 SCCR 571.
[27] 1986 SCCR 215.

time, though this may be thought to be an unnecessarily cumbersome way of going about things.

Under both solemn and summary procedure, the application for the appeal will be passed to the trial judge. Under solemn procedure, in terms of section 113(1) of the 1995 Act that judge is required, as soon as is reasonably practicable thereafter, to provide a written report giving an opinion on the case generally and on the grounds contained in the note of appeal in particular. The equivalent, under summary procedure, section 178 of the 1995 Act which requires the sheriff (or clerk to the district court) to issue a draft stated case within three weeks of final determination of the proceedings. The form requires the trial judge to 'state concisely and without argument the nature of the cause and the facts if any admitted or proved in evidence, any objections to the admission or rejection of evidence taken in the proof, the grounds of the decision and any other matters necessary to be stated for the information of the superior court'.

Accordingly, the draft will set out the facts which the trial judge has found to be admitted or proved and not merely the statements of the witnesses[28] nor the questions and answers which were the subject of the objection.[29]

Gordon v *Allan*[30] is a particularly clear example of how a stated case should not be drafted. In that case, the appellant was convicted in a district court of assault. The case prepared was, according to Lord Justice-General Emslie, 'woefully deficient in that it contained no findings in fact but merely a narration of evidence without any indication of the extent to which the justice accepted or rejected it'. The High Court at first remitted the case to the justice to prepare a proper stated case but his second effort was no better than his first and the court simply quashed the conviction, observing that 'it is no good writing a stated case and pretending that facts found can be discovered by a recitation of evidence. Findings in fact ought to be crisp, clear and certain, and if discussion of the evidence is relevant for the purposes of an appeal the place for that discussion is in the note which follows the findings which, upon the evidence, the justice has found himself able to make'. It was made clear in *Bowman* v *Jessop*[31] that it is incorrect, in a case in which there has been a conviction, to confine the material in the stated case to that which is derived from the Crown case.

The grounds of the decision should be stated distinctly in the stated case so as to avoid the problem which occurred in *Lyon* v *Don Brothers Buist & Co*[32] in which the sheriff substitute, after setting forth the facts which were proved, stated merely that upon these facts he found the accused not guilty. In a prosecution under the Factories Acts, as that was, with somewhat complex relevant legislation, the High Court's difficulties may be imagined.

The ground of decision is likely to be particularly important when evidence has been disallowed.[33]

---

[28] *Gordon* v *Hansen* (1914) 7 Adam 441; *Pert* v *Robinson* 1955 SLT 23.
[29] *Waddell* v *Kinnaird* 1922 JC 40.
[30] 1987 SLT 400.
[31] 1989 SCCR 597.
[32] 1944 JC 1.
[33] *Falconer* v *Brown* (1893) 1 Adam 96.

There is provision for adjustment of the stated case, which is to be found in section 178 of the 1995 Act. The parties have three weeks from the issue of the draft to propose adjustments or to state that they have no adjustments to propose. If the appellant fails to do either of these things he is deemed to have abandoned his appeal.

Where adjustments are proposed, the procedure is governed by section 179 of the 1995 Act. There is a hearing at which the parties may make representations to the trial judge. Thereafter, the stated case must be issued in its final form, within two weeks of the date of the hearing. There must be appended to it a note of any adjustment which has been proposed and which the trial judge has rejected, together with a note of any evidence rejected by the trial judge which is alleged to support the adjustment concerned and a note of the trial judge's reasons for rejecting that adjustment and evidence. There is also to be appended a note of the evidence on which the trial judge bases any finding in fact challenged as unsupported by the evidence.

The appellant must then lodge the stated case with the Clerk of Justiciary.

Leave to appeal

Before the appeal can go forward, leave is required. The procedure for obtaining that leave is set out in sections 107 and 180 of the 1995 Act. Essentially it involves a 'sift' by a single judge of the High Court.

In terms of these provisions, a judge of the High Court is to consider the content of certain documents and, if he considers that the documents disclose arguable grounds of appeal, he is to grant leave to appeal. In any other case, he is to refuse leave to appeal, giving his reasons in writing (and granting warrant for arrest if the appellant is on bail pending appeal). A further application for leave may be made to the High Court within fourteen days of refusal of leave by a single judge and, in that case, the application is dealt with by three judges.

Applications for leave either to a single judge or to three judges are dealt with in chambers and without the parties being present.

The documents which are to be considered upon an application for leave are set out in each subsection (2). In an appeal under solemn procedure, they are the note of appeal, a certified copy or the original of the record of proceedings, the trial judge's report and a transcript of the judge's charge to the jury if the notes have been extended. Under summary procedure, they are the stated case as issued and the complaint, productions and 'other proceedings'.

The test to be applied is whether the documents disclose arguable grounds of appeal and this is not a high hurdle. The legislation does not require the judge considering whether or not to grant leave to form any view on the likelihood that the appeal will succeed. It is enough that it is stateable. If the test is passed, the judge is to grant leave and 'make such comments in writing as he considers appropriate'. In any other case, he is to refuse leave, giving his reasons in writing, and, where the appellant is on bail and the sentence in the case appealed is one of imprisonment, grant a warrant for arrest. The warrant does not take effect for fourteen days to allow for appeal to a Bench of three judges.

The legislation is silent on the purpose of the written comments which may be made in the event of leave being granted but they will presumably afford an opportunity to a judge who has required to do research in the course of considering whether to grant leave to give the benefit of that work to the bench which hears the appeal.

Additional evidence

In some cases, under both solemn and summary procedure, the defence desires to lay further evidence before the court in support of the appeal. It is competent for the High Court to hear such evidence but the circumstances in which it will choose to do so are rather limited.

The starting-point is section 106(3) of the 1995 Act and section 175(5) of the 1995 Act, which make identical provision for solemn and summary procedure respectively. In terms of these sections, a person may bring under review of the High Court any alleged miscarriage of justice, including any such miscarriage 'on the basis of the existence and significance of fresh evidence which was not heard at the trial and which was not available and could not reasonably have been made available at the trial'.

It is evident that there are three criteria to be met in this. First, the evidence must not have been heard at the trial. This on the face of it is obvious, but the court has had to deal with certain refinements. The first of these is the meaning of the word 'evidence', and in *White* v *HM Advocate*[34] the question related to a person referred to in appellant's defence at the trial who had not been available to be identified by witnesses. The same person was later traced. The appeal court held that since what was in issue was not the person's evidence but his presence at the trial there was no question of his evidence having a bearing on the verdict and it was not in the interests of justice to allow his evidence to be led.

Assuming that what is proffered actually is evidence, it was made clear in *Maitland* v *HM Advocate*[35] that the court will decline to hear it if it merely adds to evidence already given. This rule was derived from *Temple* v *HM Advocate*[36] in which the court had refused to allow additional evidence to be led to supplement evidence given at trial in support of an alibi.

The court has, however, also had to deal with the situation in which witnesses who have given evidence at the trial wish to change that evidence. This arose in *Mitchell* v *HM Advocate*,[37] in which a man called Doig, who had been a Crown witness at the trial giving evidence of some importance, had given an affidavit that the evidence which he had given at the trial was false, though the Crown investigation of that did not persuade the court that it was. As to this, the Lord Justice-General said:

'We are in no doubt that we may not entertain this appeal on the basis of evidence from Doig on the lines of his affidavit or otherwise. This evidence can in no circumstances be described as additional evidence within the meaning of [the relevant section] of the statute. It is merely evidence from a witness for the Crown at the appellant's trial which on its face is different evidence from that which he gave at the trial. It is obvious too, that this new version of Doig's evidence was evidence which could have been given at the trial. Putting the matter shortly we shall say that the court will never entertain an appeal upon the proposition that a witness who has given evidence at a trial merely wishes to change his story.'

[34] 1989 SCCR 553.
[35] 1992 SCCR 759.
[36] 1971 JC 1.
[37] 1989 SCCR 502.

This is to be distinguished from the position in *Marshall* v *MacDougall*[38] in which evidence emerged that a Crown witness was heard to admit after the trial that he had lied; that allegation was investigated and the conviction ultimately quashed.

The *Mitchell* approach was followed in *Jones* v *HM Advocate*[39] in which the additional evidence was to come from the appellant himself and would have directly contradicted what he had said in his evidence at trial. Lord Justice-Clerk Ross, under reference to *Mitchell,* said that this was 'in no proper sense of the words additional evidence; it is merely evidence which is different from evidence which was given at the trial. It is not sufficient to justify an application to have additional evidence allowed that a witness, and in particular an accused, has changed his story'. The court in *Jones* did not allow the additional evidence to be led.

The second and third criteria are that the evidence must not have been available at the trial and that the evidence must have been incapable of reasonably being made available at the trial. Obviously, these two are closely related.

The best starting-point is probably *Salusbury-Hughes* v *HM Advocate.*[40] In that case the appellant was convicted of causing death by reckless driving. His defence had been that the presence of his vehicle on the wrong side of the road could only be accounted for by a mechanical defect, such as the sudden deflation of a tyre. On appeal he sought to lead evidence from an engineer who had examined the tyre and prepared a report some three weeks after the accused had been sentenced. That report claimed that there had been such a mechanical defect. The court took the view, however, that there appeared to be 'no good reason why such evidence could not have been obtained prior to the trial and why it could not have been heard at the trial'. The court said that

'The truth appears to be that no efforts were made to obtain this evidence until after the appellant had been convicted and sentenced. No good reason has been advanced to explain why no steps were taken to obtain the evidence in time for the trial. No good reason has been advanced to explain why no motion was made to adjourn the trial to enable such evidence to be obtained so that it could be led at the trial. . . . The appellant may have neglected to make proper preparations for the trial but for that he has only himself to blame. The time for an accused to put forward his full defence is at his trial, not after his trial . . . it would be contrary to the clear intent of the statute for the court to hear additional evidence where the appellant has failed to demonstrate that such evidence could not reasonably have been made available at the trial.'

A similarly robust line was taken by the court in *Williamson* v *HM Advocate.*[41] There, the appellant proposed to lead additional evidence to support a special defence of incrimination (of a Crown witness) although no such defence had been offered at trial. Essentially, the appellant's complaint was that his defence had been conducted along the wrong lines. He claimed to have given his solicitor the information which should have led to the lodging of a special defence but that had not been passed

[38] 1986 SCCR 376.
[39] 1989 SCCR 726.
[40] 1987 SCCR 38.
[41] 1988 SCCR 56.

on to defence counsel. The High Court characterised the appeal as 'simply designed to give the appellant an opportunity to put forward, in a new trial, a full defence which could and should have been put forward at his original trial'. Again, in *Craven* v *Macphail*[42] an appellant who tried to bring fresh evidence from his mother as to the timing of a telephone call by him to her which he now regarded as having been crucial to his defence was unsuccessful. He had thought that she was not a competent witness on his behalf and did not tell his solicitor about the evidence she might be able to give but the appeal court held that the proposed additional evidence could have been available at the trial and that the appellant, having failed to seek advice on an important point of law, could not now pray in aid his own error.

If the criteria are satisfied, before allowing additional evidence the High Court will apply the test set out in *Cameron* v *HM Advocate*.[43] In that case, the appeal court held, after some hesitation, that the statutory tests as to availability of the evidence were met. They examined the evidence in considerable detail and the defence argued that, although it could not be said that on the basis of the new evidence the jury would have reached a different result, it was enough if it could be said that the new evidence was reliable and had a material bearing on the critical question in the case. The appellant invited the court to quash the conviction and grant authority for a new prosecution.

The court took the opportunity to consider the approach which should be taken in such an appeal. The judgment contained the following important passage.

> 'In the first place, it is clear that the court may allow an appeal against conviction on any ground only if it is satisfied that there has been a miscarriage of justice. In the case of an appeal in which it is contended that there has been a miscarriage of justice on the basis of the existence and significance of certain additional evidence which was not heard at the trial, it is obvious that the court will be in a position to give effect to that contention if it is satisfied that, if the original jury had heard the new evidence, its significance was such that the jury would have been bound to acquit. In such a case the appeal court will quash the conviction. The problem arises, however, where ... the court cannot be so satisfied. ... Plainly, the court will require to be satisfied not merely that the additional evidence was relevant for consideration by the trial jury. Setting aside the verdict of a jury is no light matter, and before the court can hold that there has been a miscarriage of justice it will ... require to be satisfied that the additional evidence is important evidence, of such a kind and quality that it was likely to have been found by a reasonable jury under proper directions of material assistance in their consideration of a critical issue which emerged at the trial.'

Applying this in *Mitchell*, the court found that there was additional evidence, from apparently credible witnesses, which contradicted a police account of a journey from the accused's house to a police car, during which the police said that an admission had been made. The new witnesses said that there had been no conversation. It was said that the existence of these witnesses had been unknown to the defence until after the trial and it was

---

[42] 1990 SCCR 558.
[43] 1987 SCCR 608.

clear to the court that, although their evidence would not inevitably have led to an acquittal, it would have had a material part to play in the jury's determination. Accordingly, the conviction was quashed and authority was granted for a new prosecution. By contrast, in *Stillie* v *HM Advocate*[44] the appellant lodged five affidavits which purported to demonstrate that he had not been the man with the knife who assaulted the victim but that the attacker had been another named man. Having read the affidavits the appeal court took the view that they contradicted one another to such an extent that it could not properly be held that the fresh evidence was reliable. That being so, the court refused the appeal.

All this was thrown into doubt by the case of *Church* v *HM Advocate*[45] in which Lord Justice-General Hope, sitting with Lord Allanbridge and Lord Brand, decided that the court was entitled to entertain an appeal where new evidence was sought to be led, even though the evidence was not evidence which was not available and could not reasonably have been made available at the trial.

In so holding, the court was disagreeing with the law as it had been stated by several High Court Benches, especially in *Salusbury-Hughes*. The approach in *Church* was, however, to be criticised by Lord Justice-Clerk Ross in *Elliott* v *HM Advocate*[46] both in terms of its procedure—he pointed out, probably correctly, that if the court in *Church* was to depart from the established case-law they should have remitted the matter to a Full Bench—and on its merits.

Having subjected the judgment in *Church* to a minute dissection, under reference to the earlier authorities, the Lord Justice-Clerk moved the court to disapprove of *Church* to the extent that it held that the power of the High Court to hear additional evidence was unrestricted and to affirm that the law is correctly stated in *Salusbury-Hughes*. With that approach Lord McCluskey, Lord Morison, Lord Morton and Lord Cowie agreed. Accordingly, the law remains as stated in the line of cases founded on *Salusbury-Hughes*.

Powers of court

The powers of the court in dealing with appeals are dealt with primarily by sections 118 and 183 of the 1995 Act. The High Court may dispose of an appeal against conviction by affirming the verdict of the trial court (namely refusing the appeal), by setting aside the verdict of the trial court and either quashing the conviction or substituting an amended verdict of guilty or by setting aside the verdict of the trial court and granting authority to bring a new prosecution. In addition, under summary procedure, the High Court may dispose of a stated case by remitting the cause to the inferior court with an opinion and a direction as to how to proceed. So, for example, in *Aitchison* v *Rizza*,[47] where a sheriff had erred in finding that there was no case to answer, the High Court remitted the case to him with a direction to proceed as accords, by which was meant that he should continue with the trial as if he had held that there *was* a case to answer.

---

[44] 1990 SCCR 719.
[45] 1995 SCCR 194.
[46] 1995 SCCR 280.
[47] 1985 SCCR 297.

If the High Court substitutes an amended verdict of guilty it must ensure that the amended verdict is one which could have been returned on the indictment or complaint before the trial court.

The setting aside of a conviction will obviously have a bearing on the sentence. Where the whole conviction on the indictment is set aside, the whole sentence will fall with it. However, where a conviction is only partly set aside, either because convictions remain on other charges on the indictment or because an amended verdict of guilty is substituted, the sentence might well become inappropriate. Accordingly, the High Court is empowered, in setting aside a verdict, to quash any sentence imposed on the appellant as respects the indictment or complaint and pass another sentence. That sentence, however, must not be more severe than the original sentence.

Authority for a new prosecution is provided for by sections 118(1)(c) and 183(1)(d) of the 1995 Act, the procedure being regulated by sections 119 and 185. Where such authority is granted, a new prosecution may be brought charging the accused with the same or any similar offence arising out of the same facts. However, by each subsection (2) the accused cannot be charged with an offence more serious than that which he was convicted in the earlier proceedings and, by each subsection (3), no sentence may be passed on conviction under the new prosecution which could not have been passed on conviction under the earlier proceedings.

Subsection (4) of each section disapplies any time-limit which would ordinarily apply to the case but by each subsection (5) the new prosecution must be commenced within two months of the date on which authority to bring the prosecution was granted, otherwise the setting aside of the conviction by the High Court operates as a complete acquittal.

It is not in every case that the court will grant authority for a new prosecution. In particular, where the Crown has contributed to the error which resulted in the miscarriage of justice, the court may be slow to give the Crown a second bite at the cherry. Where, however, the mistake was solely that of the trial judge there is a greater chance of authority being granted. So in *McGhee* v *HM Advocate*[48] the appeal court said that as the miscarriage of justice arose from comments made by the judge and as there was no suggestion that there was any insufficiency of evidence, authority should be given for a new prosecution.

Greater detail was given of the reasoning which led to the granting of authority to bring a new prosecution in *Wilkinson* v *HM Advocate*.[49] There, Lord Justice-General Hope said:

'This was a case where the misdirection arose solely out of a decision taken by the sheriff himself. There was nothing done by the Crown, so far as we have been told, which in any way contributed to his decision. The events which were the subject of the charge . . . are of relatively recent happening. There is nothing in the facts or circumstances to suggest that it would be contrary to the public interest that a fresh prosecution should be brought.'

This should not, of course, be construed as an exhaustive list of the criteria which the High Court will regard as relevant but it is probably a good working guide.

[48] 1991 SCCR 510.
[49] 1991 SCCR 856.

Appeals against sentence alone

In an appeal by a convicted person against sentence (but not conviction), the issues are much simpler than those involved in an appeal against conviction and the procedure to some extent reflects that relative simplicity.

Under solemn procedure, by section 110(1)(a) of the 1995 Act, an appeal against sentence alone commences with the lodging of a written note of appeal with the Clerk of Justiciary within two weeks of the passing of sentence. The preliminary step of lodging intimation of intention to appeal does not apply. Thereafter, the appeal proceeds under the same rules as an appeal against conviction or conviction and sentence.

Under summary procedure, an appeal against sentence alone does not proceed by stated case. Instead, sections 175(9), 186, 187, 189, 190 and 192 of the 1995 Act provide for a note of appeal against sentence. The form of the note is set out in Form 19.3–A and the note must, by section 186(2), be lodged with the clerk of the court which passed sentence within one week of the passing of the sentence or of the order deferring sentence which is appealed against. The sentencer then prepares a report for the High Court. Section 187 makes provision as to leave to appeal which is equivalent to that for appeals against conviction.

By sections 118(4) and 189 of the 1995 Act the High Court may dispose of an appeal against sentence by affirming the sentence or, if it thinks that, having regard to all the circumstances, a different sentence should have been passed, by quashing the sentence and passing another sentence. However, it is very important to note that the sentence will not necessarily be reduced in such a case. The High Court has the power to increase it. In *Donnelly* v *HM Advocate*[50] a sheriff had dealt with a sixteen-year-old first offender who had pleaded guilty to possession of a CS gas canister at a football match, during which the canister had been thrown into a group of rival supporters by someone else (who was sentenced to four years' detention), by imposing eighteen months' detention. On appeal against sentence, during which it was argued that the sentence was excessive, the court held that the sentence by the sheriff was in fact inadequate and substituted a sentence of two years' detention.

Crown appeals

There are two situations in which the Lord Advocate can bring a matter before the appeal court under solemn procedure. Under summary procedure the prosecutor (who is, of course, almost always the procurator fiscal) can appeal by stated case on a point of law against either an acquittal or the sentence passed. All these Crown rights of appeal are used very sparingly.

Lord Advocate's reference

The first situation is provided for by section 123 of the 1995 Act which permits the Lord Advocate to refer to the High Court a point of law which has arisen in relation to a charge (on indictment) of which the accused has been acquitted. A copy of the reference is to be sent by the Clerk of

---

[50] 1988 SCCR 386.

Justiciary to the accused and to his solicitor and the accused is entitled to be represented. However, in terms of subsection (5) the opinion on the point of law does not affect the acquittal at the trial.

The procedure has been used to establish, for example, that the law relating to admissibility of alleged confessions by an accused is irrelevant to the matter of admissibility in a perjury trial[51] and that to brandish an imitation firearm and demand money is assault even if it had been as a joke.[52] We have already noticed *Lord Advocate's Reference (No 1 of 1992)*[53] when dealing with hearsay and documentary evidence.

Lord Advocate's appeal against sentence

The second situation concerns the Lord Advocate's appeal against sentence under section 108 of the 1995 Act. In terms of that section, where a person has been convicted on indictment, the Lord Advocate may appeal against the sentence passed on conviction (or against probation, etc) if it appears to him that the disposal is unduly lenient or on a point of law. The first reported example of the use of the procedure is *HM Advocate* v *McPhee*[54] in which a community service order was quashed and a sentence of three years' detention imposed in its place in respect of supplying Class A drugs to children.

Stated case

So far as summary procedure is concerned, the procurator fiscal's right to apply for a stated case may be used where the Crown considers that, on the facts established, the sheriff has acquitted incorrectly as a result of misdirecting himself in law. The Crown can also appeal where the sheriff has failed to comply with the requirements of the law in relation to the sentence imposed. Provision is made in section 175(4) of the 1995 Act for the Crown to appeal against an unduly lenient sentence but only in relation to classes of case specified by Order in Council. No such classes have been specified at the time of writing and such appeals are, therefore, not further considered in this book.

Many summary appeals by the Crown relate to cases in which it has been held that there is no case to answer, since such a decision is a matter of pure law which has resulted in an acquittal. In such cases, as *Keane* v *Bathgate*[55] makes clear, the traditional approach to stated cases, described above, by which findings in fact are made, is inappropriate. As the High Court noted in that case, the decision in relation to a submission of no case to answer does not in itself require the sheriff to decide the facts. As will be recalled, the effect of *Williamson* v *Wither*[56] is that the question for the court is whether there is no evidence which if accepted will entitle the court to proceed to conviction. Reflecting this, the High Court said in *Keane* that 'in setting out the case for an appeal where the [no case to answer] procedure has been successfully invoked the proper thing for the court to do is simply to set out the evidence which has been adduced by the

---

[51] *Lord Advocate's Reference (No 1 of 1985)* 1987 SLT 187.
[52] *Lord Advocate's Reference (No 2 of 1992)* 1992 SCCR 960.
[53] 1992 SCCR 724.
[54] 1994 SCCR 830. For a consideration of the facts of that case, see (1995) 63 SLG 20.
[55] 1983 SLT 651.
[56] 1981 SCCR 216.

prosecution and any inferences drawn therefrom for arriving at the decision'.

Bills of advocation and bills of suspension

Bills of advocation and bills of suspension are remedies which are directed essentially to procedural disasters, usually of a fairly fundamental kind (though this is a working guide and not a proposition of law). Although often regarded as mirror images of one another, they in fact have differing scope and are available at different stages.

Advocation

The bill of advocation is available to both prosecution and defence[57] and in both solemn and summary proceedings. The prosecutor can use it even in relation to the High Court itself, where it sits as a court of first instance. It is also available at any stage of proceedings. Advocation is the calling up or removal of a cause from an inferior court to a superior court but its sphere is limited to the correction of irregularities in the preliminary stages of a case.[58] Although the judicial view in the late 1960s seems to have been that the bill of advocation was falling into disuse as a result of the introduction of the stated case, the remedy has since enjoyed something of a renaissance, with the Crown using it, for example, where a warrant has been wrongfully refused.[59] It has been used by the defence where a sheriff continued a part-heard trial for eight days with the accused in custody even though the forty-day time-limit for commencing the trial had expired,[60] where a sheriff adjourned a trial partly heard by another sheriff who had been taken seriously ill[61] and where it was sought to challenge a sheriff's decision to allow an amendment of the complaint so as to insert the accused's correct name.[62] In none of these cases was it said that the competency of the procedure was in doubt, though the outcomes cannot be said to be encouraging for defence use of the procedure.

Suspension

The classic definition of a bill of suspension was given by Lord Wheatley in *McGregor v MacNeill*.[63]

'Suspension is a competent method of review, available in summary proceedings only[64] when some step in the procedure has gone wrong or some factor has emerged which satisfies the court that a miscarriage of justice has taken place resulting in a failure to do justice to the accused.'

Suspension, then, is available only to the accused and, in terms of section 130 of the 1995 Act, only in summary cases. It is a process whereby a warrant, conviction or judgment issued by an inferior judge may be reviewed. It follows that such a warrant, conviction or judgment must exist

[57] See *Durant v Lockhart* 1985 SCCR 72.
[58] *MacLeod v Levitt* 1969 JC 16.
[59] *MacNeill* 1984 SLT 157.
[60] *Grugen v Jessop* 1988 SCCR 182.
[61] *Platt v Lockhart* 1988 SCCR 308.
[62] *Hoyers (UK) Ltd v Houston* 1991 SCCR 919.
[63] 1975 JC 57.
[64] Section 130 of the 1995 Act gives statutory form to this restriction.

and that suspension is incompetent before such a warrant, conviction of judgment actually exists. This was the issue in *Durant* v *Lockhart*[65] in which an attempt was made to take a bill of suspension against a sheriff's decision to adjourn a trial diet, but was refused as incompetent. This is not to say, however, that it is only available after the final determination of proceedings. It was used in *Stuart* v *Crowe*[66] to attack search warrants obtained by the police and upon which the Crown intended to found at the forthcoming trial and, although the attack failed on its merits, the appropriateness of the procedure was not disputed.

Procedure

The procedure under bills of suspension and bills of advocation is the same. The bill is lodged at the Justiciary Office and then placed before a single judge of the High Court for an order for service. If that judge thinks that the bill discloses no substantial ground of appeal, he is entitled to remit the bill to a quorum of the High Court who may, if they agree with the single judge, refuse the bill then and there. Where, however, the single judge considers that the bill is not clearly without substance he will grant an order for service and the bill is then served upon the opponent. The clerk will also send a copy to the judge whose decision is being challenged. The opponent will then lodge answers and, as in civil pleadings, the effect of those answers will be to identify the areas of disagreement (if any) as to the facts. Lord Justice-General Emslie said in *Neilands* v *Leslie*[67] that where there is a conflict between the bill and the answers, the court will usually accept the answers. In this regard it is appropriate to recall that, although the High Court is not bound to follow the Lord Advocate's account of the facts of a matter, it does treat his opinion with considerable respect, as appears from the judgment in *Bennett* v *HM Advocate*.[68]

There is no time-limit for the lodging of a bill of advocation or suspension but it should be noted that undue delay in so doing is likely to found a plea that the complainer has acquiesced in the order complained of, especially if it imposes a sentence and that sentence has been served.[69]

---

[65] 1985 SCCR 72.
[66] 1992 SCCR 181.
[67] 1973 SLT (Notes) 332.
[68] 1994 SCCR 902.
[69] *Macfarlan* v *Pringle* (1904) 4 Adam 403.